Learning Resource Centre

Email: LRC@swindon.ac.uk   Tel: (01793) 491591 ext.1500

Please re~ ~~~ ~~~ ~~ ~~e last date stamped below

SKILLS-BASED SOCIOLOGY

Series Editors: Tony Lawson and Tim Heaton

The *Skills-based Sociology* series is designed to cover all the key concepts, issues and debates in Sociology. The books take a critical look at contemporary developments in sociological knowledge as well as essential social theories. Each title examines a key topic area within sociology, offering relevant examples and student-focused pedagogical features to aid learning and develop essential study skills.

THEORY AND METHOD (second edition)
Mel Churton and Anne Brown

RELIGION AND BELIEF
Joan Garrod and Marsha Jones

MASS MEDIA
Marsha Jones and Emma Jones

CULTURE AND IDENTITY (second edition)
Warren Kidd and Alison Teagle

POLITICS AND POWER
Warren Kidd, Karen Legge and Philippe Harari

STRATIFICATION AND DIFFERENCE
Mark Kirby

CRIME AND DEVIANCE (second edition)
Tony Lawson and Tim Heaton

EDUCATION AND TRAINING (second edition)
Tony Lawson, Tim Heaton and Anne Brown

HEALTH AND ILLNESS
Michael Senior and Bruce Viveash

THE FAMILY (second edition)
Liz Steel, Warren Kidd and Anne Brown

Skills-based Sociology
Series Standing Order ISBN 0–333–69350–7
(*outside North America only*)

You can receive future titles in this series as they are published. To place a standing order please contact your bookseller or, in the case of difficulty, write to us at the address below with your name and address, the title of the series and the ISBN quoted above.

Customer Service Department, Macmillan Distribution Ltd, Houndmills, Basingstoke, Hampshire RG21 6XS, England, UK

Culture and Identity

Second Edition

Warren Kidd

and

Alison Teagle

palgrave
macmillan

First edition 2002
Second edition 2012

Published by
PALGRAVE MACMILLAN

Palgrave Macmillan in the UK is an imprint of Macmillan Publishers Limited, registered in England, company number 785998, of Houndmills, Basingstoke, Hampshire RG21 6XS.

Palgrave Macmillan in the US is a division of St Martin's Press LLC, 175 Fifth Avenue, New York, NY 10010.

Palgrave Macmillan is the global academic imprint of the above companies and has companies and representatives throughout the world.

Palgrave® and Macmillan® are registered trademarks in the United States, the United Kingdom, Europe and other countries.

ISBN 978–0–230–28102–8

This book is printed on paper suitable for recycling and made from fully managed and sustained forest sources. Logging, pulping and manufacturing processes are expected to conform to the environmental regulations of the country of origin.

A catalogue record for this book is available from the British Library.

A catalog record for this book is available from the Library of Congress.

10   9   8   7   6   5   4   3   2   1
21   20   19   18   17   16   15   14   13   12

Printed and bound in Great Britain by
CPI Antony Rowe, Chippenham and Eastbourne

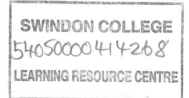

For Jane, Joan, Eddie, Fred and Barbara.
Thank you for your love and support.
Warren Kidd

To all of the students I have taught over the years. Thank you for your good
humour, inspiration and determination to seek answers to the important
questions about the world around us.

Above all, this is for my family. Thank you for your support,
encouragement and love. For Scott, Freya and Anwyn.
Alison Teagle

Contents

List of Figures and Tables

Figures

Tables

Acknowledgements

The authors would like to thank Tony Lawson, Anna Marie Reeve and Esther Croom for their editorial help with this book.

Every effort has been made to trace all copyright-holders, but if any have inadvertently been overlooked, the publishers will be pleased to make the necessary arrangements at the earliest opportunity.

Chapter 1

Introduction

THE PHILOSOPHY BEHIND THE BOOK

The aims of this book are twofold: to give you a good understanding of the study of culture and identity within sociology, but in particular to involve you in your own learning and develop your skills as a sociologist. There are activities and exercises throughout to help you develop sociological skills and apply them to this topic area. The world of sociology is a rapidly-changing and ever-expanding one. Each month, new trends are established, old traditions are continued, and recent fads and fashions are replaced by newer ones. Each month, new research is completed, and new articles, journals and books are published. There is a wealth and rich variety of sociological information 'out there' for the interested consumer. Sociology is a subject enlivened by the 'now'. With your development of sociological skills comes the pleasure and challenge of applying them to current events, of looking at the world around you in a different way.

Given that the use of theory is at the heart of what sociology does, a key feature of this book is its emphasis on the newer sociological theories, which are given an equal footing with more traditional ideas and concepts. There is an overview of classical theories, but the book does not attempt to cover them in great depth: this has been capably covered by many other texts. This book focuses on recent theoretical developments, comparing them with classical theory and focusing on critical issues and awareness of current debate. Given its current popularity and issues in society today, this is especially important in the case of 'culture and identity'.

WHAT ARE CULTURE AND IDENTITY?

By culture, sociologists generally mean 'the way of life of a group', and by identity they usually mean 'knowing who you are', though, as Chapter 2 will illustrate, there is much controversy over the precise definition of these key concepts. The study of culture and identity therefore involves debates on a wide range of important issues:

- The relationship of the individual to the wider group.
- The degree of freedom individuals have in their day-to-day life.
- The type and degree of self-consciousness individuals have in respect of the way they behave.
- The amount of control that the wider social framework into which individuals are born has over their lives.

THE IMPORTANCE AND ORIGINS OF CULTURE AND IDENTITY

The adoption of the topic of 'culture and identity' is a major theoretical and empirical development in contemporary sociology. One of the aims of this book is to demonstrate that sociology has, since its beginning and the work of its founders, been concerned with the relationship between the individual and society, the role of culture in social life, and how identity develops in a social context.

The study of culture and identity is not just within the domain of sociology, however: this book will also refer to psychology, biology, anthropology and the broader areas of cultural and media studies where these are relevant. Culture and identity are central issues for a number of academic disciplines.

However, as well as acknowledging the traditional roots of culture and identity in older theories, it is also important to pay attention to newer ideas. Hence this book will not consider only the ideas of Durkheim, Marx and Weber, but will also look at the theories that developed after their time (the interactionist schools, neo-Marxism, the various branches of feminism and the Frankfurt School), relating these older ideas to post-structuralism, postmodernism, the new right, structurational sociology, and the idea of reflexive modernity and the risk society, among other recent developments.

USING THE SKILLS OF SOCIOLOGY

Sociology is not just about having knowledge of, understanding and remembering ideas and concepts – though memory is, of course, an important aspect of revising for examinations. In order to be successful at sociology you have to be able to analyse debates and arguments, apply sociological and non-sociological ideas in appropriate ways, to interpret questions correctly and to develop the skill of evaluation – to be able to discuss both the strengths and weaknesses of the ideas contained within the sociological 'world view' after discussing the evidence and the claims made by the proponents of various theoretical positions. It involves a particular way of thinking about the world around you.

To help you develop these skills, practical exercises are provided in each chapter of this book. Each exercise is accompanied by symbols denoting the particular skill, or skills, it aims to help you develop:

- Knowledge Ⓚ
- Understanding Ⓤ
- Interpretation Ⓘ
- Application Ⓐ
- Analysis Ⓐⁿ
- Evaluation Ⓔ

Chapters conclude with a list of important concepts, an exam focus section and critical thinking questions.

EXAM FOCUS

The exam focus sections give you a range of sample essay questions. These provide you with an opportunity to apply your knowledge and understanding, and to develop your skills when responding to essay questions. See the exam guidance section in the Appendix of this book for further guidance on planning and writing essays.

STUDY GUIDANCE

As well as completing the exercises throughout the text, here are some suggestions to aid your use of the text and develop your sociological understanding:

- Compile a glossary of important terms and concepts to refer back to.
- Approach the text critically. Ask questions throughout. Discuss the issues raised with friends and colleagues.
- Note down research and theorists you would like to consider in more detail and then seek out the original texts.
- Reflect on your own experiences. Reflexive consideration will develop your skills as a sociologist.
- Be an active learner. Take a critical thinking question and ponder it as you go out for a walk, or talk to friends about it.
- When making notes, be creative. Compile summary tables, lists of key points, chapter summaries. Try using different coloured pens to highlight different skills. When evaluating, use red for weaknesses and green for strengths, use a different colour for research studies.
- Creating forms of spider diagrams for different topics gives you the opportunity to make links between different concepts, theories and ideas. Look at the visual 'concept map' for the class and consumption topic Figure 1.1 as a starting point and the guidance below on how to use them.
- Try to put research and theories in their social and historical context. Keep in mind when they were published and where research is conducted. For example, identity and culture in the twenty-first century has been influenced by global terrorist activity, the internet and instant global communications.
- Always give yourself time to think. This will help you to mentally organize the knowledge, and give it some structure, both of which will aid memory.

USING CONCEPT MAPS

The concept maps within the text aim to aid your understanding of key ideas within the historical and theoretical frame in which they were conceived. In addition, we hope they encourage you to make links between different theories and ideas. For example, the concept map for class and consumption (see Figure 1.1 and Chapter 11) enables you to make the links between, for example, the ideas of Marx on 'false idols' and postmodern analysis of consumption. Visual representations can help you to gain a clear overview of a topic and prompt you to summarize key ideas. Here are some suggestions for using concept maps:

- Copy and enlarge the maps and add summaries, dates, and make links between theories and ideas.
- Add strengths and weaknesses of theories and research in different colours.

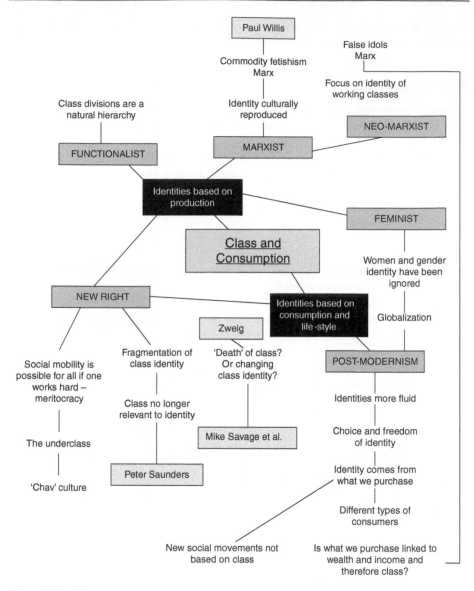

Figure 1.1   Class and consumption concept map

- Highlight central ideas.
- Use them to help you plan essay responses.
- Create a concept map for any idea or section of text you find challenging; the process of creating one and reflecting on which areas are most significant will deepen your understanding.
- If you are learn best when being creative, add cartoons and images.

- Chronological concept maps are useful to gain an overview of the developments of theories and ideas over time (such as the impact of feminism on gender identity in Chapter 12, or classical theory in Chapter 3).
- Create your own concept maps for other sections of the text – the bigger, the better (try using A1 size paper and sticking them on your wall when revising).

THE CONTENT OF THE BOOK

Chapter 2 introduces key issues in the study of culture and identity, plus the relevant definitions and concepts.

Chapters 3–6 outline various key theoretical perspectives that sociologists draw on to consider matters of culture and identity, including functionalism, Marxism, neo-Marxism, interactionist sociologies, late modernism and postmodernism, poststructuralism, feminisms and structurational sociology.

After this review of theory, Chapters 7–14 take these theories and apply them to related topics and debates, including mass culture, youth culture, work and class, gender, sexuality and the body, ethnicity, and nationality and globalization.

Chapter 2

Key Issues in the Study of Culture and Identity

After studying this chapter you should be able to:

- define the concepts of culture and identity
- evaluate the problems involved in the definition of the concepts of culture and identity
- understand why issues of culture and identity are of importance in sociology
- compare sociological and non-sociological ideas on culture and identity

INTRODUCTION

Consider for a moment how you came to be reading this book. Glad though we obviously are that you are reading it, the act of purchasing and reading a book is not as 'normal' or 'simplistic' as it might at first seem. Did you buy the book, or was it bought for you? Was it ordered by post, over the telephone or via the internet, or was it bought in a bookshop? Is it an electronic version? Was the book recommended to you by a teacher or lecturer? Are you expected to use it in lectures, lessons, or at home as part of your private study? Why are you studying this subject – assuming of course that you are not simply an interested reader, or even a teacher? Is it 'normal' or 'natural' to conduct one's life in this way? Why do we take these patterns of behaviour for granted in our day-to-day lives? Do we read books in order to obtain knowledge, pass an examination, help us get a job, earn money and so on? Could society – and therefore our lives – be organized in any other way?

By thinking about our lives in this way, we bring ourselves to the sociological study of what we call 'culture' and 'identity'.

WHAT IS CULTURE?

To start with a simple definition, culture means 'the way of life of a group of people'. In other words – how they live their lives. The patterns of social organization and the 'normal' ways in which we are expected to behave in society touch all aspects of our daily lives. It includes the customs, attitudes, beliefs, traditions and rituals of a society. However, we should not assume that all cultures are the same. For example, simply because social life, for us, happens to be structured in a particular way, does not mean that it *has* to be like this, nor that it was like this in the past – or is even like this in other societies around the world. Given its importance in every aspect of our social life, the concept of culture is central to the subject of sociology.

Exercise 2.1

Consider what we mean by the phrase 'way of life'. Copy out and complete the following table, and then answer the question that follows it.

Way of life on an average Sunday	
Myself	
Someone of my age living 100 years ago	
Someone living today who is elderly	
Someone living in a poor area of India	

How do 'ways of life' vary among cultural groups? Answer this question in about 300 words.

Now consider what you have done since you awoke this morning. Consider the reasons, or rather the 'motivations' – the 'meanings' – that lie behind the acts you have performed. Why do you behave as you do? Who says you should act as you do? How do you know how to behave? These questions relate to our culture and prompt other questions that are seemingly simple but sociologically vital:

- How is culture patterned?
- How is culture maintained?
- Who shares the same culture? Why?
- Do you have control over this? If not, who does?
- Why is culture as it is – could it be any different?

These questions run through the topic of 'culture and identity', and answers to them are to be found throughout this book. They are also fundamental to sociology in general and sociological theories in particular. The study of culture is therefore vital to sociology, and to our lives as a whole. Culture is part and parcel of all that we do, all that we are, and all that we can and might become. We shall return later to consider different attempts to define culture within sociology and other disciplines.

WHAT IS IDENTITY?

If culture is how we behave as a member of a group, then the word 'identity' relates to how we think about ourselves as people, how we think about other people around us, and what we imagine others think of us. 'Identity' means being able to 'fix' or 'figure out' who we are as people. Identity can be expressed through culture.

Exercise 2.2

Before reading any further, describe yourself in 100 words as you would to a stranger. This should be an informal introduction, as if you were meeting someone for the first time.

How have you defined yourself? Identify which characteristics are biological in nature (gender, age, appearance). Have you used any geographical characteristics to identify your-self (where you live, nationality, where you were born)? Have you referred to interests, leisure activities, employment or personal qualities? Any links to status, your role in a family, your marital status? What you have not mentioned is perhaps as important as what you have. Consider why some areas were omitted. Do you not see yourself in that way?

Exercise 2.3

Using the internet, find pictures of five different youth cultural groups – such as skinheads, heavy metal, indie-kids, nu-metal, punk, hip-hop, emo and so on. For each picture, describe how you think they see themselves – what you think their identity is, based on the cultural groups to which they belong. Consider to what extent their identity differs from yours. Describe each one in about 100 words.

Culture and identity are frequently linked – but they should not be seen as exactly the same. While our culture often establishes our sense of identity, or even identities (often people have more than one identity, while others may classify individuals' identity differ-ently from their self-concept, how individuals see themselves), sociologists usually separate the two concepts, with 'culture' representing the 'macro' pattern – the 'big picture' – and 'identity' representing the smaller, more 'micro' meanings we have as individuals.

Exercise 2.4

Look up the definition of 'culture' in any good English language dictionary. Take a note of all the different meanings this concept has – you might be surprised at how many there are! When you have completed your list of meanings, divide them into four types, according to the four ways in which the word 'culture' tends to be used:

1. Social scientific uses – these, as in sociology, tend to look at group behaviour and patterns	
2. Artistic uses	
3. Scientific uses	
4. Any others	

It is from the definitions in your first group that a sociological definition of the word 'culture' will come. Using these to help you, and the brief introductory discussion, write your own definition of the concept of 'culture'. Use your own words, and try to write a definition that you think might be of use to sociologists.

In his famous book, *The Sociological Imagination*, C. Wright Mills (1959: 5) writes:

The sociological imagination enables its possessor to understand the larger historical scene in terms of its meaning for the inner life and the external career of a variety of individuals... The sociological imagination enables us to grasp history and biography and the relations between the two within society. That is its task and its promise.

By 'the sociological imagination', Mills means that a key feature of all sociological thinking is the ability not to take ordinary life for granted – not to allow the culture we are brought up in to affect how we understand the world as sociologists. Yet while we should try to step back from our culture, sociology can help us to understand our own life better if we think in a detached fashion about how culture operates. We can, as sociologists, reflect on the function that culture performs for society, and therefore think about how it has shaped our own lives. Later in the same book, C. Wright Mills (1959: 6) suggests that 'No social study that does not come back to the problems of biography, of history and of their intersections within a society, has completed its intellectual journey.' Here we have a very clear statement about the key role that both culture and identity should have in sociology. Mills suggests that the task and purpose of sociology is to study the way in which individuals fit into the cultures that produce them, and that they themselves maintain and re-create over time.

We are thus shaped by culture: who we think we are – our 'identity' – is related to what society says we should do and be. During the course of our lives – our 'biography' – we should be able to look at what we do and how we behave, and attempt to see how our identities and the social structure, or culture, fit together. By 'biography' sociologists tend to mean the history of who we have become, and how we have become who we are – the process and experiences of socialization. One's self-identity or biography (who we think we are) is developed over a long period of time and seen by many sociologists as a resource: we can draw on it to determine how to act in particular situations. It is something we can reflect upon.

Exercise 2.5

Consider the ideas of C. Wright Mills above. Key features of the 'sociological imagination' are the ability to be critical about social life, and when studying it, to detach yourself from the values you have been brought up to believe in. Brainstorm why it is important for the sociologist to be as critical as possible about society. Is it possible for sociologists to detach themselves from their own values?

ATTEMPTS TO DEFINE CULTURE

The sociologist Raymond Williams (1983: 87), in his book *Key Words: A Vocabulary of Culture and Society*, says:

Culture is one of the two or three most complicated words in the English language. This is partly so because of its intricate historical development, in several European languages, but mainly because it has now come to be used for important concepts in several distinct intellectual disciplines and in several distinct and incompatible systems of thought.

From your work in Exercise 2.5, you may have already come to the same conclusion as Williams regarding the word 'culture'. While for sociologists 'culture' is often taken to mean 'the way of life of a group', this shorthand definition hardly does the concept justice, given that what it stands for is often regarded as a vital, if not the most vital, feature of all social life. For example, the 'way of life of a group' would need to include:

- The dominant values of a society.
- The views of smaller groups within society.
- The values that guide the direction that social change might take.
- Shared linguistic symbols (language).
- Religious beliefs.
- What is considered to be the correct way for people to behave in their day-to-day lives.
- What is considered to be the highest intellectual and artistic achievements of a group, including science, art, literature, music and so on.
- Formal behavioural traditions and rituals.
- Dominant patterns of living, including styles of architecture and patterns of land use.

As can be seen from this list, the way of life of a group – its culture – is the product of a massive social undertaking: the result of the collective, combined and interrelated efforts of all its members. The role taken by individuals is also important to consider.

Exercise 2.6

To explore the idea of what culture means in more detail, write a list of examples of each of the above characteristics of the 'way of life of a group'. Base your list on what happens in your own society at the moment.

To use the concept of culture in a detailed, precise and fruitful way we need to take our basic definition and expand it. Consider the following interpretations.

Culture as a 'system'

In this interpretation, culture is seen as the cement that bonds individuals together. It is made up of shared or collective symbols and it shapes our lives. It gives us the rules by which to live our lives. It hovers over us, structuring the world around us.

Exercise 2.7

One way of looking at culture is to see it as providing rules by which to live. In a group, write a list of your college/workplace rules. Then produce a written answer to each of the following questions:

1. Do you agree with your college/workplace rules? Why? Why not?
2. Does everyone follow the rules? What happens if they do not?
3. How do these rules create a shared 'identity' in the college/workplace?
4. How does the college/workplace encourage you to feel as though you belong to a group?

Culture as a 'map of meaning'

In this view, culture is what we carry around inside us, created by our interactions with others. It still provides us with symbols and rules, but we have a much more active role in its creation. Culture creates the world we live in. It also allows us to understand and interpret our own actions and the actions of others. These two interpretations of culture (culture as a system, and culture as a map of meaning) offer different yet related views on what culture is, what it does, and why it is important.

- Cultures allow us to build the reality we live in, usually through the meanings we give to symbols, passed down in language. Do we consciously choose these meanings?
- Cultures are shared and are also a form of constraint, since they pre-date those who are brought up in them. None the less, they are a 'human enterprise' – they exist because of humans.
- Culture allows us to interact with others, to share common meanings, patterns of behaviour and ways of communicating.
- Cultures exist both objectively and subjectively: they are objective because they are concerned with material things – they shape styles of dress, food, art, music and so on; and they are subjective because they are concerned with individuals' interpretations – they exist in the mind and allow us to make sense of the world around us.

Though culture is shared, in any given society there may be more than one culture or many small subcultures, the sum of which influences the individual. For many sociologists, humans are both cultural beings and social beings: we are shaped by our culture, and we shape it and perpetuate it in our day-to-day lives when we interact with others.

Exercise 2.8

In the eyes of many sociologists, culture creates a 'bond' between people in society. How might this be achieved? Write down as many examples as you can think of. To start you off, here are two examples:

- Culture gives shared rules.
- Culture provides a shared language.

A key question for sociologists and other interested commentators – such as sociobiologists, anthropologists and psychologists – is: to what extent does our culture constrain us? Or to put it another way: are humans the subjects of culture or do they have free will?

These questions are very profound and have preoccupied philosophers since the beginning of intellectual inquiry. In sociology we can make a very rough and simplistic division into two basic positions, between which a whole range of other views might exist (see Figure 2.1):

View one: 'structural sociology'	View two: 'action sociology'
Culture as constraint/order	Culture as meaning
Looks at the 'big picture' (macro/positivism)	Looks at the 'small picture' (micro/phenomenology)
Humans are subjects of society	Humans have 'agency', or free will
Humans are passive	Humans are active
Concerned with the wider system or social structure	More concerned with looking at action and interaction
Determinism (humans are made, or 'determined' by social forces)	Voluntarism (humans can think for themselves)
More interested in 'culture'	More interested in 'identity'

Figure 2.1   Two views of sociology

On the one hand we have a sociological view that sees humans as being manipulated by their culture, while the other view suggests that humans themselves manipulate their own identities in an active way. While these are extreme views, they are reflected in the differences between the structural sociology (View one) of perspectives such as functionalism and some forms of Marxism, and the action sociology (View two) of the various interactionist or interpretive schools of thought. These distinctions will be explored in more depth in later chapters, as will theories that attempt to bridge this divide and reflect on culture and identity in society today.

Exercise 2.9

Copy out the following passage and fill in the gaps with the words provided at the end.

Many sociologists have studied culture and how it operates in society, though they often ....its role in different ways. While it can be seen in different ways, it is usually regarded within sociology as a vital aspect of social.........– providing meaning,........., socialization and so on. For some, culture is what.........us together and constrains our actions – it is vital for the effective running of society, it is essential for social order. Others give more.........to humans and describe them as 'actors'. In this view, culture is created by.........in order to create a stable sense of reality in everyday life, full of meaning that is shared.

Missing words

• interpret • humans • reality • norms • free will • bonds

NON-SOCIOLOGICAL USES OF THE CONCEPT OF CULTURE

Since culture plays an important role in social life, the concept should have an equally important place in sociological study. There has been renewed interest in these ideas as a result of changes in the theories used by sociologists to make sense of society – in particular the rise of ideas known under the rather broad heading of 'postmodernism'. Postmodernists (see Chapter 7) argue that the traditionally accepted theories of sociology (and other disciplines) no longer apply in a society characterized by individual choice and diversity resulting from the wide range of beliefs, attitudes and identities on offer through the global media. Culture is characterized by 'choice'. Sociology is not, however, the only academic discipline to be interested in such ideas.

Biological explanations of identity

Biological explanations of identity (and to a lesser extent of culture) are often seen as being at odds with sociological explanations, believing firmly that identity comes from 'nature' as opposed to 'nurture'. Evolutionary theory within biology (sociobiology) and psychology explains our commitment to the group in terms of survival, and has the potential to explain our shared identity and cultural values. These are seen as being beneficial to the survival of the human race, or sections of it.

Biological theories, unsurprisingly, focus on our biological make-up, what we inherit, and how this impacts on our identity. Sociology can be seen as a challenge to the ideas of sociobiology. The latter, which dates back to the ideas put forward by Charles Darwin (1871) in *The Descent of Man and Selection in Relation to Sex* on the evolution of the human species, suggests that everything that humans do is the result of their biological make-up. As a species evolves, its biological needs may change, and therefore too might the culture of the species. For example, Tiger and Fox (1972) claim that social action is the direct result of the satisfying of pre-programmed biological needs and appetites. Equally, Desmond Morris (1968), a noted zoologist of whom you may have heard through his television documentary work, claims in his book, *The Naked Ape*, that while culture is a human creation and is shared, the need for culture is primarily the inbuilt biological need to continue the life of the group over time. In this sense, humans – the 'naked apes' – are no less animal-like than are other apes: our biology rules our culture. Our gender identity, and particularly different identities and roles for men and women, arising from our reproductive needs and priorities, is one example of a sociobiological explanation of identity.

An example of this type of theorizing is to be found in the work of Goldschmidt (1990), who claims that the human sense of self-identity, given by the cultures to which we belong, is the result of humans' neurophysical impulses and their drive for self-gratification. In other words, identity is a biological need to seek pleasure, to satisfy our own needs in order to survive, and we compete with others to do so. Evolutionary theory is applied within psychology to explain our commitment to the group, potentially our shared identity and cultural values. These are seen as beneficial to the survival of the human race, or sections of it.

(An)(E) | **Exercise 2.10**

Note down four strengths and four weaknesses of the sociobiological approach.

Anthropology

Anthropologists take a similar approach to sociologists in studying the world around them by focusing on specific societies or subcultures in detail. Traditionally, these cultures were viewed as 'developing' but in the world today anthropologists are working to understand urban subcultures in parts of Europe and the USA as much as they are in more isolated communities in Africa or Asia. For anthropologists, their focus is primarily on the role of culture and how it is learnt and relative to the individuals and the situation. They are keen to find out how people view their own culture and identity, and aim to see the world 'through the eyes of those who live it'. Cultures are seen to be created by their members, and because they may be based on different ideas compared to the researcher's about the world, the researcher should suspend his/her own beliefs, values and preconceptions.

The anthropologist Kate Fox, in *Watching the English* (2004: 2), uses participant observation 'to discover the hidden, unspoken rules of English behaviour, and what these rules tell us about our national identity'. She spent time participating in everyday experiences in pubs and train stations. While participating she consciously broke norms of behaviour – for example, by queue jumping and bumping into people, and observing how the people responded. Her goal was to understand what she calls the 'grammar' of Englishness, the underlying structures influencing behaviour. Fox is interested in 'some common core, a set of underlying basic patterns that might help us to define Englishness'. Thus, Fox (2004: 11) is interested in the micro level of everyday behaviour and action as well as relating this to the structure of British society – for example, social class. These experiments could be carried out in any society to 'reveal' the taken-for-granted rules. Do you think that it is possible for researchers to study the social world (particularly their own culture) objectively?

Psychological explanations of identity

A great deal of sociology and social anthropology seriously questions the notion that humans act according to instincts and in response to inborn stimuli. Psychology and sociology have generally taken very different paths to understanding identity. As Côté and Levine (2002: 11) note, 'In spite of their common roots...over the past several decades the psychological and sociological approaches to identity have constituted independent frameworks. Indeed, they have operated in virtual isolation from one another.'

Within psychology, identity has been looked at as an aspect of personality development in the work of Sigmund Freud (1856–1939), and Erik Erikson (1902–94) within social psychology. It has also been studied in terms of abnormality, focusing on individuals who have not developed an identity or personality, resulting in them being unable to function in society, which has been termed an 'identity crisis' (Erikson, 1970: 17). These theorists tend to see development in stages, with the formation of identity being one of these stages.

Pychoanalytic theory

The tradition of psychological thought known as 'psychoanalysis' looks at how instinct might affect how we think and act. This view, developed by Freud (1923), suggests that throughout life all human action is based on the interrelationship between natural biological needs and learnt social or cultural rules. Freud divided the human mind into three separate but interrelated elements: the id, the ego and the superego. The id represents humans as we naturally are – having biological drives that seek to maximize pleasure; in the ego we reflect on who we are and how we behave; and in the superego we learn to follow the cultural rules of the particular society in which we have been brought up.

Freud claimed that psychological disorders and problems result from culture and biology clashing in the individual's mind. Freud saw the tension between culture – or what he called 'civilization' – and natural needs and drives as often producing neuroses and 'perversions'. This is where humans act according to their unconscious biological needs, yet the culture they have learnt might define such behaviour as wrong or immoral. Erikson (1970) developed Freud's theory, and focused on the development of personality and identity (which he termed 'ego identity') over a lifetime. Ego identity is the sense of identity we hold that is developed through our interactions with others. He incorporated social and cultural aspects into his theory (partly a result of his own experiences of national and religious identity conflict in his youth) and anthropological research. Erikson is unusual in that respect. He developed his theory of identity concept in the 1940s and argued that people have a number of identities. Whereas identity used to be proscribed it is now chosen, leaving a childlike identity behind, and it forms a part of his stages of psychosocial development. Identity and a sense of self are developed primarily during adolescence. There is a marked difference between the identities of a child and an adult, moving from a time of powerlessness with lack of responsibility, to gaining power combined with the responsibilities of adulthood. Our identity is a mix of what we are born with and inherit, with what we learn from society around us. In our identities 'we see emerge a unique unification of what is irreversibly given – that is, body type and temperament, giftedness and vulnerability, infantile models and acquired ideals – with the open choices provided in available roles, occupational possibilities, values offered, mentors met, friendships made, and first sexual encounters' (Erikson, 1970: 15).

Without these things, we are likely to experience role confusion, meaning an uncertainty about our place in society and the world. When an adolescent is faced with role confusion, Erikson says he or she is suffering from an 'identity crisis'. Erikson points to many of the questions asked and issues faced by adolescents as being traced to a straightforward question of identity: 'Who am I?' Erikson's social psychological approach to identity is one mixing biological, evolutionary and social stimuli.

The social psychologist James Marcia (1966) extended Erikson's work and saw personality development as a progression through a continuum from childhood to adulthood, from the lack of maturity in childhood to making a commitment to a complex identity in adulthood. He focused on the development of different forms of identity deriving from our values, norms, occupation, religion, gender and relationships. An identity crisis refers to the stage where young people are re-evaluating their choices. There are obvious and specific links to the sociological study of culture and identity here, where sociologists look at the choices people make, whether these choices are free and made solely individually, or whether aspects of social structures are limiting their choices.

Henri Tajfel's (1982, 1986) social identity theory looked at how groups impact on social identity, focusing on structure and its effect on individuals in terms of identity. Individuals use group behaviour to develop their own identities. Tajfel recognized the interaction between individual and group identity and the structures of wider society (class, gender, ethnicity), and that people would search for a more satisfactory individual identity from the group. Tajfel tried to integrate an understanding of individual identity with the wider social picture of power, wealth and status, arguing that individuals would use groups to search for a better individual identity. Here, there is more of an integration with sociology, where social processes have to become part of individual identity formulation and development.

ⓀⓊ
ⒶⒶⁿ

Exercise 2.11

Identify which of the following statements are (a) sociological; (b) sociobiological; (c) psychoanalytic; (d) psychological; (e) anthropological; or (f) a combination of two or all three.

1. Culture exists because it is a product of how we behave as humans: it is natural.
2. Culture allows us to create a stable reality in which to act.
3. Humans are in a constant state of tension between learnt behaviour and natural instincts.
4. Society and culture are only real inasmuch as humans act as though they are real.
5. Culture bonds individuals to the group, but each group may have its own rules, customs and identity.
6. All cultures perform the same functions – even if they appear to be different in content – since they all serve human nature.
7. Identity development is a process, progressing in stages from childhood to adulthood.
8. The study of identity and culture is best done from the perspective of the individuals involved.

Are sociologists influenced by other disciplines?

The closest links in terms of theory and research are with social anthropology. Côté and Levine's (2002) critique of sociology and psychology as taking completely different paths reflects on the reality that the links between the study of identity are not fully established in the two disciplines. However, an increasing body of work, including their own, is now making the link. Within psychology, the closest links are with social psychology. The prominence of the scientific paradigm in psychology means that the two paths have not crossed as often as they could, or are likely to do in the future.

Though many sociologists take issue with Freud's notion of the id in respect of human biological instincts, some have been influenced by his ideas on the theme of civilization. In *Civilization and its Discontents* (1930), Freud argued that while humans, by their nature, seek pleasure (known as the 'pleasure principle'), many people in modern society are in fact unhappy. Freud asked why this should be, given that humans instinctually seek pleasure. The answer to this question lies in the idea of 'civilization' (or 'culture'): modern living has placed new demands on humans and set new rules for how they should live their lives. The rules of supposedly 'civilized' societies are in fact massive social constraints that lead to unhappiness – or 'discontents' – since they prevent people from acting in 'truly human' ways. This theme of civilization has influenced the work of some sociologists in very different ways.

What can sociologists studying culture and identity learn from psychology, biology and anthropology? Is it beneficial to study culture and identity in a cross-disciplinary way?

Norbert Elias

In his book, *The Civilizing Process* (originally written in 1939), Elias (1978) provides a history of how manners have changed and developed over time. Elias argues that manners are a clear indication of cultural tastes and standards, and that they provide a clear insight into the personalities and psychologies of the individuals who live in society in particular times, and who are expected to behave in particular ways. Elias's central thesis is that, as time goes by, society becomes increasingly more 'civilized'. There is increased pressure to conform to a larger set of rules, and this pressure changes and affects personality and identity. Elias argues that this evolutionary civilizing process has its modern expression in the regulation by the state of many aspects of day-to-day life. This view appears to reflect Freud's concern that modern life constrains the nature of the individual through cultural change. Elias uses the development of rules in sport as evidence for his views. Elias and Dunning (1986) suggest that the organization of both sport and government have experienced a similar and historically parallel cultural evolution away from violence and towards rules to control and outlaw violence.

The Frankfurt School: Herbert Marcuse

Many writers at the Institute of Social Research at Frankfurt University, Germany (established in 1923), adopted an interdisciplinary approach to social theorizing; that is, they combined the different ideas of various thinkers, including Karl Marx (see Chapter 3) and Freud. In *Eros and Civilization*, Herbert Marcuse (1969: 87) wrote, with the Second World War in mind:

> the fact that the destruction of life (human and animal) has progressed with the progress of civilization, that cruelty and hatred and the scientific extermination of men have increased in relation to the real possibility of the elimination of oppression – this feature of late industrial civilization would have instinctual roots which perpetuate destructiveness beyond all rationality.

This is a more pessimistic use of Freud's notion of civilization than that of Elias. For Marcuse, the so-called civilized culture of the modern age had simply resulted in technological developments meaning that humans could kill with ever-increasing efficiency. This pessimistic and critical view of science, technology and other aspects of the cultural 'civilizing process' was echoed in Max Weber's famous declaration that modern times would unleash an 'iron cage of bureaucracy' from which it would be very hard to escape. For Marcuse and other members of the Frankfurt School, civilization had resulted in capitalist exploitation of the masses and their alienation. The natural need of humans for pleasure-seeking had been stripped away by the factory – depriving them of their humanity in the search for profit by the capitalist class. Thus culture only serves the interests of the powerful, and in doing so it suppresses the instinctual human need for work as a source of pleasure, not profit – a key idea in the work of Marx himself. Marcuse's concern that culture and its developments – technology and science – might lead to further destruction as a result of the instinctual nature of humans is reflected in the work of Freud (1930: 18): 'The fateful question for the human species seems to me to be whether and to what extent their cultural development will succeed in mastering the disturbance of their communal life by the human instinct of aggression and self-destruction.'

SOCIALIZATION, NORMS AND VALUES

The learning of a culture – the process whereby the traditions of a community are passed down the generations – is known as 'socialization'. This process is usually seen as involving the transmission of the norms and values of a given culture.

- Norms are the culturally prescribed ways or patterns of behaviour that a society expects of its members. Going against the norm is usually referred to as 'deviant' behaviour.
- Values are the ends that 'normal' behavioural patterns attempt to achieve. For example, queuing for a bus in British society is a norm designed to achieve an 'orderly' society.

Exercise 2.13

Copy out the table below and complete it by listing some examples of norms and values in your day-to-day life. One example has been provided to start you off.

Examples of norms	Examples of values
1. We should queue for the bus.	1.
2.	2.
3.	3.
4.	4.
5.	5.
6.	6.
7.	7.
8.	8.

Exercise 2.14

Why is socialization important for (i) the individual, (ii) society, and (iii) how sociologists understand what goes on in society? Write your answers in a table copied from the one below.

The individual	Society	Sociology

Perspectives on socialization

Sociological perspectives differ in how they interpret the role of socialization in society. Whereas some sociologists emphasize the passivity of humans in the socialization of their culture, and regard individuals as 'cultural robots', others emphasize the more active part played by humans in the creation of the reality in which they live. The latter sociologists claim that humans are not subjects of society, but are endowed with 'agency'. To summarize:

- Functionalist sociologists tend to see socialization as a positive means by which to ensure that the individual conforms to the rules of the wider group (see Chapter 3).
- Marxist sociologists see socialization as a form of social control whereby the masses are expected to conform to dominant rules of the capitalist class (see Chapter 3).
- Interactionist sociologists see socialization as the process by which a symbolic set of meanings about what social reality is like for those involved come to be shared (see Chapter 4).
- In a more contemporary argument, Anthony Giddens' 'structurational sociology' suggests that while the existing culture is instilled in individuals through the socialization process, these same individuals contribute to the changing nature of this reality through their daily lives. For Giddens (1984) both structure and action should be combined if sociologists are to see the bigger picture of the relationship of the individual to society – to see how both cultural socialization and individual free will contribute to the lives of those in society (see Chapters 5 and 6).

Exercise 2.15

Identify the theoretical view associated with each of the statements (functionalists, Marxists, interactionists and structurational sociology):

Statement	Theoretical view
Culture is created by social actors, yet it also constrains them.	
Norms and values tell us how to live – we do not decide them, and we are punished if we do not follow them.	
Humans have agency or 'free will', they are not passive victims of culture.	
Individuals need to create a culture in order to interact with others.	
Culture and socialization are tools designed and used by the powerful to retain their dominance over society.	
Norms and values are created through a process of agreement.	
Socialization bonds individuals together.	

The nature versus nurture debate

When comparing the ideas of sociologists with those of biology and psychology we can glimpse a key intellectual debate within many disciplines in the social sciences – the 'nature versus nurture debate'. Central questions are:

- Are we the product of culture or instinct?
- Do we learn how to behave, or is behaviour inborn?
- What features of our identity relate to nature or nurture?

Exercise 2.16

Which aspects of our identity relate to nature or nurture? Complete the table below. To start you off, consider factors such as eye colour, sense of humour, nationality and so on.

Nature, Heredity, Environment	Nurture, Socialization	Potentially both nature and nurture

Within this debate we can identify two positions, as illustrated in Figure 2.2.

This debate is of central concern within sociology. Even if individual sociologists disagree over whether cultural constraint is positive or negative, all-embracing or limited, they all tend to favour the idea of culture over instinct, and focus on the idea of socialization. We shall return to a more detailed discussion of socialization in Chapter 5.

Feminism and 'being a woman'

Early feminist thinker and philosopher Simone de Beauvoir wrote in her book, *The Second Sex* (1972: 295; first published 1953) that 'One is not born, but rather, becomes a woman.' What this means is that women are taught how to behave; that what we understand by 'femininity' is the product of culturally learnt behaviour rather than the result of biological

| Nature
This position is held by biologists, some psychologists, sociobiologists | Nurture
This position is held by sociologists, anthropologists (although in different ways) and some psychologists |
| --- | --- |
| Action is inborn | Action is learnt/taught |
| Instincts shape culture | Culture is learnt and therefore changes and varies a great deal between societies |
| Behaviour is pre-programmed | Behaviour is socialized (learnt) |
| Known as 'biological determinism' | Known as 'social determinism' |

Figure 2.2   The Nature versus Nurture debate

pre-programming. This inspired a key theme in feminist thinking: that men and women might be biologically different in terms of their reproductive organs (their 'sex'), but the behavioural differences between men and women (called 'gender') are cultural creations, and can therefore be challenged and eventually changed. Feminist views on the divide between 'sex' and 'gender' – between nature and culture – places feminist thought in direct opposition to the claims made by sociobiologists.

Ⓤ①
Ⓐ⒜

Exercise 2.17

The following statements are traditionally associated with either masculinity or femininity. Copy out the table and identify which statement is associated with masculinity and which with femininity.

Statement	Traditionally associated with masculinity or femininity?
Over-emotional	
More interested in sex than in love	
Concerned about their appearance	
Unable to make decisions	
Caring	
Good leaders	
Better at solving problems	
Better at making objects/products	
Physically strong	

Sociobiological ideas on the superiority of nature over nurture continue to this day, especially among some in the social scientific community, despite many years of feminist intellectual thought. Steve Jones (1994), in his book, *The Language of the Genes*, suggests that what we often call the 'battle of the sexes' is not only real but is also rooted in the human genetic code: it is a fundamental feature of all animal species and is the basis of many features of evolution. Jones argues that conflicts over sex are behind all human society:

▨ Males and females are the result of a complex biological conflict within the womb of the biological mother.
▨ There is conflict between men to find a sex partner; and equally between women to find a sex partner.
▨ Men and women themselves conflict in society since they seek different things from life.

While Jones warns against comparing humans too closely with animals, he stresses that the fact that humans are animals should not be forgotten: nature is still more important than nurture (also see Buss, 2003). It is this type of argument against which many feminist thinkers protest. To state that the social and behavioural differences between men and women are natural is to justify male dominance and female subordination – known as 'patriarchy'.

Understanding the individual and society

Many modern sociological thinkers have suggested that the central issue or problem for sociological study is the relationship between the individual and society. In other words, the point of much sociological inquiry is to investigate the following questions:

- How is collective culture possible, given that we are all individual beings?
- How is individuality possible, given that we share a common culture?
- Or, to use the terms used previously in this chapter, how does structure – the social system – control individuality?

In the words of Margaret Archer (1995: 1), 'Necessarily then, the problem of the relationship between individual and society was the central sociological problem from the beginning. The...task of understanding the linkage between "structure and agency" will always retain this centrality because it derives from what society intrinsically is.' This means that studying both culture and identity is vital for the sociologist:

- Studying culture allows an insight into the bigger picture, the social structure, how society is patterned and is thought of as a 'thing' by those who live in it.
- Studying identity, or rather identities, allows us to think about the meaningful role of humans as thinking beings who make up society.

Issues of 'structure' and 'action' or 'agency' have been the focus of much sociology since its foundation. This is because, as Archer states above, of this being the prime concern of many early sociologists. For example, Bryan Turner (1984) suggests that early sociologists such as Émile Durkheim (see Chapter 3) operated with a view of the individual and society in which humans were seen as a product of natural desires that needed to be controlled by culture – not dissimilar, perhaps, from some of the themes that run through the work of Freud. 'Since man is both a member of nature by virtue of being an organism and a member of society by virtue of culture, some solution has to be found to this Jekyll-and-Hyde duplexity' (Turner, 1984: 52). Turner suggests that, just like Freud and his psychoanalytic theory, many founding sociologists – including Durkheim (1982) – were interested in the possible tensions between 'nature' and 'culture':

- For Freud, if culture prevents people behaving according to their nature this may lead to many psychological problems for the individual.
- For Durkheim, the function of culture is to act as a vital form of social constraint, keeping the individual bonded to the wider social group by suppressing the natural desire for individuality.

As Durkheim argued in his classic text, *The Elementary Forms of the Religious Life* (1982; originally published in 1912), 'Man is double. There are two beings in him: an individual being … and a social being which represents the highest reality in the intellectual and moral order that we can know by observation – I mean society.'

EVALUATING THE CONCEPT OF CULTURE: THREE PROBLEMS

Problem 1: Value judgement

In *The Myth of Mass Culture*, Alan Swingewood (1977, p. 26) suggests that 'Culture is not a neutral concept; it is historical, specific and ideological.' What Swingewood means by this is that, when using the concept of culture we must be sure to consider whether all sociologists take the word to mean the same thing, even if they are using it in a similar way. Sociologists tend to look at the social world in different ways and therefore draw some very different conclusions. Often the concept of culture (like many others in sociology) has a political orientation or value judgement attached to its use. For example, whereas functionalists might see culture as vital since it bonds social members together, Marxists might see it as a mechanism by which some groups maintain power over others. We should therefore be very careful when considering any sociological debate to ask ourselves the following question: what political values are used by this thinker, and how might this affect how he or she sees the world?

Exercise 2.18

The next chapter (Chapter 3) deals in more detail with different theoretical interpretations of culture and identity (we shall also return to the subject later on in this chapter). For the time being, think about the two theoretical interpretations of culture raised in the text above:

- Culture as social bond.
- Culture as social control.

For each of the two, describe in writing how culture might act in this way. Then state which interpretation you favour the most and explain why. Complete this exercise in about 300 words.

Problem 2: Choosing between cultures

When discussing the role of culture in society, and in particular when comparing different cultures and subcultures, sociologists tend to adopt one of two positions.

First, one might believe there are absolute standards of taste, and that some values are better than others. According to this view, some cultures and subcultures are better, more elite or more advanced/developed than others because they are based on higher standards. This absolutism often leads to quite controversial political positions, since if one culture is judged to be better than another, should the lesser culture be taught better values? In the past this argument was used to justify the Western world's colonial expansion and even slavery. It also has parallels in modern forms of racism (and even ethnic cleansing in modern Eastern Europe), where one group of people object to another group simply because they have different values. It is problematic to 'prove' in an objective fashion that one set of cultural ideas are better than another, since who is to say which cultural values are superior, and on what basis is the judgement made?

Second, the political and moral problems involved in valuing some cultures above others has led many sociologists to adopt a more relativistic position when thinking about and comparing cultures. In this view, no single culture is 'correct' – rather, different cultures are simply different and should be tolerated as such. However this relativist position also raises many political and moral questions: if a culture is based on the oppression of a minority group, should we still value that culture as much as one based on tolerance and freedom? Or are we simply judging other cultures by standards that should not be applied to them?

Problem 3: The myth of cultural integration

Archer (1996), echoing some of Raymond Williams' (1963) concerns about the word 'culture', suggests that the concept suffers from two main problems in modern sociological thought:

- The concept is too vague: there are too many unclear definitions and it means different things to different thinkers.
- The concept is interpreted by thinkers in two very different, extreme ways: either as a supreme power ruling over all and controlling all actions; or as shared meanings which individuals have the power to manipulate as they wish.

Archer suggests that modern sociology should clarify what it means by culture, and what it thinks culture does. It is time to think again about the classical problem of the relationship of the individual to society. Archer argues that this problem stems from a wider problem, which she calls the 'myth of cultural integration'. What she means by this is that while the various sociological theories interpret the role of culture in society differently, they all agree that culture is unifying, bonding everyone together into an integrated whole. Archer suggests that this assumed integration is a core myth of sociology, and it is a myth that has been perpetuated over time by many different sociologists and types of sociological theory: Marxism, functionalism and interactionism, to name but a few, though they use the idea of integration in different ways. We shall be considering the role of conflicting and competing subcultures in Chapter 9.

| Exercise 2.19 |

Archers' ideas are important for two reasons:

- They identify a key theme that runs through the whole of sociology.
- They serve as a good criticism of the idea that we are all 'swamped' by our culture and are totally integrated into it.

Since her ideas are quite difficult to understand at first, re-read the above passage and carry out the following tasks:

1. Write out Archer's ideas in your own words (approximately 100 words).
2. Describe how Archer's ideas can be seen as a criticism of functionalism and Marxism (approximately 100 words).

UNDERSTANDING THE CONCEPT OF IDENTITY: DO NOT LOSE SIGHT OF THE INDIVIDUAL

When we, as sociologists, talk about the culture of a whole society and about the subcultures of the smaller groups who make up this whole, we are in danger of losing sight of the role of the individual in society. In order to consider what individuals themselves think – both about themselves and about others – sociologists employ the concept of 'identity': the characteristics of thinking, reflection and self-perception that are held by people in society.

Defining identity

A useful starting point when thinking about what 'identity', or rather 'social identity' might mean, is to view it as simply being able to 'know who you are'.

Exercise 2.20

Consider the paragraph you wrote in Exercise 2.2 outlining your identity. Review what you wrote then. Why is it important to know who you are?
  Now ask a friend to write a similar paragraph. Compare your notes.

1. How similar and how different are they?
2. What do you consider to be important to 'who you are as a person'?

Knowing who you are is a massive undertaking, requiring great mental reflection and contemplation, yet most of us probably 'know who we are'. That this can happen, that humans have a sense of who they are as people, can be seen as vital for all social life. Without knowing who I am, how can I begin to understand what I do, and therefore what others around me do?

Richard Jenkins (1996: 5) takes this theme of 'knowing who we are' further and defines social identity as:

> our understanding of who we are and of who other people are, and, reciprocally, other people's understanding of themselves and of others (which includes us). Social identity is, therefore, no more essential than meaning; it too is the product of agreement and disagreement, it too is negotiable.

Jenkins suggests that social identity is so important to society that social life is unimaginable without it: we simply need to know who we are:

> Whether in the abstract or the concrete, with reference to ourselves or to others, in personal depth or during superficial casual chat, with reference to individuality, nationality, social class, gender or age … it seems that we cannot do without some concepts with which to think about social identity, with which to query and confirm who we are and who others are … Without frameworks for delineating social identity and identities, I would be the same as you and neither of us could relate to the other meaningfully or consistently. Without social identity, there is, in fact, no society. (Ibid.: 6)

Identity as an active construction

What is important about Jenkins' definition is his claim that identity is negotiable. The importance of the concept of identity for modern sociology is that it allows us to see humans as active, thinking beings, rather than the passive victims or 'robots' of the culture that controls them.

It is possible to distinguish between three related but subtly different forms of identity:

- *Individual identity*. Though in one sense this sort of identity is social since it is believed by many to be created through social interaction with others, individual identity is the unique sense of personhood held by each social actor in her or his own right.
- *Social identity*. By 'social identity' many sociologists mean a collective sense of belonging to a group, of individuals identifying themselves as being similar to or having something in common with the other members of the group.
- *Cultural identity*. This concept refers to a sense of belonging to a distinct ethnic, cultural or subcultural group.

Exercise 2.21

Some sociologists think that we cannot act as we wish to – that we do not have free will or the right to make choices. Others insist that we are not controlled by society and are free to make choices. Which view do you find the most realistic, and why?

1. List the situations in society where you are free to make choices (for example, choosing your own clothes, but is this true in all societies?).
2. Now list the situations where you can make choices but they are very limited (for example choosing a school for your children).
3. Now make a final list of situations where you are forced to act in a certain way and have no choice in the matter (for example, conforming to the law or religious rules).
4. Which is the longer list? Write down what you think this might mean for the degree of freedom you do or do not have as a member of your society.

Stuart Hall (1990: 222) notes that 'Identity is not as transparent or un-problematic as we think. Perhaps instead of thinking of identity as an already accomplished fact, which the new cultural practices then represent, we should think, instead, of identity as a "production", which is never complete'. This image of a moving, fluid and dynamic identity is far removed from the idea held by some of the more traditional schools of sociological thought that humans are 'subjects of culture'. In Hall's view, identity is as much a process of becoming, as it is about what one is.

Identity and 'difference'

In 'knowing who we are' we not only call up notions of 'similarity' with others, but also notions of 'difference' from others. By noting that difference is as important an aspect of identity as similarity, we are able to draw an important distinction between what Kathryn Woodward (1997) refers to as 'essentialist' and 'non-essentialist' definitions of identity:

- *Essentialist definitions*. Such definitions suggest that each ethnic/cultural group has an absolute and rigidly fixed set of historical characteristics that make up its identity and are shared by all members of the group. Furthermore, each cultural identity has one important and essential defining characteristic.
- *Non-essentialist definitions*. These focus on the characteristics shared by those in an ethnic/cultural group and the differences within the group – and between this group and others. These definitions also take into consideration the fact that identities change over time.

Imagined communities and postmodernism

Identity has been taken to mean 'knowing who one is' – having a sense of similarity with some people and a sense of difference from others. Because of the instilling of cultural values, we can speak of identity as giving one a sense of belonging to a 'symbolic community' or an 'imagined community'. As Anthony Cohen (1989) argues, the notions of 'community' that give rise to a sense of identity cannot be plotted on a geographical map, nor can a community be understood as a common group of people controlled by the same state. Instead, the identification with a community is largely a symbolic process. It is based not on territorial lines but on the establishment of shared sets of meaning, the use of which enables people to act and interact with others, and with whom they can identify.

Some sociologists and philosophers, under the banner of post-modernism, claim that, in the contemporary age, identities are changing and are very different from those in the past. Postmodern writers – and writers who reject some of the claims of postmodernism, such as Anthony Giddens (1991) – have suggested that identities are become increasingly freer, more ambiguous and plural in the postmodern age (see Chapters 5 and 6). Many postmodernist writers suggest that the 'master identities' (as David Harris, 1996, calls them) of class, age, gender and ethnicity are 'decomposing': they are falling away, to be replaced by new identities based on a whole range of sources, including consumerism, the body and sexuality.

Exercise 2.22

Either enlarge on a photocopier or draw your own version of the concept map on understanding culture and identity (see Figure 2.3). Using this chapter to help you, add definitions and explanations of all terms and concepts you are not familiar with. Add the names of the following theorists and terms to the appropriate sections of the concept map. This will be a useful aid to your memory and a visual representation of the key issues when defining culture and identity.

- Margaret Archer
- Émile Durkheim
- Norbert Elias
- Anthony Giddens
- Richard Jenkins
- Herbert Marcuse

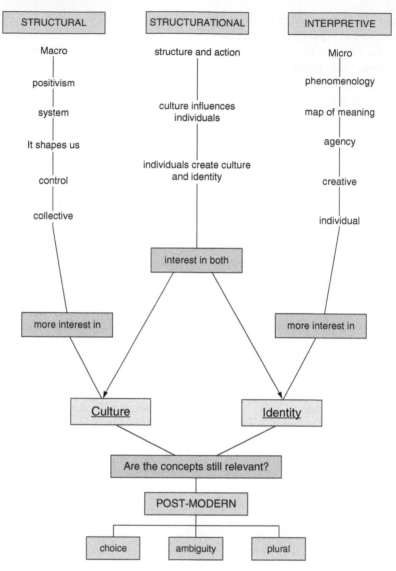

Figure 2.3 Understanding culture and identity concept map

CONCLUSION

Culture and identity have been key issues in sociology since its inception. They allow sociologists to discuss who we think we are and how we behave as individuals and groups. The concept of culture allows us to explain how and why different societies behave in different and unfamiliar ways. It also allows us to think about what it means to be human – are we the product of biology or of socialization? Do we have free will or are we subjects of our culture? In what way are humans 'symbolic creatures'?

When discussing culture and identity we can engage in a debate with the 'ghosts' of the founders of sociology. We can look at the ideas that led to the birth of the subject and at the newer ideas that challenge many of the assumptions held by the founders. This postmodern challenge to the traditional sociology of identity will be explored later in this book, but first we need to consider how classical sociology and its founders viewed culture and identity.

Important concepts

Culture • Identity • Macro • Micro • Nature • Norms • Nurture • Relativism • Socialization • Subculture • Values

---

Exam focus

(a) How important is socialization for human societies?
(b) Evaluate the usefulness of the idea of 'culture' in helping us to understand the role of the individual within society.
(c) Assess the view of Jenkins (1996) that social identity is so important to society that social life is unimaginable without it: we simply need to know who we are, 'without social identity, there is, in fact, no society'.

Critical thinking

1. What implications does the concept of 'culture' have for how we behave as humans?
2. Are we born 'ready-made' as humans, or do we learn to become human?
3. Is it possible for sociologists to step back from their own culture to study it objectively?
4. Does culture enhance our lives, or can it limit them?
5. Does the internet and global media and communications technology mean that a global culture now exists?

Chapter 3

Classical Views on Culture and Identity

After studying this chapter you should:

- be familiar with the classical/founding ideas of Marx and Durkheim
- be able to discuss the importance of the ideas of Marx and Durkheim to a modern sociology of culture and identity
- be able to apply functionalist and Marxist ideas to the modern world
- be able to evaluate functionalism and Marxism

INTRODUCTION

The French thinker, Auguste Comte (1798–1857), writing in the mid-1800s, is credited with coining the term 'sociology' to describe the scientific study of society. However, the modern discipline with which we are familiar owes a great deal to the legacy of another three key thinkers, known collectively as the 'founders': the German political philosopher and economist, Karl Marx (1818–83); the French sociologist, Émile Durkheim (1858–1917), who was influenced by Comte's version of sociology; and the German social historian, Max Weber (1864–1920), whose intellectual legacy we shall discuss in Chapter 4. Another important influence who has until recently been ignored in analyses of the founding figures of sociology is Harriet Martineau (1802–76) who translated Comte's text 'Positive Philosophy' into English in 1855 and wrote on gender inequality.

When first conceived, sociology was both macro (looking at the 'big picture') and scientific in nature. It was concerned with studying the whole of social life: society was seen as a living, growing system made up of parts or elements that all contributed towards the whole in some way. The study of such a system, in order to understand the larger structure and pattern, was originally intended by Comte and Durkheim to be scientific in nature. This early sociology was known as 'positivism' – a term that still exists today. As Comte (1957: 3) suggested in *A General View of Positivism*, first published in France in the mid-1800s, 'The primary object ... of Positivism is two-fold: to generalize our scientific conceptions, and to systematize the art of social life.'

From its earliest days, the purpose of sociology was to understand how society operates as a whole in order to help society itself to progress and develop further. According to Comte, his sociology was both philosophy and polity: both a scientific intellectual endeavour and a means of suggesting ways forward to policy-makers. This sociology was born out of the Industrial Revolution and the general personal, moral and intellectual upheavals this dramatic social change left in its wake.

Marx suggested that his particular system of intellectual thought (he would not have used the word 'sociology' himself) was a scientific means by which to understand the key currents of social change that move the whole structure of society through history. As Marx noted in one of his numerous letters, the work by Darwin on the evolution of the human species (see Chapter 2) 'serves me as a natural scientific basis for the class-struggle in history' (Marx, quoted in Beer, 1985: 51). Equally, standing at Marx's grave at Highgate, London, in 1883 Friedrich Engels – Marx's friend and intellectual companion – said, 'just as Darwin discovered the law of development of organic nature, so Marx discovered the law of development of human history' (Engels, quoted in Kumar, 1986). Marx believed, like Comte, that intellectual study of the ways in which societies evolve and develop could be used to improve the nature of society. However, the two writers drew very different conclusions as to how society could best be helped, given their very different political value judgements.

Exercise 3.1

The ideas of Marx and Durkheim are central to modern sociology and they influenced many sociologists who came after them. In a two-column table, list what you can remember from your studies so far of the ideas of Marx (column 1) and Durkheim (column 2).

The 'classical sociology' of the founders had the following key features:

- A belief in social progress.
- An image of society as a system.
- The view that societies evolve through history.
- The idea that sociology can understand and solve social problems by scientific means.

These features have been labelled 'modernist', since the founders believed that modern industrial society represented the end achievement of all human history: the ultimate social progression.

Exercise 3.2

Sociology was born at the time of what historians refer to as the 'Industrial Revolution', which brought about major social change. Conduct some research on the Industrial Revolution using history books, other sociology books, the internet and any other sources.

1. Take some notes on what happened.
2. How do you think this social change might have influenced the origins of sociology?

Modernist scientific sociology, which looked at the overall pattern of society as a system, and at how structures controlled the individual, might seem far removed from the study of culture and identity. But this is not the case. Within these classical traditions of early sociological thought we find the basis of all of modern sociology. Most, if not all, contemporary thinkers have felt the need to 'debate with the ghosts of the founders'. Whether or not such debate might lead to agreement with the classical ideas, modern sociology owes a huge debt to the ideas of Marx and Durkheim, and their views on culture and identity. However, many of today's thinkers believe that society has moved on and changed in significant ways that were not foreseen by the founders, and that this social change has discredited a great deal of what the founders represented. Some of these critics of the founders' 'modernity' use the term 'postmodern' for their particular type of theorizing. Through the use of this term they are trying to indicate that profound change has recently taken place, especially with regard to culture and identity (see Chapter 7).

INTRODUCING TWO CLASSICAL VIEWS ON CULTURE

By studying first Durkheim and then Marx it is possible to identify two 'classical' or 'modernist' interpretations of the role that culture plays in social life – both from a position of structural sociology.

Interpretation 1: Émile Durkheim

- Culture bonds the individual to the wider group through the socialization process.
- Culture keeps potentially disruptive individuality at bay.
- A collective group identity is more important than an individual identity for society to 'work' in a state of consensus.
- Collective identity and culture are necessary for social order to be established and maintained.

Exercise 3.3

The ideas of Durkheim are essential to sociology, despite the fact that they were written a long time ago. Rephrase the above list in your own words, in detail.

Interpretation 2: Karl Marx

- Culture – or 'ruling ideas and values' – is produced by a ruling group in order to justify its dominance over others.
- Culture acts as a constraint on the individual, leading to social order and control.
- Individuals must realize their true class identity to enable them to break free from ruling-class oppression.

▓ Class consciousness and identity lead to revolutionary social change, and to the creation of a new social type and a new social culture.

Ⓤ① Ⓐ

Exercise 3.4

Like those of Durkheim, Marx's ideas are still essential to sociology. Rephrase the above list in your own words, in detail.

ⓀⓊ ⒶⒺ

Exercise 3.5

On the basis of the ideas presented so far in this chapter, and your answers to Exercises 3.3 and 3.4, which theory do you think is the most realistic – that of Durkheim or that of Marx? To help you decide, complete the table below.

List the ideas of Durkheim that you find most satisfactory.	List the ideas of Marx that you find most satisfactory.
1	1
2	2
3	3
4	4
5	5
Explain why:	Explain why:
What do you find unsatisfactory about the ideas of Durkheim?	What do you find unsatisfactory about the ideas of Marx?
Which of the two theories do you prefer, and why?	

The ideas of Durkheim and Marx: similarities and differences

Similarities

- Both Durkheim and Marx adopted a structural position – they saw society as a system made up of smaller parts.
- They both saw society as characterized by the existence of order, control and the constraint of individuals.
- Individuals were viewed as being less important than groups.
- Individuals were seen as the 'puppets' of culture.

Differences

- Whereas Durkheim saw order as a necessary part of society, Marx believed that order was established through unequal power relations between the ruling class and the masses.
- Durkheim saw individual identity as a 'problem' (that is, it was disruptive) for the group to solve so that order and harmony could continue, whereas Marx thought that individual identity should be replaced by class identity so that class groups could overthrow the oppressive ruling elite through revolutionary struggle and conflict.
- Both believed that the social structure controlled the individual through the socialization of values, but for Durkheim this was a positive situation, whereas for Marx it was a negative one.

Ⓚ Ⓤ
Ⓘ

Exercise 3.6

Copy the following table and decide for each statement whether Marx, Durkheim or both would be most associated with it.

Statement	Marx, Durkheim or both?
a. Culture is a form of constraint	
b. Elite rules and values lead to power inequality in society	
c. Identity is most associated with one's role in the productive process and the economy	
d. People need to be bonded together	
e. Culture is a form of social control	
f. Cultural constraint is necessary for society	
g. Culture is a form of social cement	
h. Culture exists as a structure over and above individuals	
i. Without culture there will be chaos	
j. Culture is simply a reflection of the rules of the powerful	

We shall now consider these two views in more detail, as well as more recent expressions of these ideas.

VIEW ONE: CULTURE AS ORDER – FUNCTIONALISM

While it is universally accepted that Émile Durkheim was the founder of the functionalist movement in sociology, there is much debate over how we should 'read' or interpret his ideas. Much of what English-speaking sociologists know of Durkheim comes from the translations by Talcott Parsons (1951) (this is also true of the ideas of Max Weber). There is considerable disagreement over whether Parsons' interpretation of Durkheim is the 'correct' one, or whether Parsons understood Durkheim only within the context of the 1950s American society in which he was living.

In current sociology there is great debate over the contemporary and future relevance of Durkheim's ideas and the wider theory of functionalism. Whereas some see the rise of Marxist theories in the 1970s, feminism in the early 1980s and postmodern ideas in the 1990s as evidence of the death of functionalism, others point to the rise of what have been known as New Right and New Left ideas (from the 1970s onwards, so not 'new' in the twenty-first century), which have points of comparison with some functionalist ideas and can even be seen as neofunctionalism (new functionalism).

Functionalism before Durkheim

The term 'functionalism' – or as it is sometimes known, 'structural functionalism' – was coined in the 1950s, but the label covers the work of a wide range of thinkers who preceded or followed Durkheim: the anthropologist Bronislaw Malinowski, Talcott Parsons and the nineteenth-century English sociologist Herbert Spencer. Like Marx, Spencer was influenced by Darwin's theory of evolution, although in a very different sense. Marx was interested in the evolution of class struggle and conflict, while Spencer was interested in how society as a living, growing 'organic' whole slowly developed and became more complex with the onset of industrialization. In fact, the phrase 'survival of the fittest', which is often credited to Darwin, was actually first used by Herbert Spencer himself.

Spencer asked 'What is a society?' in his book, *The Principles of Sociology* (2003, first published in 1898. His answer (and others like it) was couched in terms of an 'organic analogy', where society was compared to a living creature: usually a human body – a highly modernist image. Spencer claimed that society is like a living body since it is more than simply the sum of its parts. The combination of all the components of society, and how they fit together, is more important than the components themselves. This is also true of the human body. Individually, the parts of a body can do nothing, but combined in the right way they work together to maintain the whole. This is what we mean by a 'system'.

Exercise 3.7

Spencer (and Durkheim) claimed that society is like a body, in that both society and the body have basic needs that must be fulfilled. Draw up a two-column table and list what you think are the basic needs of the body (column 1) and the basic needs of society (column 2). Try to identify six examples of each.

Spencer suggests that society is a living thing, as it:

- Grows in size (this was especially true with the arrival of industrialization).
- Develops additional component parts over time ('differentiation').
- Each separate part of the whole develops and performs a specific function or task for the whole.
- The various parts are mutually dependent on each other – they are of no use on their own.

Exercise 3.8

Further to your answer to Exercise 3.7, how might culture meet the needs of society? Draw up a list, then compare your list with that of someone else.

Exercise 3.9

Spencer (and a number of others since him) viewed society as a huge, interlinked entity where individuals are controlled by wider forces. How realistic is this notion? Draw up a list of the weaknesses of this 'organic analogy'.

Since all the parts of the living system of society fit together and perform a function for the whole, order and solidarity (being 'bonded together') are vital to the smooth operation of the system. Culture is that which cements individuals to the whole, a form of 'social glue', through the socialization of norms and values and a collective identity. Individualism is potentially damaging to such a system. Spencer's 'organic analogy' has been taken up by other writers, including Durkheim.

The historical context of Durkheim's work

To understand Durkheim's views on the orderly function of culture – the key feature of his sociology – we must think for a moment about the sort of society in which Durkheim lived. Not only was Durkhiem's sociology instrumental to the creation of modernist sociology, but Durkheim the person was the product of the rapidly developing modernity of the French society around him.

As Colin Sumner (1994) notes, a number of key social events occurred in France in Durkheim's time:

- The governmental system was changing and the Third Republic was established.
- The early stages of industrialization were taking place.
- This industrialization was followed by a period of economic depression.
- France was rapidly expanding as a colonial power.
- French culture (art, music, literature and so on) was flourishing.
- The death sentence for criminals (public execution by guillotine) was replaced by more 'humane' imprisonment.

According to Sumner, 'the old sat uneasily with the new. Times were changing and consequently so were ways of seeing' (1994:8).

Exercise 3.10

It is often useful to consider sociologists themselves as people who live in society and are therefore influenced by what happens around them. Look again at the list of changes that took place in France during Durkheim's lifetime. How do you think these might have influenced his ideas? Make a table with the following heading, and respond to the six bullet points above.

How might these historical events have influenced Durkheim's views on the nature of society?

In light of the above, Durkheim's views on the relationship between culture, social order and the individual can only be understood by considering Durkheim as a theorist of social change.

Exercise 3.11

Like Durkheim, Marx lived in a period of change and this probably influenced his ideas. With the help of history books, biographies and the internet, investigate the period in which Marx was writing and draw up a list of the historical changes you think would have most influenced his sociological ideas.

Durkheim: looking at order in a time of social change

Durkheim can be seen as trying to provide a solution to what is known as the 'Hobbesian problem of order'. This 'problem', first posed by the English philosopher Thomas Hobbes, asks: how is order possible, given that by nature humans are greedy, competitive and do not live in harmony with each other? Durkheim answered this question by turning his thoughts to the role that culture plays in society: culture socializes the individual into the group, and in so doing creates social order. We might suggest that Durkheim was directed to think about the problems of order because French society, at the time when he was writing, was experiencing rapid social change.

Exercise 3.12

How might identity be threatened by social change? Present your answer to this question as a list of examples.

Durkheim suggested that the socialization process instils a 'conscience collective' in the minds of the social group. This is made up of 'collective representations': shared norms and values that place special significance on the group, and in so doing create a group identity. According to Durkheim (quoted in Giddens, 1972: 228):

> When individual minds are not isolated, but enter into close relation with, and act upon, each other, from their synthesis arises a new kind of psychic life. It is clearly distinct from that led by the solitary individual because of its unusual intensity. Sentiments created and developed in the group have a greater energy than purely individual sentiments.

Identity and the group

In *The Elementary Forms of the Religious Life* (1982; originally published in 1912), Durkheim suggested that group rituals are essential for the socialization process to work. He claimed, using ideas on the psychology of crowd behaviour borrowed from fellow French thinker, Gustave Le Bon, that group membership creates the psychologically correct atmosphere for the successful socialization of cultural norms and values. In such situations – for example, tribal religious ceremonies – individuality is submerged in a collective sense of identity.

Exercise 3.13

Durkheim's views on group identity can be applied to many more groups than the religious groups in his own example. Consider the supporters at a football match. How do the home team's supporters identify themselves as a group, separate from the opposing team's supporters? Discuss your ideas with someone else and draw up a list of your answers.

Durkheim argued that a 'division of labour' exists in modern social life, which has changed significantly as a result of industrialization. A division of labour is when tasks are divided between many different people. Durkheim noted that in 'traditional' societies, solidarity – individuals being bonded together – was based on their essential similarity, yet in an industrial society this similarity gives way to job specialization and therefore people become dissimilar. How, then, asked Durkheim, could order – solidarity – still be possible? Durkheim drew a distinction between two types of solidarity:

- *organic solidarity*: this is found in 'traditional societies' and is based on similarity between members; and
- *mechanical solidarity*: this is found in industrial/'modernist' societies, where a specialized division of labour exists. Solidarity is ensured as the members of the group become increasingly interdependent: they have to rely on each other.

Therefore social order is maintained in the industrial age through the creation of a whole range of identities, based on one's position in the division of labour, but these identities are integrated into a common culture and a 'value consensus' because of increasing interdependence.

Norms, anomie and freedom

As we have seen, culture acts as a form of 'social glue'. However, if order breaks down, and if the norms are not followed, we have a state of what Durkheim called 'anomie' – normlessness:

> [with anomie]... since the conscience collective is weaker, the frictions which are thus created can no longer be so completely nullified. Common sentiments no longer have the same capacity to keep the individual attached to the group under any circumstances. Subversive tendencies, no longer having the same counterweight, occur more frequently. (Durkheim, 1972: 183)

Durkheim was particularly worried about the potential for increased anomie with the rise of organic forms of solidarity. He was also worried about the increase of suicide at times of social change caused by the rise of anomie and loss of the order normally provided by the socialization of cultural values. Durkheim believed that order and control through culture ultimately leads to human freedom. What he meant by this is that, if human desires are not checked – if humans are allowed to exist in their 'natural' state without culture to constrain them, then they are open to irrational individualism. However, if their nature is controlled by culture, they are able to think rationally about the world they inhabit. This nature/culture duality in human beings, and humanity's need for the constraint of culture, is a key theme in all of Durkheim's work.

Durkheim suggested that the individual is made up of two elements:

- the individual being with selfish, 'natural' desires; and
- the collective social being – the product of control by culture and socialization, giving up natural desires in favour of collective moral sentiments.

This shows that, since its early days, sociology has been concerned with the problems of the relationship of individuals to society (see Chapters 1 and 6).

Functionalism after Durkheim: Talcott Parsons

The American sociologist, Talcott Parsons – like Durkheim and Spencer before him – saw society as a system of interrelated parts. It is culture that keeps the individuals who make up this system in order, through the creation of 'value consensus' by socialization. Our identity is affected by the value consensus that most in society share. Parsons argues that we internalize what society says is important and make it part of us.

Exercise 3.14

Consider what new parents might wish for in terms of personal qualities for a girl and a boy. Note down your thoughts.

Reflect on your list. How many of the factors you have listed are useful to society and the state in general? Have you identified qualities that would lead to efficient workers? Would these qualities make them valuable and productive members of society? Personal qualities that would be valuable for boys to have include; being competitive, having a good career, functional relationships with others, contribute something to society, be independent, and have a good education. For girls, many of the same factors would apply, but Parsons (writing in a time of segregated or differentiated gender roles) would argue that parents would also wish for their daughter to be a good carer and display sensitivity to others. In this sense, through socialization, we are taking on board what society values.

This social system is made up of four key elements, or rather four key functions that must be performed by the subsystems to ensure the survival of the whole:

- *Adaptation*: fitting into the environment and delivering the basic necessities of life. Fulfilled by the economic subsystem.
- *Goal-attainment*: providing standards for behaviour and the direction of social development and change. Fulfilled by religious and political subsystems.
- *Integration*: ensuring that everyone follows the rules and fits into the wider group. Fulfilled by the legal subsystem.
- *Latent pattern maintenance (latency)*: keeping the whole together through collective sentiments. Fulfilled by the cultural subsystem.

According to Parsons, culture performs the function of 'pattern maintenance' – it creates the collective symbols (for example, religious symbols) that people internalize through socialization and that help to bring about a shared sense of identity in a harmonious society.

Exercise 3.15

Copy out the following passage and fill in the blanks with the words listed below.

Functionalism is often associated with the ideas of Spencer, Durkheim and........., though there is some disagreement about the interpretation of what Durkheim 'really meant'. Functionalism, although there are some similarities, is usually viewed as the opposite of........., in the sense that functionalists see society as stable and in........., whereas Marxists concentrate on the existence of class conflict. Culture is seen by functionalists to........., the individual to the group, often through what is called value consensus. Individuality is often seen as a........., for the smooth running of a........., society, and the........., brought together by 'moral unity', is seen as the most suitable way for society to function. This moral unity creates a sense of........., identity, which helps to avoid the problem of anomie or 'normlessness'.

Missing words:

• bond • stable • harmony • group • Parsons • problem • collective • Marxism

Neofunctionalism and the 'radical Durkheim'?

Jeffrey Alexander (1985) suggests that it might be time for sociological analysis to return to functionalist ideas, though what he is suggesting is more of a reworking of Parsons' work – a kind of neo-Parsonianism – than of the whole of functionalism. According to Alexander:

> No one knows where such developments will lead, whether a neofunctionalist school will shape contemporary sociology in less conspicuous ways. In the past, Parsons' controversial reputation meant that even some of the participants in this revival were loathe [*sic*] to acknowledge his influence. The movement to reappropriate Parsons in a neofunctionalist way is gaining momentum. Whether it is simply old wine in new bottles, or a new brew, is something history will decide. (Ibid.: 16)

This reworking would reject some elements of Parsons' work and retain others. In particular, Alexander wishes to reject the notion that the life and actions of people are totally shaped by structural forces. In this sense ,Alexander is rejecting the traditional argument that culture shapes the destiny of the individual via the internalization of values through socialization, in favour of a model where society is still seen as a system, but one that is in a state of change or flux. In *The Radical Durkheim*, Pearce (1989) suggests a reworking not of Parsons' work but of Durkheim's. In this 'new Durkheimianism', Pearce suggests that Durkheim was not a theorist of consensus but of conflict, and in this sense his work can be seen as paralleling that of Marx. Despite – mainly from Parsons – there being an interpretation of Durkheim as a theorist of the harmony and solidarity of society through culture, he does consider the problems of disorder, conflict and deviance – through his idea of anomie and his concern for the growth of individualism. This new 'radical' Durkheim would not be writing from a right-wing political position as Parsons did, but much more from a liberal or even a socialist stance – advocating the morality of the community for the good of the whole. This version of Durkheim has many parallels with the ideas of what has been called the 'New Left'(though it is no longer new), such as those views held in the UK by the Labour Party under Tony Blair, and to some extent by the coalition government under David Cameron. It is interesting to note that Durkheim's work is so wide-ranging that it has influenced not only the New Left but also the 'New' Right (again, not so 'new' today, but it is referred to as 'new' in many texts of the time). The term New Right is a label given to the political thinking of the British Conservative Party from the 1970s onwards, and during the 'Reagan years' in American politics. The New Right are often seen as inheriting the intellectual legacy of functionalism, because both theories stress the role of collective moral sentiments in the creation of harmony, order and discipline in society. The New Right claim that a moral rejuvenation of society is needed, otherwise order and 'traditional moral values' will collapse, to be replaced by a rising tide of normlessness – not too far from Durkhiem's own concern about the rise of anomie in society.

The strengths of functionalism

The strengths of functionalism are that:

- it allows us to think about the nature of the social system as a whole; and
- it explains the process of socialization and how culture can create order in society.

(An)(E)

Exercise 3.16

Consider the two strengths of functionalism listed above. Draw up a list of further strengths.

The weaknesses of functionalism

The weaknesses of functionalism are:

- Marxist sociologists would suggest that functionalism overemphasizes the role played by consensus in society at the expense of conflict;
- it treats humans as puppets or victims of their culture;
- it is often described as having an 'oversocialized' conception of the individual, since it assumes that the socialization process is able to subsume everyone into the group;
- it treats society as a living thing, more important than the individual; and
- interactionist sociologists would criticize the fact that functionalists see individuals as passive, ignoring their active role in creating culture through meaningful interaction.

VIEW TWO: CULTURE AS IDEOLOGICAL CONTROL – MARXISM

Whereas Durkheim and the wider functionalist movement see society as a system based on harmony, consensus and order, for Marxists society is structured as a pattern of conflict – even if, for a great deal of the time, the individuals who live in a society might not consciously recognize this. According to this 'conflict structural' perspective, the existence of conflict and power inequalities in society are caused by the existence of different classes and the struggle for power among these. For Marx, writing in the mid-1800s, the single most important feature of society was the existence of class. The opening line of his famous *The Communist Manifesto* (1985), written in 1872 with Friedrich Engels, states: 'The history of all hitherto existing society is the history of class struggles.'

Marx's social theory was based on the prediction that class conflict would disappear after the fall of capitalism. Marx's ideas proved to be very powerful, not just in sociology, philosophy and economics, but also in the world as a whole: governments were toppled, monarchies were overthrown and whole societies were created that claimed to be 'Marxist' or 'communist' in character.

Class and conflict

Class is an economic category and usually refers to the amount of economic power and material wealth an individual has. Those who share a position of power in common with others – based on their material and economic wealth – can be said to be in the same class as each other. Marx himself defined class in a very succinct way: there are only two class groups – those who own 'the means of production', and those who do not. The latter have no choice but to sell their labour power to (work for) the former. Marx referred to the ruling class as the 'bourgeoisie' and the working class as the 'proletariat'. He saw the relationship between the classes as one of inequality: the oppression of the powerless masses by the powerful ruling class. Marx suggested that class forces move and shape the direction taken by the history of any given society. This was a highly 'modernist' claim (see Chapter 7), based on three key ideas:

- evolution;
- 'teleology'; and
- 'dialectical force'.

Marx was influenced by the ideas of Charles Darwin and his theory of evolution. When Marx was formulating his economic and philosophical ideas, the concept of evolution – which is generally taken for granted today – was new and revolutionary. Darwin proposed that the historical evolution of all species is based on the principle of 'natural selection'. Individuals compete with each other for the resources required for survival, and only those with characteristics most suited to their environment will survive and pass on these favourable characteristics to their offspring. This process continues incrementally over time, with each new species gradually developing out of earlier forms. Marx borrowed this notion of slow evolutionary change, where one change leads to the development of a second, and so on, and applied it to the evolution of human societies over time. He claimed that, as class power changes, so does the nature of the society in question. Essentially, social change is the result of the conflict between class groupings.

Marx's views on how societies change over time were highly 'teleological'. This concept was formulated by religious thinkers, who saw the direction of universal change as a purposeful (rather than causal) movement towards a defined goal, usually directed by a God or gods. Marx's view of history was teleological in the sense that he saw change as having a purpose and a direction. Marx divided human social history into five stages, or social types, called 'modes of production':

- primitive communism;
- slavery;
- feudalism;
- capitalism; and
- communism.

Marx argued that it was conflict between classes that governed these changes and the direction they took. To explain this, Marx borrowed an idea from the German philosopher Hegel – an idea known as the 'dialectic'. A dialectical force is when two opposites come together, experience conflict and produce a new outcome – a change.

For Hegel:

Thesis + antithesis = synthesis

or

One idea + another idea = conflict/debate = new idea.

For Marx:

Ruling class + subordinate class = class conflict = revolution.

Marx suggested that those who own the means of production conflict with those who do not. The result of this conflict is dramatic or 'revolutionary' change and the creation of a new social type, where the previous subordinate class becomes the dominant class. The process continues until, finally, communism is reached. For Marx, the word 'communism' meant the collective or communal ownership of the means of production. Since in this social type there is no dominant class – in fact, there is no class at all – there can be no more social change through dialectical forces. This social type is therefore seen as the ultimate type, the evolutionary result of the march of history: a very teleological image.

Class consciousness and social identity

Marx argued that revolutionary change can occur only when the working classes become fully aware of the oppressive conditions in which they live. In other words, the working classes are exploited by the ruling or 'capitalist' class to the point where they simply cannot endure hardship and inequality any longer: 'What the bourgeoisie, therefore, produces, above all, is its own grave-diggers. Its fall and the victory of the proletariat are equally inevitable' (Marx and Engels, 1985).

This revolutionary change occurs only as a result of a change in consciousness and identity on the part of the working classes themselves. Marx referred to this as a movement from a class 'in itself' to a class 'for itself'. In other words, the members of the working classes realize the nature of their situation and begin to develop a class identity that allows them to develop solidarity with their fellow members and act against their oppressors. Before the working class becomes a 'class for itself' with the development of a class identity, the realities and problems of society are largely hidden from them. This state of deluded consciousness, this illusory world in which they live, is referred to as a state of 'false class consciousness'. Marx believed culture serves to create and perpetuate this state of 'false consciousness' in society. The aim of Marxist sociology is therefore to expose society for what it really is, and in doing so to create 'true class consciousness'.

Economic forces and culture

Marx's views on class are known by the term 'historical materialism', since he believed that economic production ('materialism') has been responsible for societal change throughout history. In terms of the structure of the social system, economic productive forces are also key. Marx divided the social system into two:

1. The economic base (also known as the 'substructure' or 'infrastructure').
2. The superstructure.

This division is based on the material and non-material components of the social system and can be further divided, as shown in Figure 3.1.

'Means of production' refers to everything needed to produce goods: factories, machinery, raw materials and so on. 'Social relations of production' refers to the nature of the relationship between those involved in the productive process – namely, the exploitation and oppression of the masses by the ruling class.

The economic base – how production is organized – shapes everything in the superstructure. This way of thinking is often referred to as 'economic determinism', since economic forces shape or 'determine' everything else – including the culture of a society. Hence those who control the productive process (the ruling classes, since they own the

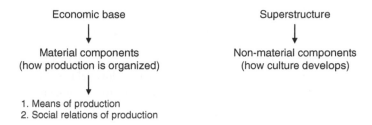

Figure 3.1 Marx's division of the social system

means of production) are those who have the power over society – the power to control and shape the nature of the values and norms of that society, its rules, religion, education and so on. Marx believed that the ruling classes use the superstructure (the culture of a society) for their own purposes: to hide the true nature of society from those they rule over. Therefore, culture has a specific purpose for the bourgeoisie or ruling class.

The dominant ideology thesis

Since those who control the economic base control the society's culture, it follows that they control the dominant values of that culture, and the socialization process is a mechanism with which to ensure the control of the working class through the creation of false consciousness. Socialization is a process of indoctrination, where identity and values are learnt and inequality is justified. In their classic work, *The German Ideology*, written between 1845 and 1846, Marx and Engels (1974: 64) stated that 'The ideas of the ruling class are in every epoch the ruling ideas, i.e. the class which is the ruling material force of society, is at the same time its ruling intellectual force.' In modern-day sociology this statement has become known as 'the dominant ideology thesis', since Marx and Engels argued that the ruling cultural ideas of a society are handed down, ready-made, by those who are dominant and powerful. They continued: 'The class which has means of material production at its disposal, has control at the same time over the means of mental production, so that thereby, generally speaking, the ideas of those who lack the means of mental production are subject to it' (ibid.). This is a theory of culture that sees culture as a form of constraint, a form of control, and individuals largely as the subjects of this control if they suffer from false consciousness.

Culture as ideology

The key Marxist concept with which to understand this cultural control by 'ruling ideas' is 'ideology'. Culture is seen to contain a ruling-class ideology that is socialized into the consciousness of the individuals living in a society. To define 'ideology' we shall look at two sociologists' considerations of the term, those of Karl Mannheim and Stuart Hall. First, Mannheim:

The particular conception of ideology is implied when the term denotes that we are sceptical of the ideas and representations advanced by our opponent. They are regarded as more or less conscious disguises of the real nature of a situation, the true recognition of which would not be in accord with his interests. (Mannheim, 1960)

In this view, ideology consists of ideas that are purposefully incorrect. These ideas are used by their formulators to control others. Ideology is thus deliberately created by the powerful to ensure their continuing domination through the manipulation of others by means of false ideas. And now Hall's view:

By ideology I mean the mental frameworks – the languages, the concepts, categories, imagery of thought, and the systems of representation – which different classes and social groups deploy in order to make sense of, define, figure out and render intelligible the way society works... the theory of ideology helps us to analyse how a particular set of ideas comes to dominate the social thinking of a historical bloc... and maintain its dominance and leadership over society as a whole. It has especially to do with the concepts and the languages of practical thought which stabilize a particular form of power and domination. (Hall, 1996: 26)

In this view, different groups (the powerful and the powerless) have their own ideologies – their own world views – and the battle between these ideologies is a struggle for power. An ideology, if it becomes dominant throughout society, gives people a language and rules, which they use to understand the world around them. Hence ideological struggle is a struggle over the 'correct' way to think.

Ⓚ Ⓤ
Ⓘ
Exercise 3.17

Consider the ideas of Karl Mannheim and Stuart Hall on ideology. Then rewrite their views in your own words and describe what 'ideology' is for each of these two writers.

In general, ideology refers to ideas, images, values and representations that justify a position of power. They are used by those in such a position to maintain their rule, at the expense of those they rule over. It is ideology that culture gives to the masses and that keeps them in a state of illusion – even self-delusion – as to the real workings of the social system. It is ideology that Marxism seeks to fight against.

Ⓚ Ⓤ
Ⓘ
Exercise 3.18

When studying sociology for the first time it is very easy to become confused and worried by the range of specialist terms and difficult language. This language is important, however, since it provides an easy way – eventually – to think about and discuss some quite difficult but important ideas. Use the above discussion of Marxist views on culture and identity to define the following key Marxist words/terms:

• Class • Superstructure • Means of production • Mode of production • Ideology
• False class consciousness

Now use these words to write a summary paragraph of the Marxist view on the role of culture in society.

Examples of ideology: religion, education and the mass media

Religion

Writing in 1844, Marx contended that 'Religion is the sigh of the oppressed creature, the heart of a heartless world, just as it is the spirit of an unspiritual situation. It is the opium of the people' (Marx and Engels, 1984). In this view, religious values are a part of culture that instils an ideological view of the world to justify capitalist oppression. Marx compares these values to a drug – opium, which prevents people from seeing the reality of inequality.

Education

Bowles and Gintis (1976) note that the values underpinning schooling in capitalist society – through what is described as the 'hidden curriculum' – are ideological, since they represent the dominant ideology of the time. These values further the power of the ruling class by creating a false consciousness in the minds of the working classes: teaching them to obey authority, not to question the need to do mundane tasks and so on. Paul Willis (1977) includes a similar theme in his book, *Learning to Labour*, where he argues that the function of schools in capitalist society is to prepare working-class children for a life of labour under capitalism. The working-class children are unaware of this process and their involvement in it.

The mass media

Adorno and Horkheimer (1993), who were members of the Frankfurt School (see Chapter 2) during the period before the Second World War, suggested that the commercial development of the mass media had led to a 'mass culture' based on intellectual sameness, which prevented critical thought and in so doing sustained capitalist ideological rule (see Chapter 8).

Exercise 3.19

This exercise requires you to consider how religion, education and the mass media might control ideas in society.

1. How does religion contribute to ideological control?
2. How does education contribute to ideological control?
3. How do the mass media contribute to ideological control?

Exercise 3.20

In a two-column table, list the places in society where ideology might be found (for example, the workplace) (column 1), and explain how each of your examples might contribute to ideological control (column 2).

Commodification and commodity fetishism

For the Frankfurt School, a key feature of modern culture was the creation of a 'culture industry', where cultural products lose their intellectual and critical value and become cheap, non-artistic and disposable. The problems of consumerism also concerned Marx. He suggested that a process of 'commodification' of culture takes place under capitalism, where cultural products are reduced to how much money they can be bought and sold for, rather than for the pleasure they can give to individuals.

Equally, Marx argued that, if society becomes too obsessed with the purchase of cultural goods, then humans enter into a state of 'fetishism' with 'things' and almost worship things for what they have come to stand for – that is, money, wealth and status. Because of this, capitalism is allowed to continue, since it is seen to 'deliver the goods'. For Marx – and for the Frankfurt School – this fetishism is based on false ideological wants, manipulated by capitalism through advertising in the media. We shall be returning to this idea of commodification of culture and consumption in Chapter 11.

The strengths and weaknesses of Marxism

Strengths

- Unlike functionalism, Marxism recognizes the role played by conflict in social life.
- It illustrates the unequal nature of social life.
- It attempts to help those without power to think about their situation more clearly.
- Like functionalism, it provides a way of thinking about the overall picture of the social system.
- Marx's predictions about the development of class consciousness did not happen, but because of mechanization and rising living standards, the working classes became more affluent and consumerist and began to choose to retain capitalism. It could be argued that capitalism has been allowed to continue because it does deliver the goods and products that people want.

Weaknesses

- Marxism assumes that people live in a state of delusion about the world they live in.
- It resorts to alienation in order to explain how power inequality continues.
- It sees society as a system made up of collectives and does not really consider the role of the individual.
- Feminists would suggest that class inequality is focused upon at the expense of gender.

(An)(E)

Exercise 3.21

Consider the above strengths and weaknesses of the Marxist position. Does one list outweigh the other? Do you see more of the strengths of Marxism or more of the weaknesses as being important? Write an explanation of which list you think is more important, and why (about 150 words).

Marxism after Marx

While Marx produced his work in the 1800s and is considered to be one of the founders of sociology, his ideas did not become a popular or established part of the sociological world-view until the 1970s. Marxist theory today covers a wide range of ideas and variations. A distinction is usually made between classical/traditional Marxism, as discussed in this chapter, and what is called neo-Marxism or new Marxism.

Within neo-Marxism there are many different varieties and versions (see Chapters 9, 10 and 12), and many Marxist ideas have been taken up by other sociological branches, such as feminism (see Chapter 12) and interactionist sociology (see Chapter 4). Neo-Marxist ideas have developed for the following reasons:

- What many see as the failure of the 1917 Russian Revolution to achieve true communism without resorting to the establishment of an oppressive regime.
- The discovery in the 1970s of previously unknown texts by Marx, which led to renewed interest in his ideas.
- Periods of economic depression in the 1970s in the West, which caused some to turn to the subject of class to explain such events.
- The predicted Marxist revolution in the UK failed to materialize.
- The constant updating and re-evaluation of ideas within academic sociology.

Exercise 3.22

Using the timeline given in Table 3.1 and data from your earlier research for activities 3.2, 3.10 and 3.11, identify which events could have contributed to which aspects of Marx and Durkheim's theories. Explain your reasoning.

Table 3.1 Timeline of theorists, publications and events from the eighteenth century to the 1920s

Century	Theorists	Publication of key works	Events in society
Eighteenth century	1798–1857 Auguste Comte	1857 *A General View of Positivism* (Comte)	Age of Enlightenment **1780s–90s** French Revolution
	1802–76 Harriet Martineau 1818–83 Karl Marx 1820–1903 Herbert Spencer		**18th–19th century** Industrial Revolution **1819** British Factory Act limiting employment of children **1825** First passenger steam train in England **1830** Revolution in France

Table 3.1 (Continued)

Century	Theorists	Publication of key works	Events in society
Nineteenth century	1858–1917 Emile Durkheim 1864–1920 Max Weber	1846 *The German Ideology* (Marx and Engels) 1848 *The Communist Manifesto* (Marx and Engels) 1867 *Capital* (Marx) 1873 *The Study Of Sociology* (Spencer)	1830s Chartism emerges in England 1833 British empire abolishes slavery 1845–52 Irish potato famine 1847 British Parliament passes 'Ten Hours Bill' limiting work for women and children to 63 hours a week 1848 Revolutionary events in Italy and France and other parts of Europe 1850s Worldwide economic crisis 1859 *On The Origin of Species* published (Charles Darwin) 1859 Peaceful picketing during a strike made legal in UK 1861 Serfs in Russia freed (end of the feudal system) 1861–65 American Civil War 1865–1900 Second industrial revolution (railways, steam, communications) 1867 Reform Act, extending vote to more men in Britain 1867 Telephone invented (Alexander Graham Bell) 1870 Franco-Prussian War 1871 Proletariat revolution in Paris
Early twentieth century	1902–79 Talcott Parsons	1893 *The Division of Labour In Society* (Durkheim) 1895 *The Rules of Sociological Method* (Durkheim) 1897 *Suicide* (Durkheim)	1872 Formation of the National Society for Women's Suffrage 1879 Light bulb invented 1895 Radio invented 1901 Queen Victoria dies; Edward VII crowned 1901 Rowntree poverty survey of York published 1903 Formation of the Women's Social and Political Union in Britain (Emmeline Pankhurst) 1908 Henry Ford produces Model T automobile

		1912 *The Elementary Forms of the Religious Life* (Durkheim)	1914 Outbreak of First World War
			1916 Einstein's General Theory of Relativity
			1917–18 Russian Revolution
			1918 End of First World War
			1920s Prohibition in USA
			1920s Television invented

Exercise 3.23

To what extent can the theories of Marx and Durkheim be used to explain the contemporary events listed below? Use appropriate terms and concepts. For each event:

- Identify which elements of Durkheim's theory can explain the event.
- Identify which elements of Marx's theory can explain the event.
- Identify which aspects of the event cannot be explained by either theorist.

1. Many European and American businesses outsource their production and customer service departments to Africa and Asia to save labour costs and boost their market competitiveness. There have been widely publicized breaches of human rights and examples of poor workplace conditions, with many of these countries having little in the way of health and safety regulations in the workplace. Many deaths in the workplace have been attributed to poor conditions or overwork. There are words in Chinese and Japanese for death from overwork (guolaosi and karoshi respectively). This often seems removed from the reality of consumers buying cheaper goods in Western societies.

2. Financial instability in America and Europe as a result of trading practices has resulted in the collapse of banks and investment companies. At the same time, many bankers have received large bonuses, and the gap between the income of the rich and the poor has actually increased. It is not just bankers that have been criticized for excessive salaries. Pay and bonuses given to heads of public organizations as well as the publication of Members of Parliament (MP's) expenses in the UK have resulted in much anger from many areas of society.

3. In France and Belgium there have been calls to ban women wearing a face-covering veil in public (the law would apply to all, but in the public consciousness it has been specifically linked to banning a form of the Islamic burqa). Immigrants to France and England have been asked to make attempts to integrate as opposed to retaining aspects of their country of origin. In England, immigrants have to show, as a criterion of their citizenship, that they have a reasonable knowledge of the language and are keen to improve their language use.

4. Some airlines and health organizations in the UK have clashed with employees over their right to wear religious symbols such as a crucifix. Workers have complained that it is a violation of their human rights.

5. Terrorist attacks such as those on the World Trade Center in New York in 2001, and the London transport system in 2004, in addition to environmental disasters such as the tsunami in the Far East in 2005, the floods in Pakistan in 2010,

and the Japanese earthquake and tsunami in 2011, have resulted in communal gatherings of mourning generating books of remembrance, commemorative statues and collective worship. Church attendance increased dramatically in New York after the terrorist attack.

6. Social networking sites have millions of members globally. Users are able to post their 'status' (mood, current state of mind), what they are doing on a daily basis, what they like or dislike, and photographs of themselves. Not all of the users use all of these functions. People can become obsessed by the number of 'friends' or 'followers' they have. Users of the sites receive information about how content and how social their 'friends' or 'followers' are being. Some argue these sites are a way of keeping in touch with friends and family in a global society, and that it can result in individuals feeling connected to a cyber community (Lenhart, 2007). Alternatively, they can result in over-familiarity, fuelling anti-social fantasy and potential stalking. Others argue that they can leave users feeling isolated and result in cyber-bullying. David Holmes (2005), a psychologist at Manchester Metropolitan University, estimates that up to 40 per cent of the information posted on social networking sites could be fabricated. This could be as a result of a wish to protect privacy, or the user is creating the identity s/he wants to present online.

Exercise 3.24

Use the concept map in Figure 3.2. Classical views on culture and identity as the start point for a visual overview of this chapter. Copy it on to a large sheet of paper or enlarge it on a photocopier. Expand and elaborate on the key elements of functionalist and Marxist thinking and link them to culture and identity. Add strengths and weaknesses in different colours.

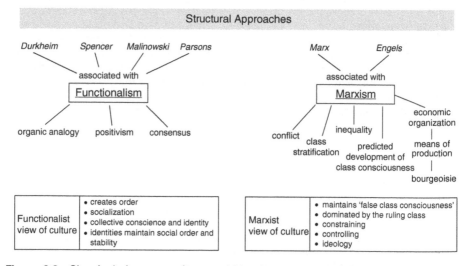

Figure 3.2   Classical views on culture and identity concept map

CONCLUSION

The 'modernist' sociologies of Marx, Durkheim and their followers tend to view humans as being manipulated by their cultures. In their writings, they focus primarily on culture and see identity as a by-product of culture; however, identity is crucial. It is seen as something given by the group rather than being created by the individual for him/herself. The influence on sociology of Marxist and Durkheimian ideas has been massive – without these ideas sociology would not be the discipline it is today. However, many of the assumptions held by these thinkers have come under attack in contemporary sociology. The most serious challenge to the popularity of Marxist ideas has been the rise of theories described as 'postmodern', as will be explained in Chapter 7. However, the ideas of Durkheim and Marx will continue to feature in sociological debates on culture and identity because of their foundational role. In Chapter 4 we turn to the ideas of the last of the three founders – Max Weber – and his attempts to evaluate Marxism.

Important concepts

Anomie • Bourgeoisie • Capitalism • Class consciousness • Collective conscience • Communism • Dialectical force • Differentiation • Division of labour • Economic base • Evolution • Functionalism • Ideology • Industrialization • Means of production • Mechanical solidarity • Modernist • Organic analogy • Organic solidarity • Positivism • Proletariat • Social relations of production • Superstructure • Structural • Teleology • Value consensus

Exam focus

(a) Evaluate the Marxist view that dominant culture always reflects the interests of the powerful.
(b) Assess the argument that common cultural values lead to stability in society.
(c) To what extent do the theories or Marx and Durkheim about culture and identity differ?
(d) How useful are structural theories of culture and identity?

Critical thinking

1. There is considerable debate within sociology about the relevance of the founders' ideas in the world today. How relevant do you think their ideas are, and why?
2. What social change occurring in the twentieth century is likely to have impacted on how sociologists see the world?

Chapter 4

The Development of 'Action' Sociology and Interactionists

After studying this chapter you should:

- be able to evaluate the ideas of Marxism and functionalism from an 'action' standpoint
- have knowledge of the contribution made by Max Weber to the understanding of culture and identity
- understand the ideas of 'action' sociology
- understand how action sociology has influenced the contemporary development of sociology as a whole

INTRODUCTION

From our discussion of Durkheim and Marx in Chapter 3 we can identify two basic views on culture and identity. The first, from Durkheim, suggests that culture binds the individual to the group and instils a collective identity. The second, from Marx, is that culture is a form of constraint, used to justify inequality and to hide the true nature of an exploitative society. Both of these views, though different, come from a sociological tradition that can be described as 'structural' or adopting a 'systems' approach to viewing and studying society. The work of the German social historian, Max Weber, in the early part of the twentieth century provided a very different interpretation of the role of culture and identity. Weber did not write from a 'structural' position; rather, he adopted what we call an 'action' or a 'micro' approach. The basis of the action approach to sociology is:

- Humans are not passive victims of the social structure.
- 'Society' does not exist as a 'thing', but rather as a series of actions and interactions by individuals.
- Social life 'makes sense' – it is meaningful to those involved in its day-to-day creation.

■ Sociology and sociologists can only study the reality of society by looking at the micro level – that is, by looking at the smaller picture: what people actually do, and what they think about what they do.

Ⓚ Ⓤ
Ⓘ

Exercise 4.1

Consider the above list of key ideas of the 'action' approach to sociology. Rewrite each one in your own words and give an example of each.

Ⓚ Ⓤ

Exercise 4.2

The ideas of Max Weber – like those of Durkheim and Marx (see Chapter 3) – are important to a great deal of sociological discussion. Brainstorm what you know about the ideas of Weber from your studies so far.

Weber was not interested in society as a 'thing', nor in humans as the subjects of culture. Rather, he believed that humans make history and society through what they do – there are no underlying rules or 'logic' to the pattern of history. In this view, culture is created by humans through the meanings and motives they hold, which allows them to make sense of what they do. Identity is important in interaction since it is the basis of how people think they should fit in, and therefore what they think they should be doing.

 Ⓤ Ⓘ
Ⓐ

Exercise 4.3

In a copy of the following table, give an example of each of the observations made by Weber.

Observations made by Weber	Example
Humans make history and society through what they do	
There are no underlying rules or 'logic' to the pattern of history	
Culture is created by humans through the meanings and motives they hold	
Culture allows people to make sense of what they do	
Identity is important in interaction since it is the basis of how people think they should fit in	

With Weber's ideas we have a third view of culture and identity – that culture is made up of meanings and motives for action, and is created by individuals in an active fashion.

THE ROLE OF MEANINGS AND MOTIVES IN SOCIETY

Though Weber's emphasis on the role of action, consciousness and meanings in culture place his ideas firmly within an 'action' sociology framework, his broader sociological ideas are less easy to label in this fashion. What makes Weber an interesting sociologist – and a powerful influence – is that many of his ideas appear to cross the divide between structure and action.

Weber argued that all sociological explanations should strive to be 'adequate' on two levels: at the level of 'meaning' – called 'Verstehen'; and at the level of 'causality' – called 'Erklären'. Put another way, Weber advocated an approach to studying the individual and society that seeks to understand what individuals do (and what they think of what they do) – Verstehen – and then to determine how this fits into the bigger picture of social life – Erklären. Weber's major contribution to sociology was the idea of trying to achieve Verstehen in social research. This idea can be described as 'seeing the world through the eyes of those involved'. Many action sociologists since Weber have taken up the idea of Verstehen. The claim is made that, to understand the reality of what society is, and how it works, we must look at how individuals make sense of what they do, in an active fashion. The task of sociology is to see how culture socializes a collective set of symbols into a group of people, who then use these symbols to gain an understanding of what they do, what others do, and what others expect them to do.

The aim of action sociology is to look at the meanings and motives of action and interaction through the eyes of those doing the acting. For Weber, individuals do not act unless they have a reason or 'motivation' for doing so. All actions make sense to those doing them, even if they might not to an outside observer. Individuals are seen to hold a 'subjective meaning' of what they do, and this meaning is created by the individual through interaction with others.

Exercise 4.4

Action sociologists – or as we sometimes call them, interactionists – are interested in the role played by individuals' meanings and motives.

1. In a two-column table, list your reasons (motivations) for attending college or work (column 1) and the reasons for completing the work expected of you (column 2).
2. How do meanings and motives make action possible?

Complete the exercise in approximately 150 words.

According to action sociology, culture is the collective sets of meanings, values and motives that together make up the 'subjective understandings' of all those involved in the creation of society. In this interpretation, culture is not a 'thing', but something that individuals do. It is a process: dynamic and fluid, and produced by individual consciousness. Individual identity is also important in the processes of action and inter-action, since without a sense of who they are it will be difficult for individuals to think about:

- how they wish to behave;
- who other people are;
- why others behave as they do; and
- how others expect them to behave towards them.

Identity is essential if meaningful interaction is to take place among a society of thinking, creative, conscious and active individuals.

Exercise 4.5

Weber proposed that we should study the meanings and motives individuals have in their minds. Why do you think it might be useful for a sociologist to study these? Explain your view in about 150 words.

To summarize the ideas of Weber:

- Society is not a 'thing' that exercises control over the individual through culture. Instead it is actively created by individuals.
- Individuals need to have motivations for what they do, and they reflect upon these – they are not simply subsumed into the group identity and stripped of all individual consciousness.
- Culture has no overall pattern that controls and moulds the individual – such patterns only exist in the minds of those who, in their day-to-day life, create culture by interacting with each other.

The role of cultural ideas in history

In *The Protestant Ethic and the Spirit of Capitalism*, first published in 1905, Weber (1985) provides us with both an account of how values and meanings work within culture, and an evaluation of Marx's ideas about how classes affect the evolution of society (see Chapter 3). Marx argued that:

- Class division is the most important factor in a society.
- Societal evolution can be divided into five key stages, through which all cultures will travel.
- Class conflict moves society ever onward towards its ultimate destiny – communism.
- This historical pattern can be predicted in advance.

Whereas, for Weber:

- Societal evolution is haphazard and accidental.
- It is human action and interaction that cause social change and societal evolution.
- The outcome of this interaction can never be predicted in advance.
- Cultural ideas and values are independent of the economy and of how production is organized (this is a key difference between Weber and Marx).

In order to evaluate Marx's contention that class conflict was the force behind social change, Weber looked at the formation of industrial capitalist societies in Western Europe. According to Marx, these were an inevitable feature of history, and had to come about through conflict between merchants and the aristocracy in the feudal mode of production. For Weber, however, capitalism developing in parts of Europe was the accidental and unintended outcome of the meaningful actions and interactions of a group of Calvinist Protestants, following their particular religious values and trying to make life meaningful.

The Calvinists were a Protestant sect who broke away from the Roman Catholic Church because they felt that Catholicism was becoming too 'decadent' – too concerned with worldly and material goods and wealth. The Calvinists had a very particular set of ideas, with which they made sense of the world around them, and which, like any other meaningful set of motivations, allowed them to make sense of their action and interaction in society. The Calvinists believed that everyone should have a 'calling' in life: a pursuit that one should follow single-mindedly in order to show one's devotion to God. In this view, hard work was a virtue. People should not waste time or be lazy, but should devote themselves to their calling. For the Calvinists, who was destined to enter heaven after his or her death had been decided at the moment of 'creation' (of the Earth) – only a select few (the 'elect') would meet God in the afterlife. Finally, success in one's calling was an indication of God's favour – a sign that one might be one of the elect.

Weber argued that the specific cultural values of this religious group led them to act in a very particular way that made sense to them: to work hard, and rather than spend their financial rewards, to plough them back into their businesses – back into their 'calling'. This meaningful set of motivations, this 'Protestant ethic', was responsible for the creation of what Weber termed 'the spirit of capitalism'. Not actually capitalist society as such, but the necessary cultural ideas needed for others to come along and use them as the basis of meaningful interaction. In this way the values of a small group – the Calvinists – accidentally led to the establishment of a whole society based on the pursuit of profit through reinvestment. Later the capitalist economic idea spread across the globe – from simple yet highly meaningful cultural values. Weber used this historical example to illustrate, in contradiction to Marx, that history cannot be predicted, and that culture is created and given meaning by those involved in its production.

Exercise 4.6

Decide whether each statement in the table below would have been said by Marx or by Weber.

Statement	Would this be said by Marx or Weber?
Class is the most important feature of society	
Culture is a structure above the individual	
We must understand the role of meanings in action	
We must understand the role of ideology in making people follow the rules of society	
History moves through five identifiable stages	
History is unpredictable	
Class causes all social change	
Capitalism will inevitably lead to communism	
Capitalism is a historical accident	
Humans cause social change through their actions	

Exercise 4.7

1. To apply Weber's thinking to a modern example, identify some of the core beliefs and values held by people today who are concerned about their impact on the physical environment. *Tip* – think about recycling, transport, community involvement and other common beliefs and values.
2. How might these values and beliefs affect the following areas of society:

   o the economy and workplace;
   o the family; and
   o religion and spirituality?

Exercise 4.7 shows how beliefs about the use of resources, how everyday life should be lived and about ethical issues might affect wider society. Weber would argue that we cannot predict social change. The meanings individuals hold create culture and, in turn, these will impact on other areas of society.

GEORG SIMMEL

Although in many respects Weber's sociology attempted to bridge the divide between action and structure, his idea of Verstehen and the role played by meanings and motives in culture and identity have been taken up by a great number of action sociologists. Before we look at these ideas we shall discuss the work of a contemporary of Weber who shared with him an image of the active and creative interactional human in culture.

Simmel (1950) also saw society as being made up of individual members who act with full consciousness. Rather than looking at society as a structure or system over and above the individual – as in Durkheim's image of the social system as a living thing – Simmel concentrated on the role played by humans in the creation of social life. To say that, for Simmel, social life did not display any sort of pattern is not true. Simmel (1955) used the term 'web of group affiliations' to denote the points of intersection between the lives of individuals which, when added together, could be seen as a giant map or web of interactions extending over the whole of society.

Simmel drew a distinction between the form and content of social life. By this he meant that some very stable patterns ('forms') appear in different cultures and within the same culture over time. In our society we call these patterns family, education, work, religion and so on. These continue to exist over time in an easily recognizable form, but within these common patterns the day-to-day lives that we live ('content') are unique. Therefore common forms exist in each culture, but the content of social life varies according to the individual in question. The key feature of this web of interactions that we call 'society' is that it is based on action and interaction. It is based on exchanges of meaning, and as such it is dynamic, open and fluid. Society is a process of exchange, a 'happening' made possible by the collective efforts of many.

For Durkheim (see Chapter 3), if social order is to be achieved, individual identity has to be subsumed into the group through the process of socialization. For Simmel, social life, for each individual involved in the wider 'web', is a tension between two forces: individual identity and social/group identity. Simmel saw individuals not as 'passive robots of culture' but as creative agents trying to work out the meaning of their lives, and in doing so, trying to retain a sense of who they are in the face of pressures from the group. This idea that the individual is split into two and needs to find a way to reconcile both identities in his or her day-to-day life is a popular theme in classical social theory, especially in the work of Freud and Durkheim. It is described as 'homo duplex': the two sides of humanity (see Chapters 2 and 3). One side is the 'natural' side, which is engaged in a struggle against the side created by culture or society.

One of the characteristics of Simmel's work was that his choice of topics was varied, and he often chose some interesting themes to study. One of these was the significance of fashion in relation to identity. Simmel (1957) suggested that social life is a struggle between individuality and group identity. Or, in other words, between acting in a unique way and copying the actions of the wider group. The first is motivated by attempts to preserve one's individual identity; and the second by attempts to 'fit in' with others. Simmel suggested that this is a tension within all of us: the tension between being authentic to one's true wishes on the one hand, and feeling accepted by others and having a place in the group on the other. 'Identity' is thus not simply something that is handed down by culture or by the group; it is also something we try to retain some control over through our actions. In this context, fashion is seen as a means of establishing who we are in an ever-changing world, a world where we engage in struggles with others on a daily basis – struggles over who we are, who we think we should be, and how we are seen by others.

Exercise 4.8

Simmel described fashion as a mask behind which we can hide – a way we can convey to others what we want them to think we are.

In the right-hand column of the table below, describe how different items of fashion might say different things about who we think we are, and who others think we are.

Fashion item	What might this say about our identity?
A brand new pair of fashionable trainers	
The latest piece of mobile communication technology or MP3 player	
A leather jacket and torn jeans	
Basketball boots	
Lots of gold jewellery	
A Japanese character tattoo	
Combat trousers and a body warmer	
A pierced navel	
A shaven head	
A designer dress	

The 'dark side' of identity in the modern age

Unlike those of some of the other early sociologists, Weber's and Simmel's versions of what 'modernity' (see Chapter 7) or industrial society might do for individual identity are at times pessimistic. For example, Weber suggested that, in the modern age, individual identity might find itself locked into an 'iron cage of bureaucracy'. Individuals could be trapped into a life of petty rules and procedures with no sense of creativity – a dreadful future for active and creative individuals.

Simmel suggested that day-to-day life in the city might have important effects on one's sense of identity. He noted that, in the city – or as he called it, the 'metropolis' – individuals can feel isolated and lonely precisely because they are surrounded by large numbers of other city dwellers, who tend not to have intimate personal relationships with all those around them: 'The feeling of isolation is rarely as decisive and intense when one actually finds oneself physically alone, as when one is a stranger, without relations, among many physically close persons, at a party, on the train, or in the traffic of a large city' (Simmel, 1950).

Hence city life poses problems for individual identity. On the one hand, one is free to be who one wants to be, since the culture of cities tends to be more cosmopolitan, forgiving and fluid. The impersonal nature of city life often means there are fewer ties to the group, so it is easier to break free. On the other hand, the increase in freedom as a result of reduced social constraint means that one's inner 'mental life' becomes even more important. With no all-encompassing group to turn to, what the individual thinks of him/herself becomes even more important. With the constant ebb and flow of city life and the rapid turnover of people, ideas and identities, individuals might find the need to withdraw into themselves to find peace. This is what Simmel refers to as 'the separation of the subjective from the objective life'. We shall be discussing Simmel's work on community in Chapter 14.

Ⓤ Ⓘ
 Ⓐn

Exercise 4.9

Both Weber and Simmel identified the effects that the 'dark side' of modern life has on identity. Write a list of examples of this dark side – of the problems encountered in modern society, such as crime, cramped housing, loneliness and so on.

Simmel and 'modernity'

Simmel's concern with identity in the city reflected themes that were common among other classical social theorists. There are links between Simmel's thoughts on the subject and

- Durkheim's idea of 'anomie' or 'normlessness', which raises problems for who we think we are;
- Marx's idea of alienation – being separated and isolated from others; and
- Freud's notion of the tension between who we want to be and the constraints of 'civilization' that are imposed upon us.

Though we might call Simmel a 'modernist thinker', many of his ideas transcend this label. 'Modernity' (see Chapters 3 and 7) was the name given to the sort of thinking about society that was popular at the time of the founders, and Marx, Durkheim and Weber were all modernist thinkers.

'Modernity' was born at the time of the industrialization of Western Europe, and the modernist outlook on society, as held by the founders and other classical theorists, tended to include the following beliefs:

- Society was heading in a particular direction.
- Social change represented the onward march of progress.
- Science and technology were of increasing benefit to humankind.
- Societies and humans were becoming more rational.
- The aim of sociology was to discover the ultimate truth of social life.

Ⓤ Ⓘ
Ⓐn Ⓔ

Exercise 4.10

How realistic were the beliefs of modernist sociology? Complete the following table. Make sure you include evidence for your view; for example, a situation which suggests that the feature in question has or has not happened in society.

Key feature of modernist sociology	How realistic do you think this was?	What evidence can you give in support of your view?
Society was heading in a particular direction		
Social change represented the onward march of progress		
Science and technology were of increasing benefit to humankind		
Societies and humans were becoming more rational		
The aim of sociology was to discover the ultimate truth of social life		

Many of the contemporary thinkers known as 'postmodernists' claim that the modernist thinking about progress, reason and rationality was nothing more than illusion. Thinkers such as Jean Baudrillard (1993) contend that the contemporary age is not characterized by absolutes, but by:

- the fragmentation of many old ideas once held true;
- chaos;
- ambivalence;
- plurality;
- the rise of relativism (no more 'truths'; no longer can we say anything absolute or certain about the nature of social life – each situation and the individuals involved are unique).

Postmodernists claim that identity in the postmodern world is very different from identity under modernity. Today there is much more freedom to do what we want and be who we want to be, to change our minds frequently and 'reinvent' ourselves from time to time. For example, postmodern thinker Zweig (1996) argues that there has been a 'death of the self':

Amid the relativism forced upon us by the experiences of living in a global civilization … we are all challenged to look again in the mirror and rethink our assumptions about who and what we are. We face the discomfort – and the depth – of living with uncertainty, paradox, ambiguity, and constant change.

Life in the postmodern age is seen as being based on playing with images, our identity being something to play games with, having games with identity and living in chaos, and there is no true sense of who we are. However, these themes are present in Simmel's writings. For example, postmodern geographer Edward Soja (1996) describes the city as a huge, sprawling, out-of-control playground where there is chaos, a multiplicity of identities and a loss of sense of purpose and meaning. Yet we can find these themes in Simmel's work on the city, and in his idea that fashion allows us to play with the surface identities we present to others. Given the fact that Simmel made his observations in the first decade of the twentieth century, we need to ask if the postmodernists really have any new insights to offer. This illustrates the continued importance of classical thinkers for sociology today. Even those who wrote over a century ago had insights that allow us to think about our own times more clearly.

Exercise 4.11

The views and aims of modernist sociology have been criticized by postmodernists. Complete the following table. Use the information on modernism and postmodernism in this chapter to identify the key features of modernism criticized by postmodernists, and what their actual criticisms would be.

Key feature of modernist sociology	How would postmodernists criticize this?
1.	
2.	
3.	
4.	
5.	

CONTEMPORARY FORMS OF ACTION SOCIOLOGY

When we consider action sociology – or any of its other labels, such as interactionism, micro sociology or interpretive sociology – we can identify three subtraditions of this approach that have been highly influential in the shaping of theory as a whole. These three are the 'modern classics' of sociological thought and date from around the 1920s through to the late 1960s in America and Britain.

Symbolic interactionism

This branch of interpretive sociology is based on the premise that humans are active agents who manipulate symbols that have meaning. The founders of this approach, which has shaped present-day views in action sociology significantly, worked at the University of Chicago in the 1920s and are referred to as the Chicago School. Symbolic interactionism sees humanity as creating – through meaningful interaction – a sense of 'society'. Culture is ready-made for us at birth. However, our sense of self and identity is not ready-made when we are born, but is created through our interactions with others. We are socialized into the dominant meanings that our culture gives to symbols such as language, and actively seek meaning in everyday life. Some symbolic interactionists acknowledge the existence of structures in society, and refer to ethnicity, social class and gender.

A key idea developed by the Chicago School is the notion that human activity is a process of interaction between self-aware, self-consciousness beings who are able to reflect on what they do. The area of the human personality devoted to reflection on who one is has become known as 'the self' or sometimes 'the self-image'. Charles Cooley (1927) described the 'self' as a 'looking-glass self'. In other words, who we think we are is a mirrored reflection of the judgements others make of us. We are, or become, what others make of us:

> Society is an interweaving and interworking of mental selves. I imagine your mind, and especially what your mind thinks about my mind, and what your mind thinks about what my mind thinks about your mind. I dress my mind before yours and expect that you will dress yours before mine. Whoever cannot or will not perform these feats is not properly in the game. (Cooley, 1927)

Interaction is actually the combined efforts of self-aware, thinking beings whose sense of identity guides not only what they do but also how they perceive others, and think others perceive them. This idea of an active, creative and thinking self-identity was taken up by George Mead (1934) in his book *Mind, Self and Society*. According to Mead, the 'self' is divided into two halves: the 'I' – the inner self, which does not think about action, but simply performs it according to the individual's inner wishes; and the 'me' – the outer self, which takes into consideration what the individual thinks are other people's wishes. The 'me' is able to reflect on the 'I' after interaction has taken place. In terms of identity and culture, symbolic interactionism looks at how meaning comes from everyday interaction. It is this 'micro' level of analysis of interaction, of symbols, signs, gestures and language that contributes to our identity. Research methods interpreting interactions and meaning are at the heart of this approach. Blumer (1969) notes that meaning is not set in stone; it can vary from situation to situation and from time to time, therefore current research is important to understand meaning and behaviour. We shall come back to symbolic interactionism and its interpretation of socialization in the next chapter.

(An)(E)

Exercise 4.12

Identify two strengths and two weaknesses of symbolic interactionism.

Phenomenology

The second form of interpretive sociology, known as 'phenomenology', was originally developed as a philosophical perspective by Edmund Husserl and later become incorporated into sociology by Alfred Schutz. Phenomenology is interested in how individuals go about the process of creating meaning, sharing meaning and classifying meaning through the use of symbols – especially language. Schutz (1967, 1970) called it the 'analysis of the world of everyday life'. Schutz suggests that we store in our minds 'typifications' and 'meaning contexts' that help us to categorize our day-to-day experiences. 'Typifications' are the mental pigeonholes into which we sort 'typical' examples of reality into similar sets. For example, in our minds, the concept 'tree' is a typical example of all trees. Through the creation of typifications we build up sets of typical examples into 'meaning contexts', which we hold, ready to be used in our daily life as a 'stock of knowledge at hand'. For example, it is likely you have a typification in your mind called 'friendship', which you can use to try to understand your actions, the actions of others around you, and your relationships with those others. Equally, you can compare the experience of 'friendship' with similar typifications such as love, sexual attraction and so on, all of which form a 'meaning context' that you can carry around with you. It is a resource you can draw on constantly to try to give meaning to life. Phenomenology is not interested in how structures shape social actors, but how individuals experience the reality of everyday life, what they pay attention to, what they learn from others, and their subjective interpretation of reality.

Phenomenologists Peter Berger and Thomas Luckmann (1967) suggest that what each culture defines as 'real' is simply the product of the meanings of that culture. In other words, cultures created by human interaction shape how those humans perceive the world. Culture becomes a filter through which they interpret their experiences. What is seen to be 'real' is actually a product of negotiated and socially created meaning. Such cultures are human made, and kept alive by human interaction. Our reality is always shared with others; Schutz calls this our 'lifeworld'. Culture is not a 'thing' that bears down on and controls the individual. We become aware of our culture when we move into a different group, when we become a stranger.

(An)(E)

Exercise 4.13

Identify two strengths and two weaknesses of phenomenology.

Ethnomethodology

Ethnomethodologists study how members of society create an ordered social reality through their everyday lives. The idea of 'ethnomethodology' was first developed by Garfinkel (1967). The term refers to the methods used by people – 'lay actors' – to understand social reality in an active fashion through common-sense thought, which is itself a cultural product. Garfinkel is especially interested in how, though we are active in establishing with others a sense of shared meaning, we largely take interaction for granted. There are various rules on how we should and should not behave in each culture, but these are generally unspoken. There are no structures in society. The rules on how to behave are ever-present yet at the same time hidden. Culture gives us our common-sense, taken-for-granted thought, and we use this to understand who we are and how we should act – our identity.

(An)(E)

Exercise 4.14

Identify two strengths and two weaknesses of ethnomethodology.

Strengths and weaknesses of the action approach

Strengths

▓ Humans are seen as active and thinking beings.
▓ The concept of 'structure' is how individuals experience a ready-made reality – it does not exist as a 'thing' that controls the individual.
▓ Individuals think about self-identity and have some control over it.
▓ Culture is seen as the outcome of shared meanings.
▓ Humans are seen as 'social beings', but ones that remain as individuals within the wider group.

Weaknesses

▓ Humans are seen as having total free will in some versions of action sociology, yet one cannot truly do as one wishes in society without experiencing external control.
▓ Action sociology ignores the role that power and inequality play in shaping the outcome of interaction.
▓ It is often not clear in action sociology whether, in establishing our self-identity, we are passive victims of others, or able to reject others' definitions of us.

(K)(U)
(I)(An)

Exercise 4.15

Construct a diagram that illustrates how the following theories fit with each other; for example, which theories agree or disagree. Try to include the names of the sociologists most associated with the theories, and some of the key concepts they might use.

• modernism
• postmodernism
• Marxism
• neo-Marxism
• functionalism
• Weberian sociology
• interactionism
• phenomenology
• ethnomethodology

Hint: start off by drawing the macro/micro divide in sociological theory and work from there.

(I)(A)
(An)

Exercise 4.16

Using the timeline shown in Table 4.1, identify which events could have contributed to which aspects of the following theories:

• Weber
• Postmodern theorists such as Baudrillard
• Symbolic interactionism (Chicago School, Cooley, Mead)
• Phenomenology
• Ethnomethodology (Garfinkel)

Table 4.1 Timeline of theorists, publications and events from the 1920s to the 1970s

Decade	Theorists	Publication of key works	Events in society
1920s	**1858–1918** Georg Simmel **1864–1920** Max Weber **1864–1929** Charles Cooley **1863–1931** George H. Mead **1899–1959** Alfred Schutz **1900–97** Herbert Blumer **1917–87** Harold Garfinkel **1929–2007** Jean Baudrillard	**1904** *The Protestant Ethic and the Spirit of Capitalism* (Weber – translated later)	**1923** Television invented **1928** Antibiotics invented Economic boom after First World War ended with the 1929 Wall Street Crash.
1930s			**1930s** Great Depression worldwide **1931** Empire State Building completed **1932** First regular BBC television broadcasts **1937** First digital computer invented **1938** Ballpoint pen invented **1939–45** Second World War Period of urbanization **1939** Release of films *The Wizard of Oz, Gone with the Wind*
1940s		**1945** *Mind, Self and Society* (Mead)	**1940** McDonald's restaurant company founded **1945** First atomic bombs dropped on Hiroshima and Nagasaki **1945** Satellite TV invented **1947** Mobile phone invented **1947** Microwave oven first sold **1949** 45rpm record invented in USA Food rationing and evacuations Start of the Cold War between nuclear powers

1950s			**1950** Invention of the credit card, USA
			1950–53 Korean War
			1953 Discovery of DNA
			1954 Deregulation of broadcasting; introduction of commercial television
			1957 First satellite orbiting Earth: Russian Sputnik 1
			1958 EEC formed
			1959 Peace protest in Trafalgar Square, London; start of 'ban the bomb' demonstrations
			Period of increasing affluence with significant rise in car ownership
1960s		**1967** *Studies in Ethnomethodology* (Garfinkel)	**1960** The Beatles formed
		1967 *The Social Construction of Reality: A Treatise in the Sociology of Knowledge* (Berger and Luckmann)	**1960** Premier of *Coronation Street* TV soap opera (UK)
			Decade of student protests
			Civil rights movements (black, feminist, lesbian and gay)
		1969 *Symbolic Interactionism: Perspective and Method* (Blumer)	**1959–75** Vietnam War
			1969 First human on the moon
			1969 Divorce Reform Act
1970s			**1970** Equal Pay Act
			1975 First video recorders sold

ⓊⒶ
ⒶⓝⒺ

Exercise 4.17

To what extent can the theories of Weber, Simmel, symbolic interactionism, phenomenology and ethnomethodology be used to explain the following contemporary events? Use appropriate terms and concepts. For each event:

• Identify which elements of each approach can explain the event.
• Identify which elements of each approach cannot explain the event.

1. Going to university for the first time or moving to a different town for a new job. Initially finding the move unsettling and scary, but after a couple of months, returning home and having difficulty adjusting back.
2. Employers spending a significant amount of money running weekend residential team-building events for their employees.

CONCLUSION

Along with Marx and Durkheim, Weber was a founder of sociology. However, with his work – and the ideas of Simmel – we have an alternative view to that espoused by the more structuralist sociologies of Marx and Durkheim. For Weber, culture and identity are underpinned by the active and creative role that humans play in society. Culture and identity are the result of meaningful action. Humans are not passive 'robots' of either class forces or group solidarity.

The ideas of Weber and the 'action' tradition he represents have been very popular in Western sociology since the 1950s and 1960s, and represent an attempt to study the individual rather than to ignore the individual in favour of the group. The approaches and explanations of symbolic interactionism, phenomenology and ethnomethodology have impacted on research methods as well as focused our attention on the role of the individual in constructing their identity. Issues of meaning, agency and socialization are still important in sociology today, as illustrated by the ideas of Bourdieu and Giddens in the following chapters.

Important concepts
Action • Causality • Erklären • Ethnomethodology • Interaction • Micro • Modern • Phenomenology • Postmodern • Symbolic interactionism • Typifications • Verstehen

Exam focus
(a) Assess the view that human society is built on a social construction of reality.   (b) How useful do you find the 'micro' 'action' sociological interpretations of the role of culture in society when compared with more 'macro' sociological insights?

Critical thinking
1. To what extent do individuals have the power to create their own identities and cultures?

2. Berger and Luckmann (1967) argue that individuals try to integrate their everyday reality into a 'symbolic universe'; that is, a larger system of meaning and a link to the belief systems of other individuals. Religion and science are examples of 'symbolic universes'. How important are 'symbolic universes' for individuals?

Chapter 5

Socialization, Self-Identity and the Life Course

After studying this chapter, you should:

- be able to understand the role of socialization in identity formation
- have knowledge of different theoretical explanations of the role of socialization
- be able to reflect on the role of socialization throughout the life course
- understand the link between age and identity development

INTRODUCTION

Sociological theory has given us an understanding of how individuals may interact with their culture and the world around them to create or be allocated identity. Formation of identity and culture is seen by many as a process that starts at birth and continues throughout our lives through socialization. Initiation into cultures and subcultures was of as much interest to classical sociologists as it is to those writing today. Our self-identity changes and develops throughout the life course. However the role of individuals and that of wider society is viewed differently by a range of theorists.

SOCIALIZATION

Socialization is the process by which individuals learn about the culture, norms, values and expectations of the society they live in. It starts at birth and continues through childhood, which has been argued to be a crucial time for socialization (the family being the agent of primary socialization). However, socialization continues throughout our lives through secondary agents of socialization: education, peer groups, the workplace, religion, the mass media and so on.

To recap, different types of sociologists see socialization differently:

- Functionalists, such as Talcott Parsons, see socialization as crucial to learning the norms and values of society, to ensure that individuals fit in with society and to guarantee social solidarity. In addition, socialization prepares people for their future role in society as well as enabling the effective functioning of society itself.

▨ Marxists argue that socialization is the means by which indoctrination of the working classes happens, to ensure that they play their part in the capitalist system. Socialization is a process reflecting the power of the bourgeoisie.

▨ Interactionist theorists focus on how individuals, from childhood, play a part in the process of socialization. Individuals experience socialization differently and interpret the social world around them differently. However, they will be socialized into the norms, symbols and language of those they interact with.

Ⓐ
Exercise 5.1

Where do you learn the following?

1. The music and books you like.
2. To respect people older than you.
3. Not to pick your nose in public.
4. What slang words mean.
5. How to deal with bullies.
6. The appropriate clothes to wear for different occasions.
7. Whether there is a God/gods.
8. Who is the current president of the USA.

Are we taught the above explicitly or implicitly? Which agents of socialization are involved? Write approximately 100 words.

Exercise 5.2

1. Are some agents of socialization more important than others?
2. Which are the most important agencies of socialization for adults?

Exercise 5.3

There are isolated examples of individuals who have grown up without human role models or company. Some of these cases are a result of war or social unrest, and have resulted in individuals being brought up by animals (such as the example of a young boy from Uganda). Alternatively, because of abuse, where individuals have been isolated in a single room with or without limited human contact (Genie*), or institutionalized with very little contact with adult humans (orphanages in some parts of Eastern Europe). When they are 'discovered', the children or adults in these circumstances often display aspects of animal behaviour, have no understanding of language and are unable to participate in everyday life. Psychologists have studied the effects of this 'institutionalization' and deprivation on development.

*'Genie', the pseudonym of a child from California, spent the first thirteen years of her life tied to her cot or toilet with only very limited contact with her father before her abuse was discovered in 1970.

Read the text in the box above and consider what the impact would be of limited or complete lack of socialization in society today. Further details of these isolated cases can be found through internet searches (try 'feral children', which they are sometimes referred to as) or in psychological research on privation.

In terms of culture and identity, socialization is a crucial process, but it has been interpreted differently by different sociological theories. We shall look at some of these theories in more detail, to focus on the link to the formation and development of identity and culture.

Symbolic interactionism and socialization

As discussed in Chapter 4, symbolic interactionists look at how individuals interpret the self in everyday situations and create their sense of self from that process of interaction. As Mead (1934, quoted in Dillon 2010) notes:

> The self is something which has a development, it is not initially there, at birth, but arises in the process of social experience and activity, that is, develops in the given individual as a result of his relations to that process as a whole and to other individuals in that process.

Our sense of self is created throughout social situations. The family is a crucial agent of socialization, but through our families we also learn what the expectations are in wider society, of the 'generalised other' (Mead, 1934; Dillon, 2010). A conflict may exist because of what society expects and what you as an individual want. This, in part, can account for the creation of subcultures, which illustrates the interaction between the individual and society, action and structure. Examples of these are youth subcultures, which will be looked at in detail in Chapter 9. Individuals also become aware that there are competing interpretations and symbols within the 'generalized other' with respect to gender, class, sexuality and ethnicity (Collins, 2004; Dillon, 2010) and the individual has to accept or reconcile these conflicting socialization influences.

SELF-IDENTITY AND THE MAP OF ONE'S LIFE

As Jenkins (1996) notes, from the moment of birth, every individual is placed into a web of identity-defining moments, interactions and processes. These include:

- The naming of the child (this might even take place before the birth).
- The establishment of its sex.
- The establishment that the child is 'healthy'.
- The legal and bureaucratic process of birth registration.

The moment of birth, in modern Western societies, brings to the individual a whole host of cultural assumptions, legal rules and laws, and subjective meanings, through the adults that interact with the individual during the early years. Yet, despite all this instilling of group identity, during the course of their lives, individuals come to define themselves as people in their own right, they achieve self-consciousness and develop a sense of identity. Though we as humans are a group of 'social' beings, we eventually become people in our own right, not simply as defined by law and legally responsible for our actions and their consequences, but 'inside our head'. The process leading to a fully self-conscious selfhood has been conceived as a series of stages initiated by others through socialization. In early infanthood, play – especially 'copying games' – is considered important to this process.

Exercise 5.4

Identify examples of games played during childhood that teach children norms and values, and explain how they help to develop a sense of self.

According to Jenkins (1996), at birth individuals are the victims of others' definitions of their identity. They learn who they are from these others. Later they gain greater 'agency'; that is, they gain greater control over their lives, and therefore over their personhood. The question is, however, how much agency do individuals really have in the overall process of knowing who they are, and when does this occur?

Exercise 5.5

'Our own sense of humanity is a hostage to the categorizing judgements of others ... the social world is always a world of others, and, in the beginning, the balance is overwhelmingly in favour of the identificatory work that they do' (Jenkins, 1996).

1. The above quotation notes that, in the early stages of our life, who we think we are is often defined for us by others. Think about this idea, and then write a list of the ways that individuals can be judged/labelled by others – the actual judgements they can make.
2. Divide your list into those that you think are powerful and long-lasting, and those that you think are not.
3. Answer the following question on the basis of your lists. Can our identity be shaped for us by others? Explain your view in a couple of paragraphs.

Dunn (1988) suggests that we start to become responsible for ourselves in early childhood. Awareness of others leads to concern for others, and through this a concern with who we ourselves might be. Just when this self-concern develops in the child is still a matter of debate within developmental psychology and sociology, but many commentators agree about the pattern of this journey of self-discovery. According to Poole (1994, cited in Jenkins, 1996):

 By seven to nine months infants have become attached to the adults who are responsible for their day-to-day care.

- At 12 months, infants begin to recognize objects around them and understand adults' categorization of these objects.
- By the age of two a basic familiarity with conversational language has been established.
- Children continue to learn about the actions of others – especially through copying play, which represents a form of 'abstract thought'.
- Between the ages of two and four, children develop and elaborate on notions of community, and identify themselves as sharing group membership with the people in question.
- At this point, cultural pressures from others make gender an important factor in the establishment of self-identity.
- From about five or six years old, children begin to develop a sense of moral responsibility for their actions and the consequences of their actions. They begin to learn to present a mask of their self to others.
- As children move towards adulthood they become members of wider and more varied groups and communities of identification.

Contained within this model of self-development are the two key features of action sociology in respect of the formation of self-identity:

- identity is created through interaction with others; and
- humans are active and reflexive in the creation of who they are.

We have, then, within action sociology a model of humanity based on a range of 'differences' or 'opposites' that make up the individual:

- humans are both individuals and members of a group;
- humans are both active and passive receivers of group stimuli; and
- humans are both socialized into culture and have agency.

In other words, self-identity is created through what might appear to be a rather contradictory process: one's individuality originally comes from others. This observation has led to a reworking of action sociology in the work of Pierre Bourdieu, and this will be further examined in Chapter 6 by looking at the ideas of Anthony Giddens.

THE LIFE COURSE

While self-identity is seen to be the product of both socialization and interaction – of the passing down of culture between individuals and self-experience – identity also changes as the individual progresses along what is referred to as the 'life course'. The best way to understand what sociologists mean by the life course is to think about all the stages of life experienced by a human being who lives a full life. The stages along this life course can be characterized as:

- early infancy;
- late infancy;
- childhood;

- youth;
- young adulthood;
- middle age;
- old age.

The characteristics associated with each stage of the life course are defined by the culture of the society in question – and this culture determines how one thinks about oneself. David Morgan (1996) uses the idea of the life course to illustrate how cultures perceive and define who individuals are in each passing stage. However, Morgan points out that the individuals themselves might use the idea of the life course in an active and reflexive fashion in order to think about their lives – past and future – and themselves. Anthropological research shows that stages and interpretations of the life course vary between cultures and subcultures. For example, attitudes towards ageing, status and roles vary from one culture to another. There has been a wealth of anthropological research into rites of passage that individuals experience as they pass through different stages of the life course. Youth culture and subcultures will be studied in more detail in Chapter 9.

Ⓘ Ⓐ
Exercise 5.6

One's culture provides individuals with ideas about what each stage of the life course might be like. These symbols and images are important, since they provide a basis for identity according to one's age.
   Look back at the list of stages of the life course, then write a description of what your own culture says about each of the stages.

Morgan notes that, while the life course is in some senses biological because it is based on the ageing of the human body, it is also cultural, since it varies between societies. Also, human beings are highly reflexive and creative in how they understand their lives and their place in the life course. This is a major source of identity formation. The moving from one stage to another is sometimes characterized by elaborate ceremonies and 'rites of passage'. We do not simply move from one stage to the next and forget all that happened before. Rather, we carry memories of our past actions and interactions and have hopes and desires for our future. We can remember who we once were. We can reflect on who we are at each new stage of the life course, and can try to influence who we become.

Ⓘ Ⓐ
Exercise 5.7

Over time, social definitions of age change. Choose any two stages of the life course and for each one write a paragraph on how our image of that stage has changed in recent times, compared with the image held in the past.

An interesting aspect of identity is that once people 'know who they are' they are sometimes dissatisfied with how they are living their life. So how do individuals cope with the suffocating, mundane routines of everyday life? Cohen and Taylor (1992) argue that because of the routines and patterns of everyday life, interaction can become predictable and lose its interest to those who crave creativity, so individuals make what Cohen and Taylor call 'escape attempts':

> The life plan maps our existence. Ahead of us run the career lines of our jobs, our marriage [or relationship or partnership], our leisure interests, our children and our economic fortunes. But sometimes when we scan these maps, traverse these routes, follow the signs, we become strangely disturbed by the predictability of the journey, the accuracy of the map, the knowledge that today's route will be much like yesterday's... What we object to is the sense that we are sinking into a patterned way of existence... that they no longer appear to us as fresh and novel. They are becoming routinized. They no longer help us to constitute our identity. (1992:46–7.)

In this view, because the life course is mapped out before us, life is too predictable. We know what roles we shall be required to take on, and when. We can predict who others might want us to be. To continue to develop a sense of identity in an active and creative way, individuals might try to shape the direction of their lives and their future in special ways. Equally, they might try to use their time – especially their private or leisure time – to establish a stronger idea of who they wish to be, to mould their identities in new ways. Such individuals might turn to a number of different activities, such as:

- 'Activity enclaves' – for example, hobbies, games, gambling, sex and sexual fantasies.
- 'New landscapes' – for example, holidays, mass culture, art.
- 'Mindscaping' – for example, drugs, therapy.

These activities might help to build a fresh, more interesting sense of identity and to escape the mundane routines of the life course.

Exercise 5.8

Think of other examples that fit into the categories provided by Cohen and Taylor. For each of your examples, explain how they might help us to escape from our old routines and to build new identities.

Type of activity	Explain how your examples might help individuals to escape from old routines and build new identities
Activity enclaves	
1.	
2.	
3.	
New landscapes	
1.	
2.	
3.	

Mindscaping	
1.	
2.	
3.	

Exercise 5.9

Using Cohen and Taylor's analysis, explain the popularity of 'gap years', where people take time out from work to travel, study or do something completely different both during early adulthood and, increasingly, for older people taking a 'career break'.

AGE AND AGEING

One aspect of the life course that is of increasing interest to sociologists is ageing and old age. Standards of living and improvement in health care are predicted to result in an increasingly 'elderly' population. As concepts of age are socially constructed, sociologists are interested in how self-conceptions of identity change as we age. Research into the area of ageing, and how identity is impacted by ageing have become more significant. Rowe and Kahn (1998) argued for a 'new gerontology', in which they identified three elements in 'successful ageing'. These were being healthy, maintaining mental and physical functions; and engaging with a wider social life.

Andrew Blaikie (1999), in *Ageing and Popular Culture*, argues that there has been a significant change in our perceptions of retirement. This is linked to the power of this older group as consumers. He refers to the increased opportunities available in the 'retirement' years, where a myriad of opportunities are available to individuals. Identity during this period is characterized by a greater sense of choice. However, Katz and Marshall (2003) counter-argue that consumerist pressures on the elderly resulted in an 'anti-ageing' ideology, in which appearing to get old becomes a 'non-choice' as the elderly are encouraged to defy time through cosmetic surgery and lifelong learning. Blaikie (1999) notes that physical decline linked to age does impact on many, and in these circumstances the range of identities from which to choose may be limited. Status gained from the role in the workplace is lost, which can result in difficulties in adjusting to this new status. The experiences of the retirement period are also dependent on social class, gender and ethnicity, and are thus characterized by diversity. For example, Andrews (2009) rejected the dichotomy of optimistic and pessimistic views of ageing, and argued for exploring of 'multiple narratives' of ageing, in which cultural settings constrain but do not limit the forms and experiences of 'being elderly'.

RETURNING TO THE RELATIONSHIP BETWEEN THE INDIVIDUAL AND SOCIETY

When trying to distinguish the ways that different sociologists think about the role of humanity in society, Hollis (1977) identified two main approaches. Structural sociologists (see Chapter 3) tend to see humans as victims of culture and structure. This is described as a 'plastic (wo)man' approach to thinking about the relationship between the individual and society, since humans are seen as being shaped, moulded and manipulated by social forces. Action sociologists tend to see humans in the completely opposite way – not as plastic but as 'autonomous': totally able to make their own decisions and to control the course of their own lives. As Hollis notes, 'Where Plastic Man [*sic*] has his [*sic*] causes, Autonomous Man [*sic*] has his [*sic*] reasons' (ibid.: 12).

Many contemporary sociologists find both these models too extreme – individuals are not the total subjects of culture, but without culture they would not become truly human. Therefore, some sociologists have attempted to find a point somewhere between the two approaches. We shall look here at the ideas of Pierre Bourdieu, who has been influenced strongly by action approaches even though ultimately he is seeking a compromise between action and structure.

Pierre Bourdieu

Bourdieu (1990, 1993) is concerned with what people in society 'do' in their everyday lives – a common interactionist focus. He points out that social practices are more structured than simply the expression of free will, but are less controlled than a simple response to structural forces. Everyday life – or as he calls it, 'practice' – is characterized by four distinctive and important elements: time, space, unorchestration and improvization. All social practices take place according to the natural rhythms of time, though it is culture that makes these rhythms significant in our lives. Practice is also associated with a rhythm: different types of practice have different tempos, and take different amounts of time to complete. Social practices also take place in cultural and physical locations – whether it is in the mind, or in an actual physical area. For example, some activities that culture has established to be acceptable in a private bathroom are not acceptable in a public street.

Social practices often appear to 'just happen' to those who live in society. The way we act is patterned, and some patterns are more common in some cultures than in others, but there is still an element of chance to the whole thing. In this sense, it is sometimes unorchestrated. Finally, since social practices are not necessarily planned in advance by those who engage in them, they are fluid in nature. Practices are dynamic, constantly changing, and in order to 'get by' and to fit into society, we sometimes need to make them up as we go along. They are based on improvization. We have to learn how to understand and cope with new situations and encounters.

According to Bourdieu, as we – the members of a culture – grow up we are instilled with some of the rules of the game of social interaction, which we experiment with and practise with others. At first these others are our immediate family group, later our peers and, later still, people of our own choosing. To become a competent social practitioner – to fit in – we have to develop the skills of interaction and we can only do this through practising interaction. Self-identity is important in becoming a competent actor in society. We need to have a sense of who we are and where we are in relation to the wider practices of those around us. Though we have to become familiar with the rules of practice through socialization, there is a sense in which we can 'just get on with it' on a day-to-day basis, and do not have to question what we do within our culture. Bourdieu calls this 'doxa'.

Bourdieu rejects both the view that humans are free, and the opposite view that they are passive victims of culture. Instead, he links these two views together through his idea of 'habitus'. This means that, while we are never totally free, we do have choices – even though we are not always aware of making such choices or conscious that we will benefit from the choices we do make. How we act is based partly on creativity and partly on habit, on familiarity. We learn the rules but can bend and adapt them as we go along. Bourdieu likens the idea of 'habitus' to a living, thinking and learning computer program. It is self-correcting, not totally pre-programmed but certainly not free either. We have the general rules and the background experiences and we can apply them to specific situations: 'It can be understood by analogy with a computer program . . . but a self-correcting program. It is constituted from a systematic set of simple and partially interchangeable principles, from which an infinity of solutions can be invented, solutions which cannot be directly deduced from its conditions of production' (Bourdieu, 1993: 87).

We learn to behave – to act with our bodies – in particular ways, out of habit and experience and requiring no conscious thought to put into practice in everyday life. Culture provides us with a routine – but one that has many possible outcomes, even if we are not aware of this at the time. Acting in society is partly determined by the culture of that society, which is beyond our control and our conscious intentions, desires and motivations. We also have a sense of everyday routine that we take for granted – that becomes a 'habit'. Finally, we all have a unique biography – all our past interactions stored in our memory – which we draw upon as a resource to help us to understand. Therefore, how we act is, at one and the same time, regular, patterned and predictable, yet also fluid, unique and unpredictable.

CONCLUSION

Socialization is seen by sociological theory as being crucial in the formation and acquisition of culture and identity. However, the roles of the individual and of society are interpreted in various ways. Pierre Bourdieu feels that we can act according to our culture and the world around us, but we are not totally free to act as we wish. The work of Bourdieu will be further developed in the next chapter with reference to Anthony Giddens, Erving Goffman and Jürgen Habermas.

Important concepts

Doxa • Habitus • Primary agent of socialization • Secondary agent of socialization • Socialization

---

Exam focus

(a) Discuss the role of socialization in identity creation.
(b) Critically consider how socialization has been explained by different sociological theories.

Critical thinking

1. Critically consider whether the role of the media as an agent of socialization has increased in importance in recent decades.
2. To what extent is our identity shaped by others?

Chapter 6

How Much Agency Do Individuals Have in Culture?

After studying this chapter you should:

- understand the concept of 'agency'
- understand the importance of the concept of agency for action sociologies
- be aware of the ideas of Goffman on the nature of humanity
- understand the ideas of Giddens and Beck on 'reflexive modernity'
- be aware of the contribution made by Habermas to the study of the relationship of the individual to society
- understand the ideas of Archer on the role of reflexivity in culture and identity

INTRODUCTION

So far, we have established that a dominant theme running throughout sociological thought is the relationship of the individual to society. Since sociologists have conceived this relationship in different ways, a variety of theories, theoretical perspectives and world views have been developed to help social theorists establish frameworks to aid our understanding of why social life is as it is.

Exercise 6.1

This chapter focuses on the idea of free will – the freedom individuals may or may not have to create culture and shape their own identities. As a reminder of the ideas presented so far in this book, write a couple of sentences on the freedom that each of the following thinkers claim that humans have to create their own culture and identity; that is, these thinkers' views on the existence of free will:

Durkheim • Parsons • Marx • Simmel • Weber • Bourdieu

An important theme we have touched on in other chapters is the notion of 'agency', which in a very limited sense means freedom to act, or having free will. However, for many sociologists the concept has a more precise meaning. Consider the following definition by Giddens (1993):

> Agency refers not to the intentions people have in doing things but to their capability of doing those things in the first place ... Agency concerns events of which an individual is the perpetrator, in the sense that the individual could, at any phase in a given sequence of conduct, have acted differently. Whatever happened would not have happened if that individual had not intervened. Action is a continuous process, a flow, in which the reflexive monitoring which the individual maintains is fundamental to the control of the body that actors ordinarily sustain throughout their day-to-day lives.

In this view, agency is about choice and the freedom to exercise that choice. It is about the ability of an individual to imagine the outcome of a social encounter and to act in such a way as to achieve that outcome. Central to this notion of agency is the idea of reflexivity, which is people's ability to think about themselves and others around them. People are the product of their experiences, but they can try to shape and mould these experiences. Whereas structural sociologists (see Chapters 2, 3 and 4) may deny that individuals have agency in society, it is a key concept in many versions of the action approach, as it is for those who have attempted to bridge the divide between structure and action sociologies.

The anthropologist, Anthony Cohen (1994), stresses that when thinking about agency we must not separate the individual totally from wider society. To do so would be to ignore the fact that humans are social beings who live within a culture. To see humans as creative and totally free in everything they do would be to ignore power and the importance of the group. It overstates the amount of freedom we have 'to be who we wish'. Cohen suggests that we should see humans as having a 'creative self', but they have been given the ability and power to be creative because of culture, not despite it, or because of its absence.

According to Cohen (1994), 'Culture requires us to think, gives us forms – metaphors, dogmas, names, "facts" – to think with, but does not tell us what to think: that is the self's work'. In other words, culture offers us a range of choices to choose from in a creative fashion. Culture provides us with the possibilities for action, but we take responsibility – through our possession of agency – for what we actually do. Such a view would attract criticism from many feminist and Marxist sociologists, who would argue that the possibilities provided to humans are extremely limited and are the outcome of power struggles in society. In this view we only have the freedom to choose between a number of situations of inequality – which is not much freedom of choice at all.

Ⓚ Ⓤ
Ⓘ

Exercise 6.2

Once you have read the relevant chapters, complete an extended version of the following table to summarize the Marxist and feminist views on culture, identity and socialization discussed in Chapters 2, 3 and 12.

	Views on the role of culture in society	**Views on how identity is created**	**Views on the role played by socialization in society**
Marxism			
Feminism			

Exercise 6.3

Refer to the previous chapters (and the index at the back of the book) to remind yourself of the following key concepts by defining each one:

Structure • Social control • Determinism • Nature • Action • Voluntarism • Habitus • Nurture

THINKING USING CULTURE: THE CREATIVE SELF

In this chapter we shall look at the contribution made by three key thinkers – Erving Goffman, Anthony Giddens and Jürgen Habermas – to the understanding of how much freedom individuals have to create their own identity.

Erving Goffman

Writing from the symbolic interactionist tradition (see Chapter 4), American thinker Erving Goffman (1968, 1971a, 1971b) presents us with a version of looking at 'thinking, creative and self-aware individuals' which he calls 'dramaturgical analogy'. In *The Presentation of Self in Everyday Life*, Goffman (1971b) states:

> The perspective employed in this report is that of the theatrical performance; the principles derived are dramaturgical ones. I shall consider the way in which the individual in ordinary work situations presents himself and his activity to others, the ways in which he guides and controls the impression they form of him, and the kinds of things he may and may not do while sustaining his performance before them.

For Goffman, humans are creative in the sense that they think about the interactions they have and the contexts in which these interactions take place, and about their and others' motives for action. In doing this, they seek to take control of the situation for their own ends by presenting a mask or impression. Goffman sees the purpose of interaction as being about control of the definition of the social situation. Goffman's 'dramaturgical analogy' is so called because he compares social life to the theatre:

- Humans play many different roles.
- They follow certain 'scripts' that are relevant in some situations but not in others.
- Individuals give 'front stage' and 'back stage' performances.
- Interaction – since it is social by nature – is a performance to an audience.

'In developing the conceptual framework employed in this report, some language of the stage was used. I spoke of performers and audiences; of routines and parts; of performances coming off or falling flat; of cues, stage settings and backstage; of dramaturgical needs, dramaturgical skills, and dramaturgical strategies' (Goffman, 1971b). This means that the public identity we convey may be no more than a mask or a performance, designed to create a specific and calculated impression in order to take control of the definition of the situation or public encounter. The implication of these ideas for self-identity is that when we are in public we wear many different masks of our self. In a calculating way we adopt many different roles, many different identities, in order to get what we want from an interaction. Goffman refers to the techniques we use in day-to-day life to convey the impression we wish as 'impression management'. We use these techniques to shape, mould and direct how we behave towards others, and how we wish others to behave towards us.

	Exercise 6.4

Re-read the above discussion and provide examples of Goffman's key ideas in a copy of the following table.

Give four examples of 'scripts' we use in society	1. 2. 3. 4.
Give two examples each of back- and front-stage activities	Back stage 1. 2. Front stage 1. 2.
Give five examples of social situations in which you might wish to manage the impression others have of you, such as a job interview	1. 2. 3. 4. 5.

Evaluating the ideas of Goffman

Goffman's ideas have proven very influential, but some writers argue that his work is unclear about the nature of 'true' self-identity. Goffman's strengths are:

- He sees humans as active and creative.
- He has conducted a variety of studies based on participant observation to back up his claims.

- The 'dramaturgical analogy' is a useful tool for thinking about everyday life.
- Goffman relates human interaction to structures of a sort. He notes in his study on life in asylums (1968) and elsewhere that interaction can be patterned and routinized by institutions (which can have power inequalities). He even thinks that people within these institutions can calculate their actions.

With regard to weaknesses, it is unclear what the precise relationship is between front-stage and back-stage performances. This confusion begs questions about identity that Goffman never clearly answers:

- Do we act in a manipulative and calculating way, yet really 'know who we are'?
- When alone, or with those with whom we are familiar, does our 'real self' come out?
- If we are always playing a role, which role do we play when alone?
- Do humans have a 'real self', or are we just a collection of masks?
- What happens when people don't follow traditional or expected roles?

Exercise 6.5

Answer the following questions (try to write a couple of paragraphs on each). Use ideas presented in previous chapters to help you, and give reasons for your views.

1. Do you ever act in a manipulative and calculating way? Be honest with yourself!
2. When alone, or with those with whom you are familiar, does your 'real self' come out?
3. Do you have a 'real self', or are you just a collection of masks or roles?

By ignoring structure altogether, some action sociologies give us a blinkered view of human identity. When we act in society, we might choose a particular type of performance for self-serving reasons, but the scripts and roles that we follow were constructed for us by others before our birth. They are a 'structure' of sorts. This observation has led some commentators to think again about the relationship between agency and structure – as seen in the work of Anthony Giddens.

Anthony Giddens

In order to understand how Giddens sees the relationship between the individual and society – between structure and action – we shall consider the following quotations from his book *The Constitution of Society* (1984: 25):

- 'Structure is not "external" to individuals... it is in a certain sense more "internal" than exterior.'
- 'Structure is not to be equated with constraint but is always both constraining and enabling.'
- 'Structure has no existence independent of the knowledge that agents have about what they do in their day-to-day activity.'

From these three quotations we can sense an attempt to unite structure and agency/action – to see them as a 'two-way street', or as being in what is known as a 'symbiotic relationship'. This means that they feed off each other, rather than one being the outcome of the other. Structure cannot exist without the human beings who create it through their actions and meanings. Equally, young humans are born into the structures of others. These unchosen structures do not simply control, they also enable action to take place. For example, while the structure of language controls us from birth, without it we would not be able to act in a creative way. We may have a great deal of choice about the language we do use, but this choice lies within a set of rules we do not decide. Humans are seen as being able to think about their position within structures and to think about their actions – they have 'knowledgeability' about themselves and their place. Equally, knowledgeable actors can change structures through their actions over time.

Structures cannot exist without agents (humans), and agents cannot have agency without structures. When thinking about the relationship between structure and action in this way, Giddens formulated what he calls 'structurational sociology'. The aims of this type of sociology are indicated by the word used to describe it. Not just 'structure', or just 'action', but 'structure-action', or, if we combine these words – 'structuration'. In his *New Rules of Sociological Method*, Giddens (1976) listed a number of new rules he wanted to see taken up by sociology, and these eventually formed the basis of structurational sociology. He argues that humans must be seen as skilled performers. They have a great deal of knowledge about the rules of society, and when using these rules they are sensitive to variations in old situations and the problems of new encounters. While humans have agency, since they can make choices, Giddens stresses that they are still in some ways controlled: 'The realm of human agency is bounded. Men produce society, but they do so as historically located actors, and not under conditions of their own choosing' (ibid.: 168). Giddens refers to these structures as both 'enabling' and 'constraining'. There are still power differences in society, yet we can work within the structures to change them over time.

ⒶⒺ
Exercise 6.6

1. How realistic do you find Giddens' claims about the interrelationship between structure and action?
2. Has this view helped to resolve previous sociologists' debates on structure and action?

Answer both these questions in detail (approximately 150 words each).

ⒶⒺ
Exercise 6.7

Identify two strengths of Giddens' arguments and explain why they should be seen as strengths.

Two criticisms of Giddens

First, Archer (1982, 1988, 1996) (see Chapter 2) argues that, contrary to Giddens' claims, Giddens actually emphasizes the role of agents more than he does structures. What this indicates is that while his intention is to bridge the gap between structure and action, ultimately he comes down on one side – the side of action. A consequence of this is that he exaggerates the degree of choice that individuals have over their own lives, and plays down the fact that often our lives are not of our own choosing. Second, New (1993) offers a somewhat opposite but complementary criticism. She suggests that Giddens ignores the fact that some individuals have more agency than others in society, since they have more power. Some people cannot be the authors of their own lives, but have to put up with lives that others have control over. Structures tend to control some people more than they do others. For example, 'If Giddens has taken the prison bars from structure, by the same token he has taken the bite from agency ... Giddens does not address the question of who can transform what aspects of social structure and how' (ibid.: 18–19).

Exercise 6.8

Giddens' work on structurational sociology is a popular topic in sociological debates and he is not without his critics. In your own words, rewrite the above criticisms by Archer and New to show that you understand them.

Exercise 6.9

In your opinion, how would Giddens himself evaluate/criticize the ideas of (i) functionalism; (ii) Marxism; and (iii) interactionism, as discussed earlier? Give reasons for your answers.

Jürgen Habermas

The German thinker, Jürgen Habermas (1981), is often regarded as a 'second generation' member of the Frankfurt School (see Chapters 2, 3 and 8), and as such he has continued the project known as 'critical theory', established by the original members of the Frankfurt School before the Second World War. Critical theory is an interdisciplinary approach to social theory that draws its inspiration from many intellectual sources, including the works of Marx, Freud and Weber. To this intellectual melting pot Habermas adds influences from the work of Durkheim and Parsons (see Chapter 3) and the more action-oriented approach found in the work of Mead (Chapter 4). Habermas is interested in how and why people act as they do, and in particular the role played by language, or rather by communication, in social relations. In *The Theory of Communicative Action*, Habermas (1981) draws an important distinction between two types of action: instrumental and rational. Whereas instrumental action is based on goals, rational action allows a more critical way of thinking that can aid the understanding of oneself and others. Habermas explains how rational thought is used by ordinary social actors to help them engage in rational action, especially when they communicate with others. This rational action can be used to break what Habermas sees as the exploitative chains of capitalist society.

Critiques of capitalism and ideology

Under capitalism, the masses are constrained by economic structures and therefore have no power. For people to break free from capitalism they have to be able to judge in a rational way their social situation and that of the wider society. They need to think about the world, and to reach agreement with others about what should be done, and how they should act. This agreement would be rational, not based on power inequalities, and would be a way for individuals to get at the 'truth' of their society. In continuing the Marxist project, Habermas (1987) takes up the concept of ideology (see Chapter 3) in his book *Toward a Rational Society*. Habermas seeks a society in which unrestricted communication can occur, a society free from domination, and free from the constraints of ideology. The existence of ideology is seen to lead to:

- falsehoods;
- a lack of critical thinking;
- inequalities of power during communication; and
- passive acceptance of society as it is.

The items listed above are seen by Habermas as characteristic of what previous Marxists referred to as 'false consciousness'. In making this critique of the role of false ideas in capitalism, Habermas's ideas link directly to those of the original members of the Frankfurt School, who were concerned with the part played by mass culture in denying critical thought to the masses (see Chapter 8). Central to Habermas's notion of the emancipation of humankind is the achievement of a truly 'ideal speech situation', where individuals are able to communicate in an active and free fashion, without the constraints of power, structure and ideology. This means that people become 'critical' in order to become free – hence the label given to the theorizing conducted by the Frankfurt School: 'critical theory'. This is a notion of agency, but by another name.

Exercise 6.10

Think about how Habermas's ideas relate to discussions of culture and identity, and how they are both formed in a capitalist society. Copy out and complete the table in this Exercise, focusing on the four observations by Habermas that are listed in the text. As a starting point there are some statements below that you can make use of:

- Control of the media and education results in only 'acceptable' cultural forms being available.
- Action is prevented. The power structure of the dominant class is retained.
- Upper classes promote certain beliefs through religion to ensure the working classes are 'in their place'. For example, the importance of hard work and deferring reward (Weber, 1985).

- Culture is not dynamic but is reproduced from one generation to the next.
- Limited language structures are available to the working classes. Success in education is limited to those with the language to succeed (Basil Bernstein, 1970, 1972, 1996).
- Individuals are not encouraged to think about the world or to promote change.
- Rational action is limited. New identities that could promote resistance are not formed. A limited range of identities and cultural forms is available.
- Individuals do not act freely.

Features of ideology in a capitalist society	What consequences might these have for the formation of culture and identity in an unequal, class-based society?
Falsehood	
A lack of critical thinking	
Inequalities of power during communication	
Passive acceptance of society as it is	

(An)(E)

Exercise 6.11

Suggest two strengths and two weaknesses of Habermas's ideas. Consider whether some of the weaknesses of structurational sociology have been resolved by Habermas.

CLARIFYING WHAT IS MEANT BY 'AGENCY'

Campbell (2009) notes that the term 'agency' is often ambiguous. While the concept has been used widely, it has been difficult for sociologists to define clearly exactly what they mean by agency. Agency itself is a variable, and as such it is then something that is not always present. It is possible to look at the factors that impact on agency, and which of these might limit its existence. Campbell identifies two types of agency:

1. The ability of an actor to 'initiate and maintain a programme of action'; this is about an individual having the free will to act.
2. The ability of an actor 'to act independently from the constraints of social structure', acting freely themselves, known as agentic power.

The first type of agency varies between individuals, over time and from place to place. Each type of agency exists independently of the other. Campbell comments that sociologists have not yet studied what factors limit human agency whereas this has been considered by social psychologists.

REFLEXIVITY

Archer's (1982, 1988, 1995, 2007) work on culture and agency reflects her aim to understand the relationship between culture and agency. Reflexivity, according to Archer, is the internal dialogue we all maintain; those conversations and discussions inside our minds that enable us to reflect, speculate, plan and 'mull over' actions, events, our roles and our identity: 'Internally, it is through self-talk that we define our ultimate concerns and thus our personal identities.' She argues that while many sociologists refer to a certain extent to this internal dialogue, it has not been studied in depth: 'Reflexivity is the "unknown soldier" of social science: hats are doffed to it but nothing is done to establish its identity.'

Archer considers how theorists such as Bourdieu (Chapter 5) and Giddens think differently about reflexivity. Bourdieu did not see reflexivity as being necessary to all, but only available to some. In contrast, Archer argues that some reflexivity is needed by all, but today, where 'global society is undergoing restructuring...these changes mean that personal reflexivity acquires an unprecedented importance in determining how we make our way through the world'. Reflexivity is a form of mediation that enables individuals to actively weigh up their concerns and the opportunities faced by groups within society. In this way individuals can reflect on and appraise their identity. However, Archer's approach is not to see identity as a work of fantasy created solely internally by individuals; it is part of humans being active agents, but a part that is also affected by context as well as by structural and cultural factors that are beyond the control of the individual.

CONCLUSION

Though the term itself is ambiguous, the ideas of action sociology have been highly influential in contemporary sociology, and have led to a number of similar yet different ways of thinking about the role of human agency in shaping the society we live in. The concern with meaning can be traced back to Weber and Simmel (Chapter 4) and has its contemporary expression in the very influential ideas of Bourdieu (Chapter 5), Giddens and Habermas.

What Giddens and Habermas have in common is a concern to continue the 'modernist' project (see Chapters 3 and 7) that characterized the birth of sociology: to unearth the truth about social life and to understand how individuals can improve their lives. However, postmodernists claim that since there is no longer a way of understanding truth because everything has become relativistic, then sociology has no more hope of providing a better understanding of social life than anything else. In the postmodern world, all claims to truth are as truthful as each other (see Chapter 7). Both Habermas and Giddens want to rescue sociology from what they see as the excesses of postmodern ideas, and it is to these ideas that we shall turn in the next chapter.

Important concepts
Dramaturgical analogy • Instrumental action • Rational action • Reflexivity • Structuration

Exam focus
(a) Assess the contribution made by Giddens to debates on culture and identity. (b) Evaluate the idea that the individual has choice in the creation of his/her own identity.

Critical thinking
1. How much freedom do individuals really have in the creation of their own identity and culture? 2. How would Marxist and feminist theorists criticize the concept of agency? 3. Identify similarities and differences between the theories of Giddens and Habermas. 4. 'The key feature of *reflexive* inner dialogue is silently to pose questions to ourselves and to answer them, to speculate about ourselves, any aspect of our environment and, above all, about the relationship between them' Archer (2007). To what extent can reflexivity contribute to identity?

Chapter 7

Modern and Postmodern Culture and Identity

After studying this chapter, you should:

- be able to compare and contrast modernist and postmodernist theories
- have an understanding of the arguments raised by different branches of postmodern thinking
- understand the postmodern view of culture and identity
- be able to evaluate postmodern ideas
- understand alternatives to postmodern thinking, in particular the idea of 'reflexive modernity'
- be able to explain theories of risk and evaluate their impact on culture and identity

INTRODUCTION

For many commentators, sociology in particular and social theory in general have undergone profound change as a result of the development of ideas referred to as 'postmodern'. Postmodernism (the theory) is based on the attempt to understand postmodernity (the time period). Though opinions vary, this change in society – and particularly in culture and identity – is said to have been taking place since the Second World War, and especially since the 1970s. Postmodernist views vary and are often complicated, uncertain, confusing and ambiguous. This is sometimes the result of a deliberate attempt to play with language, style and meaning, since this sense of 'uncertainty' is an important part of 'the postmodern condition'. In terms of actual changes in society and the way in which we live our lives, there are three main attitudes towards the state of postmodernity:

- Postmodernity has occurred.
- Postmodernity is occurring in society at present.
- Postmodernity will occur in the future.

Added to this is concern about the usefulness of the idea of postmodernity. For some, it should happen, for others it should not, and for yet others it will not happen and the theory should be replaced by other ideas. As Featherstone (1994: 1) comments: 'Any reference to the term "postmodernism" immediately exposes one to the risk of being accused of jumping on a bandwagon, of perpetuating a rather shallow and meaningless intellectual fad. One of the problems is that the term is at once fashionable yet irritatingly elusive to define.' Another point of confusion is whether postmodernity (the time period) represents a dramatic, sudden break with the past, or whether it is a more gradual extension of what went before. The prefix 'post' indicates, regardless of its definition, that postmodernity occurred, is occurring or will occur after the era of 'modernity' (see Chapter 3), and it is this idea we must examine first.

WHAT IS MODERNITY?

Though it is difficult to pinpoint exactly, what we call 'modernity' is usually associated with the era of industrialization and the time when sociology was being developed by its founders (see Chapter 3). Modernity – the period of the modern – comes from the Latin word *modo*, meaning 'just now', and this is a key feature in the modernist spirit: the founders' idea that life and society had changed. Their times – their 'just now' – were totally different from those of the traditional pre-industrial societies of the past.

| Exercise 7.1 |

The work of the founders of sociology is often seen as the starting point for the discussion of all sociological topics in all syllabus areas. Given the importance of the founders' ideas, brainstorm all that you can remember about them from your studies so far, before continuing with the rest of this chapter. Highlight elements of their theories that could be referring to 'modern' society.

Taking place in a time of rapid and massive change, modernity was characterized by the following elements:

- industrialization;
- urbanization;
- a rise in the importance of science;
- the growth of the manufacturing industry;
- secularization (the decline of religion);
- the invention of more advanced technology; and
- rationalization.

This was the age of science, based on the belief that human beings could understand and control everything. The world of nature was the slave and humanity was now in charge. The goals of these scientists – sociologists included – were to:

- Find the absolute truth.
- Develop universal general laws.

- Control the present.
- Predict the future.
- Control the shape and direction of the future.

Do you think that the founders got it right with their view of modernity, or has it become out of date? Copy out and complete the following table.

Features of modernity as described by the founders	To what extent has sociology met these goals?	Is this view dated or not? Explain your answer
To find the absolute truth		
To develop universal general laws		
To control the present		
To predict the future		
To control the shape and direction of the future		

At its inception, modernity was based on what is called the spirit of the 'Enlightenment' – the eighteenth-century philosophical movement that stressed the importance of reason and the replacement of religion and superstition with science and rationality. An excellent illustration of the modernists' preoccupation with rationalization is the work of Max Weber, and in particular his 'sociology of music' (1968; originally written in 1910–11). Weber saw the historical development of society as the development of rationality in all spheres of social life and social organization. In this context, 'rationalization' means the breaking down of an object of study into its constituent parts to better understand the whole. Rationality is thus seen as a fundamental part of the rise of both science and technology in the industrial era, and as providing the momentum for industrialization itself – a highly modernist image of social change.

Weber illustrated the historical development of rationality with reference to musical notation. For example, in pre-industrial 'traditional' society, music was passed down the generations as part of 'folk culture'. Songs were passed down by word of mouth and instrument-making was the task of skilled individuals. With the onset of rationalization a concern developed to analyse what music actually was – to break it down in order to better control it. Hence the creation of a universal system of notation, scales and so on. Similarly, the making of instruments became a matter of mass production. The rationalization process was seen as aiding humans to control the world around them: to seek out absolute truth and make order out of the chaos of nature.

Exercise 7.3

In a similar format to the table below, list the aspects of society that you think have become more 'rational' over time, as in Weber's example of music. For example, knowledge can now be 'broken down' and analysed (rationality) as a result of the growth of computer technology.

Area of social life that has become rational	How and why has this happened?
1. The role of knowledge in society	Advances in computer technology mean that knowledge can be collected more easily and swapped between groups of people.
2.	
3.	
4.	
5.	

This process of rationalization can also be seen as being responsible for the creation of sociology itself, since its aim was to develop a 'truthful' account of the social world. This modernist sociology project – the search for truth, absolute certainty and progression in society – is now under challenge from writers who suggest that society has moved away from and beyond this. We no longer live in modernity, but in postmodernity.

Exercise 7.4

While the founders of sociology were all theorists of the impact of industrialization on society, they each interpreted the process of modernity slightly differently, paying more attention to some aspects of it than others. Match each of the aspects listed below to the classical sociologist most associated with it. To do this you may need to refer back to the previous chapters.

Contribution to sociology

1. The role of class forces in society.
2. The dark side of the city for social identity.
3. The process of rationalization.
4. How solidarity changes with industrialization.
5. The decline of religion in society.
6. The decline of community with urbanization.
7. The importance of science for society and sociology.
8. The growth of an iron cage of bureaucracy.
9. How the group deals with the problems of individuality.

Classical sociologists
Marx • Durkheim • Weber • Simmel • Comte • Spencer

WHAT IS POSTMODERNITY?

Postmodernity is what comes after modernity. For many postmodernists, this era is characterized by a shift away from production and towards an economy, culture, identities and life-styles based on consumption. Postmodernity has brought the aims and spirit of modernity crashing down, especially the Enlightenment preoccupation with absolute truth and certainty.

As Anderson (1996) notes, 'We are living in a new world, a world that does not know how to define itself by what it is, but only by what it has just-now ceased to be.' In this view, the world has changed rapidly, so rapidly that confusion has taken over from certainty. The modernist world was fixed – it had a definite character. The postmodern world is based on the collapse of all that modernity held to be true and fixed. In postmodernity, truth, certainty and reality are provisional and relativistic. There are no more absolutes – no more definite standards. This is the case not only for morality but also for the knowledge we have about the world around us. There are too many choices on offer, all claiming to be the 'real' version of the 'truth'. Religion, politics, the sciences and so on all claim special access to the truth, but how can we tell which is correct? Knowledge has become a commodity and a form of power, rather than an absolute, a truth. Just as truth fragments into a plurality of truths, so the traditional means of identity formation based on class, gender, ethnicity and so on has been replaced by a plurality of sources of identity. In this way, dominant cultural meaning has been replaced by an individual search for meaning, and life-style has becomes a matter of choice. Ultimately, uncertainty, confusion, ambiguity and plurality will be all that is left.

Exercise 7.5

Consider the characteristics of the postmodern world. Do they all apply to present-day society? Taking each of the six points in turn, in a copy of the following table write a couple sentences on whether or not you think it is a realistic description of the times in which we live. Provide an example of each one.

Feature of postmodernity	Is this true of present-day society?	Example
The world has changed so rapidly that confusion has taken over from certainty		
In postmodernity, truth, certainty and reality have become provisional and relativistic. There are no more absolutes, no more definite standards		
There are too many choices on offer – religion, politics, the sciences and so on all claim special access to the truth, but how can we tell which is correct?		
Knowledge has become a commodity and a form of power, rather than an absolute, a truth		

The traditional means of identity formation, based on class, gender, ethnicity and so on, have been replaced by a plurality of sources of identity		
Dominant cultural meaning has been replaced by an individual search for meaning, and lifestyle has become a matter of choice		

As Featherstone (1992) observes: 'Despite the oft-remarked looseness and imprecision of the term postmodernism, it does have the merit of directing our attention towards the nature of contemporary cultural change.' Rather than postmodernism, Zygmunt Bauman (2000) uses the phrase 'liquid modernity' to refer to a period at the end of 'solid' modernity, where institutions have become more fluid and individuals have to be more flexible – some of the characteristics other theorists attribute to postmodernism. Liquid modernity is characterized by 'precarious uncertainty, short-term planning, instant gratification, the weakening of institutions, ephemeral relationships, struggles to manage risk, volatile consumerist identities and the collapse of viable communities' (Jay, 2010). Modernity is seen by postmodernists as a mistaken project. Investment in it is shown to have been illusory. No absolutes are possible in an age when 'anything goes'.

According to Anderson (1996), postmodernity has occurred in four key areas of social life:

- Our self-concepts have become more malleable – we are able to be who we want to be and there are innumerable choices on offer.
- Morality has dissolved – there are no fixed and absolute moral standards.
- As there are no rules or set ways to behave, in art and culture there is no way of telling if one tradition or style is 'better' than any other. The distinction between 'high' and 'low' culture no longer exists (see Chapter 8). All there is left to do is to play with styles – to mix and match.
- The process of globalization has had a dramatic effect on the world. The world appears a much smaller place as a result of global communications, world travel and tourism, and the spread of ideas across the globe.

'Postmodernity, then, is the age of over-exposure to otherness – because, in travelling, you put yourself into a different reality; because, as a result of immigration, a different reality comes to you; because, with no physical movement at all, only the relentless and ever-increasing flow of information, cultures interpenetrate' (ibid.: 6).

This means that what we once thought was true is now exposed as simply one truth among many. The more contact we have with other peoples and once distant cultures, the more we question the way we are. Space and time have changed – we can contact people on the other side of the world in an instant via mobile phones, the internet or video-conferencing. We can travel to anywhere we wish, and can experience and appreciate other cultures, art forms and music.

①⑳

Exercise 7.6

Consider the four aspects of postmodernity identified by Anderson and listed below. In your own words explain what each means and list as many examples of it as you can.

1. We can be who we wish to be.
2. Moral standards are no longer fixed.
3. The distinction between high and low culture has dissolved.
4. Globalization has made the world feel smaller.

Varieties of postmodernism

Postmodernists themselves disagree about how the condition of postmodernity can and should be interpreted. Some suggest that the fragmentation of truth and the rapid growth of possibilities will cause chaos and ambiguity, and are a threat to civilization as we know it, while others suggest that the collapse of absolutes is liberating – providing freedom and allowing us to be who we want to be.

⑪①

Exercise 7.7

In what respect might some postmodernists be correct when they claim that self-identity is now freer and more liberating than ever before? Give examples of all the sources of personal identity currently available to the individual – for example, sexuality, class and so on.

The French thinker, Jean-François Lyotard, in his book *The Postmodern Condition* (1984: xxiv–xxv), defines 'postmodern' as 'incredulity toward metanarratives'. What he means by this is that, in the postmodern age, knowledge has become provisional and as humans we see the old claims to truth for what they really are – fictions, stories or 'narratives'. Knowledge itself has undergone a profound change, and we have changed our uses of it and response towards it. Lyotard suggests that science and scientific knowledge have been exposed for what they are – once-powerful illusions that have lost their dominance. Hope can no longer be placed on the highly modernist notions of progress or reason, since what is considered as 'knowledge' depends on where a person is, and how s/he chooses to see what is around him/her. There is no such thing as a single truth, only a multiplicity of truths, and knowledge – which was once thought to give us access to the truth – is nothing more than a commodity. Knowledge can be bought and sold, and, in the age of communications technology, those who have the most knowledge also have the most power.

①Ⓐ

Exercise 7.8

Lyotard (1984) suggests that, in the postmodern age, knowledge is no longer about the search for 'truth', but is instead a form of power. Copy out and complete the following table, basing your answers on this claim by Lyotard. A few examples are provided to start you off.

Organization that might hold information (knowledge) about you	What sorts of information might they have about your life?	How might this situation lead to inequality of power?
1. Your bank		
2. Your supermarket		
3. Your local council		
4.		
5.		
6.		
7.		
8.		

According to another French postmodernist thinker, Jean Baudrillard (1981, 1988), under postmodernity, the nature of consumption has changed fundamentally (see Chapters 8, 10 and 11). When we buy objects and products – commodities – we no longer consume them as 'objects' but as 'signs' or 'symbols'. In other words, when we consume it is not the actual physical 'thing' – the material object – that matters, but what the object stands for in our culture. In other words, for most people, buying a pair of Nike trainers says less about the physical activity they will be involved in, and more about the image they wish to project to others. The consumption of signs in this way is considered by Baudrillard to be the basis of identity formation and life-style construction.

Exercise 7.9

Baudrillard claims that, when buying a product, one is really consuming the image or sign that the product stands for, which in turn leads to identity and life-style formation.

1. Choose any four designer logos from clothing companies. Find the logos (online or in magazines) or draw copies of them.
2. When we see each logo, what images come to mind?
3. What might people be trying to say about themselves by wearing these logos?

Baudrillard goes further still and suggests that the signs and symbols used by the media – their 'simulations of reality' – have become so powerful in postmodern society that the audience has come to depend on and use these media-generated symbols more than their sensory experiences. This makes the media 'more real than real', or 'hyper-real'.

Postmodernity and truth

A great deal of postmodern thinking is characterized by a belief in what is called 'relativism': the view that there are no absolute standards of truth, correctness, reality or morality. Instead, everything comes down to a matter of choice. This claim is in direct opposition to the modernist thinking discussed at the start of this chapter (see also Chapter 3). The founders believed in progress, development and objectivity, but these are seen by many postmodernists as nothing but games people once played – nothing but stories, which in their time were powerful and shaped human thinking, but do so no longer.

Rorty (1989, 1996), a postmodern philosopher, suggests that what we see as 'truth' is created rather than found. It is not 'just there', rather it is the result of how we see what is around us, and who it is doing the seeing. Rorty distinguishes between the responses of two groups' to 'the truth' – one is essentially modernist, the other postmodernist:

- *Metaphysicians.* These people base how they see the world on common-sense thought. They believe that there are ultimate truths – absolutes – and that their own approach to understanding the world is true, correct, right and just. This is highly modernist, since it does not see that truth is a matter of where you happen to be standing. These people are convinced – they know – they are right.
- *Ironicists.* Postmodern people accept that truth and reality are relative, and that any claim to truth is as good as any other. Since there are only variations, these people accept that all one can do is to play with the variety of truth claims on offer.

POSTMODERN IDENTITIES

Because of the emphasis on plurality, divergence and freedom in some versions of postmodernism, it makes more sense to talk about the rapid expansion of identities rather than a single postmodern identity. Postmodern identities are often described as 'fragmented' or 'fractured' – meaning that the dominant, absolute and rigid traditional sources of identity have been replaced by new sources. In other words, the modernist sources of identity such as class, gender and ethnicity have become much looser, much freer – able to be manipulated and played with as never before.

Anagnostou (2009) explains the theoretical impact of the postmodern period on identity: 'In contrast to the relatively stable and fixed identities sustained by modernity, postmodern identities have been theorized as reflexive constructs, products of choice, playful mixing of codes, fluid multiplicity, blurring of categories and surface eclecticism.'

Crook *et al.* (1992) suggest that, with the decline of modernist sources of identity, the media is often turned to, since it allows us to see, understand and perhaps copy a whole range of new identities. They refer to the media as providing 'symbolic communities' which, if we so desire, we can incorporate into our own sense of self. Kellner (1992) characterizes postmodern identities as:

- accelerated;
- extended;
- unstable;

- disintegrated;
- fragile;
- superficial; and
- illusory.

In the postmodern age, identity is both a problem and a 'project'. Our sense of who we are is not given to us, handed down in a fixed and stable form – it is up to us to construct or create it. Individuals can create their own narrative, including the outward symbols, of how they wish to be perceived. Postmodernists claim that it is through the consumption of popular culture, especially media products, that we are able to construct a sense of identity (see Chapters 8 and 9). As Miles (2001: 95) notes, 'the overwhelming theme of post-modern conceptions of identity in general is that the onus for the construction of such identities increasingly falls on the shoulders of the individual'.

Tara Chittenden's (2009) research into fashion blogs created by teenage girls gives us evidence of many elements of postmodern identity. The girls, through their blogs, develop their ideas of fashion and appearance, and 'the blogs support a fluid notion of identity' (2009: 513). Chittenden writes that the blogs themselves are 'a studied interaction, as bloggers consider audience attention, feedback, and feelings as they write' (2009: 518); 'By controlling their information disclosure, bloggers are able to decide where to draw the boundary between themselves and others, gatekeeping access to their personal field of identity formation. Thus, managing the shifting public/private continuum is also an important part of a blogger's experience' (2009: 213).

Bauman (1996) interprets identity formation in a postmodern society in a slightly different way. He agrees that individuals do have the ability to form their own identities, but they spend a lot of time trying to avoid particular ones from 'sticking' and becoming permanent. Culture and identities are in a perpetual state of change, they are provisional, and individuals want their own identity to be subject to change in response. To quote from Bauman (2004): 'The frailty and the forever provisional status of identity can no longer be concealed. The secret is out'.

However, Kellner (1992) rejects this particular version of postmodernism as it is too different from and opposed to the modernity that came before it. Kellner objects to the simplistic division between:

- *modernist identity*: fixed, passive, stable, certain; and
- *postmodernist identities*: open, active/creative, fragmented, illusory.

Kellner argues that this differentiation between modernity and postmodernity ignores the fact that identity was/is also a problem in modernity. He argues that, ever since pre-industrial 'traditional' society, identity has been expanding with the opening up of new possibilities, requiring choices to be made and therefore causing anxiety and uncertainty. Kellner suggests that it is a mistake to see these as exclusively new aspects of a new era. In this view, postmodernity is an extension of modernity, not a complete challenge to it and a change from it. Postmodernity starts where modernity ended, leading to even more uncertainty and fragmentation – but this was a condition of late modernity in the first place.

Evaluating the politics of postmodern identities

Kobena Mercer (1990, 1994) is concerned about the effects on identity formation in a postmodern age, where the subject has been 'decentred'. In other words, if there are no more absolutes, no more dominant meanings, this might set us free to be who we want to be (we have control over our own 'centre'), but it is also a form of enslavement – enslavement to darkness and chaos:

> Like 'identity', difference, diversity and fragmentation are keywords in the postmodern vocabulary where they are saturated with groovy connotations. But it should be clear that there is nothing particularly groovy about the postmodern condition at all. As a bestseller ideology in artistic and intellectual circles the postmodern paradigm has been and gone, but as a pervasive sensibility in everyday life its smelly ideological effect lingers on. (Ibid., 1994: 205)

We can now make more choices about our lives and life-styles than ever before. We can decide what kinds of people we want to be and build the sorts of lives we wish. We can change and remould ourselves over time. If there are no absolute standards then no one is able to say that who we are and how we behave is wrong. This is a tremendous amount of freedom. For example, many postmodernists claim that class is no longer the basis of individual or group identity. It was a key feature of modernity, but with the shift from production to consumption, 'who we think we are' is based not on what we do or make, but rather on what goods we buy and use, and how we use those goods. However, with no standards to turn to, there is much more uncertainty. How can we tell if we really are who we think we are? How can we tell if how we are behaving is really the best way for us?

Those who are critical of the postmodern proclamation of the 'death of class', such as Mercer (1990) and Hall (1988), note that the concern with freedom through consumption echoes a great deal of the New Right thinking of the Thatcher governments during the 1980s in the UK. It is not so much that everyone is free, but rather that some people can afford to be freer than others. Martin (2009) argues that postmodernism doesn't identify that consumption is not available to all; that it is an indicator of inequality. The consequence is that the state is freed from its traditional responsibility to provide welfare support for those in need. From a political viewpoint, if 'anything goes' in the postmodern era and there are no rational grounds upon which to establish truth, reality, morality and identity, then it is hard to make the sort of absolute moral judgements upon which anti-racism and anti-sexism are based. Mercer (1994) notes that postmodernity's emphasis on the immediate, the illusory, the meaningless and the ambiguous not only denies the existence of a 'truth', but also encourages us to forget our pasts. If we can be who we want to be, we might as well forget who we once were! Politically, this 'active forgetting' of the past can be dangerous, since it tends to lead to some aspects of our history being ignored while others are redefined and restored. For example, class conflict is at present just a distant memory, and a hazy one at that, but the New Right, New Labour and the 2011 UK coalition government have asked us to return to the basics and to embrace 'traditional values'. Hence it seems that we are not moving away from traditional absolutes completely, merely leaving behind those that do not fit in with the dominant values and world view of dominant groups.

EVALUATION OF POSTMODERNISM

While many have embraced postmodern ideas, others have rejected them. Some argue that postmodernists have exaggerated the extent of social change and its impact on people's life experiences, and that ascribed forms of identity are still important. In addition, the approach raises more questions than it answers. In querying 'grand narratives' it argues against its own existence and relevance. However, postmodernism could be seen not as a theory in itself, but as a collection of ideas that help us to understand the recent changes in society. In this sense it has provoked much research and debate within sociology and other disciplines, so in this sense it has been immensely valuable.

The critics of postmodernism are particularly concerned about the implications of these ideas for the future of sociology itself. If there is no such thing as truth, then what is the point of sociology trying to determine what the world is like?

The strengths of postmodernism are:

- It allows us to update the sociology of the founders and to reassess their image of the future – our present.
- It allows us to consider the importance of globalization for culture and identity in society.
- Since postmodernism sees identity as pluralistic, we can think about how people try to define themselves in the present age in the wide variety of contexts in which they will move.
- Individuals are seen as having an element of choice in their identity creation.
- Individuals have plural identities.
- It gives the actor a role without a script. It sees individuals as active in the creation of their identities.
- The observation that society has moved from production to consumption allows us to think about the nature of work and of class formation (see Chapter 11).
- It gives a central place to the role of the mass media and popular culture in society.

However, there are four main and powerful criticisms of postmodern ideas. First, Norris (1992, 1993) considers that postmodernism is far too sceptical and relativistic to be of any use. Norris (1992) quotes an observation made by Tony Bennett (1991: 51): 'if narratives are all that we can have and if all narratives are, in principle, of equal value – as it seems they must be if there is no touchstone of "reality" to which they can be referred for the adjudication of their truth-claims – then rational debate would seem to be pointless'.

Second, Giddens (1990, 1991) notes with some concern that postmodernism does not give sociology a future; in fact it denies the very Enlightenment spirit that led to the creation of sociology in the first place. For Giddens, the postmodern denial of truth and reason leaves us with nothing upon which to build knowledge about the world – knowledge that over time may help to inform our lives – personally and at the level of social policy.

Third, many Marxists point out that postmodernism may preach about the individual's liberation from the past. This freedom is an illusion, since it is based on consumption. Given that consumption involves expenditure, then surely some people are going to be freer than others? Is postmodernism a reflection of freedom among the middle classes? Postmodernism is said to provide a thinly veiled justification for the false needs created by the capitalist economy – these simply provide more profits for the capitalists themselves and thus ensure the perpetuation of an exploitative and unequal society. Postmodernism appears to take an uncritical approach to the consumer culture. Martin (2009) concludes that ' "traditional" issues such as social division, exclusion and inequality have not simply gone away just because relations of consumption increasingly replace relations of production'.

Finally, if in terms of morality 'anything goes' – everything is relative – this leaves us with no means of challenging discrimination and prejudice in society.

	Exercise 7.11

Complete the following table as a summary of the ideas of modernity and postmodernity.

	Modernity	Postmodernity
Key thinkers		
Basic characteristics of this sort of society		
Possible evidence		
Possible criticisms		

When rejecting the claims of postmodernism, some authors have adopted the terms 'high modernism' or 'late modernism' to suggest that fundamental change has taken place in contemporary society, but that this change has extended the features developed under modernity, rather than replaced them. Giddens (1990, 1991) describes society as being in a period of 'reflexive modernity' or 'high modernity', where culture and identity are based on individuals' awareness that decisions about life are less restricted than ever before. Therefore we must become 'reflexive' about who we are, what we want and how we want to live.

THEORIES OF RISK

A similar approach to the idea of 'reflexive modernity' is contained in the book *Risk Society* by German sociologist Ulrich Beck (1992). Beck claims that the current era of 'late' or 'high' modernity is characterized by the development of what he sees as a 'risk society', where life-style and identity are based on assessment of the risks of everyday life and their avoidance through careful action. These life-styles and identities are rational and active responses to the dangerous challenges of the age, such as AIDS, skin cancer, environmental disasters such as pollution, genetically modified (GM) food, global terrorism, identity theft, the collapse of banks and financial institutions and so on. The new risks people face are not natural risks, but manufactured ones, in particular those associated with a globalizing world. These risks are not easy to resolve and are less predictable. Risk avoidance can be seen as a political act that enables individuals to think about who they are and what sort of world they live in.

Theories of risk are a result of modernity not achieving its goals. Science and rationality have not provided the society people hoped for, and they have resulted in risk. In a postmodern society, tradition has been undermined and we are left with uncertainty and fragmentation. The media-saturated society in which humankind now lives ensures that we are well of aware of these risks and this results in risks being heavily exaggerated. We have become sceptical of science and its benefits. Institutions that used to help at times of risk and provided a buffer to risk are not as effective as they were in the past (such as the family, religion and the welfare state). Though people now have greater individualism, they are still dependent on institutions such as medicine and science, while remaining aware of the risks these institutions pose.

Beck (1999) argues that we are now in a global risk society. Risks and uncertainty have replaced aspects of our identity that used to be more concrete, such as inequalities caused by race, class and gender. Giddens (1991: 27) also talks about the risks created by science and technology, 'science and technology are double-edged, creating new parameters of risk and danger as well as offering beneficient possibilities for humankind'. Giddens argues that individuals and society as a whole have been forced to become more reflexive and this has had an impact on people's identities. Individuals are forced to deal with uncertainty and to make decisions from the seemingly limitless range of possibilities available in an attempt to reduce risk.

Critics of risk theory query whether individuals in society today are truly faced with such a high level of risk. If this is the case, it is a very pessimistic and disheartening proposal. Individuals are conscious of the role of the media in fuelling and perpetuating moral panics and therefore make judgements about the likelihood of each risk impacting on them. The free choice and individuality that a post- or late modern society has given us has opened up more than just greater risk. Individuals can actively participate in, and make positive decisions about, their culture and identity. Miles (2001: 139) concludes that:

the world may not be any riskier than it was in the past, it's just that the means of communicating that risk are now more omnipresent ... The risk society arguably has very little to do with actual changes in the nature of social life, but more to do with unsubstantiated fears about the rapidity of social change.

The speed of social change has impacted on our culture and identity, resulting in the fear of risk. Risk will affect different sectors of the population in different ways, with some being able to manage it better than others. This is a parallel observation to the one made above regarding the freedoms offered by postmodernism. The middle classes are those most able to cope with the freedoms offered and to manage their risk. Risk theory highlights the individualized nature of identity and the subsequent individual response to risk. It assumes that people respond to risk as individuals without the support, resources and backing of social institutions such as family, peer groups and religion.

Exercise 7.12

1. Identify five events from the timeline given in Table 7.1 that could indicate that we live in a risk society. If any events are unfamiliar, conduct online research to make an informed decision. Explain why you have chosen each example.
2. Which factors indicate that we could be living in a postmodern society? Incorporate the following terms into your answer:

- Relativism • Fragmentation • Plurality • Fragile • Superficial • Illusory • Ambiguity
- Relative morality

Table 7.1 Timeline of theorists, publications and events during the late twentieth- and early twenty-first centuries

Year	Theorists	Publication of key works	Events in society
Twentieth century	Jean-Francois Lyotard **1924–1998** Zygmunt Bauman **1925** Jean Baudrillard **1929–2007** Pierre Bourdieu **1930–2002** Ulrick Beck **1944–** Anthony Giddens **1938–**	**1977** *Outline of a Theory of Practice* (Bourdieu) **1979** *The Postmodern Condition* (Lyotard) **1981** *For a Critique of the Political Economy of the Sign* (Baudrillard) **1983** *In the Shadow of the Silent Majorities* (Baudrillard) **1984** *The Constitution of Society: Outline of the Theory of Structuration* (Giddens) **1990** *Thinking Sociologically* (Bauman) **1990** *The Consequences of Modernity* (Giddens) **1991** *Modernity and Self-Identity: Self and Society in the Late Modern Age* (Giddens) **1992** *Risk Society: Towards a New Modernity* (Beck) **1993** *Sociology in Question* (Bourdieu) **1999** *World Risk Society* (Beck)	Increase in expected life expectancy in Western societies throughout the twentieth century **1986** Start of the BSE (Bovine spongiform encephalopathy – known as 'mad cow disease') crisis over the safety of British beef **1997** Cloning of Dolly the sheep

Twenty-first century		**2000** *Liquid Modernity* (Bauman)	**2001** World Trade Center terrorist attacks, September (9/11)
			2001 Start of 'war on global terrorism'
		2007 *Liquid Times: Living in an Age of Uncertainty* (Bauman)	**2006** Execution of Iraqi leader Saddam Hussein
			2007 Apple releases first iPhone
			2008 First beam circulated through the Large Hadron Collider
			2008–11 Banking collapse (Lehman Brothers USA; Northern Rock and others UK)
			2010 Start of the 'Arab spring'; protest and revolution against government regimes
			2010 Apple releases first iPad tablet
			2010 on Eurozone financial crisis (scale of government debt)
			2011 Al-Qaeda leader Osama Bin Laden killed by US forces, May
			2011 Rioting in UK cities, August
			2011–12 Leveson enquiry (UK) into phone hacking by media organisations

Exercise 7.13

Do you think the ideas of modernity or of postmodernity best describe the society we live in at the present time? Answer this question in approximately 150 words and provide examples.

Exercise 7.14

Copy the concept map in Figure 7.1 on to a large sheet of paper or enlarge it on a photocopier. At each stage, explain and expand the elements of modernity and postmodernity in your own words, radiating out from the centre. Note the impact each element has on identity. You can add relevant theorists and strengths and weaknesses in different colours. Elaborate and explain the alternative views and criticisms.

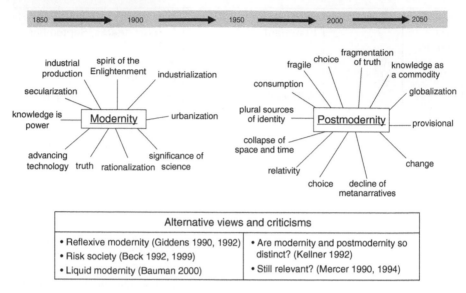

Figure 7.1 Modernity and postmodernity concept map

CONCLUSION

Postmodernism has provided sociology with many important and influential ideas, but it has also provoked controversy and criticism. Taken to its logical conclusion, postmodernism attacks the very origins of sociology. It denies absolute knowledge and instead suggests a reality based on fragmentation, relativism and plurality. Postmodernism has, however, allowed previously 'invisible' groups within sociology and society to have their say. It has illustrated the relationship between power and knowledge, and has embraced plurality – 'anything goes'. Some see this as liberating, but for others the result can only be chaos.

Important concepts
Fragmentation • Globalization • Late modernity • Meta-narrative • Modernity • Narrative • Postmodernity • Rationalization • Reflexive modernity • Reflexivity • Relativism • Risk

Exam focus
(a) To what extent are the ideas of a postmodern identity useful when thinking about modern-day society?   (b) Critically evaluate the idea that we can choose who we want to be.

(c) Evaluate the impact globalization has had on culture and identity.
(d) Discuss the view that 'to the postmodern sociologist, identity is everything'.

Critical thinking

1. Do individuals have the freedom to 'pick and mix' their identity? What freedom have you had to choose your lifestyle and identity?
2. Is globalization a new phenomenon? How does a global society differ from society in the past?
3. Lyotard (1984) argues that knowledge is less about truth in contemporary society than it is about power. Do those with knowledge have power?
4. 'It could be argued that the recent focus on post-modernity ... represents an extremely damaging trend for social theory. You might even go as far to say that it amounts to a theoretical bandwagon upon which social theorists have jumped. Unfortunately, many of them have fallen off the other side.' Miles (2001:82) To what extent do you agree or disagree with this statement?

Chapter 8

Mass Culture and Popular Culture

After studying this chapter, you should:

- understand the differences between the key concepts of mass culture, mass society, high culture, low culture and popular culture
- understand Marxist and neo-Marxist discussions of popular culture in modern society
- be able to evaluate Marxist ideas on popular culture using the perspectives of interactionism, pluralism and postmodernism
- be able to reflect on recent technological developments and their impact on cultural consumption

INTRODUCTION

Consider the amount and types of media you encounter in an average day. Perhaps as you wake up you turn on the radio, or you may even wake up to a radio alarm clock. Do you listen to podcasts? Do you watch breakfast television before leaving home or on your phone while travelling? Do you read a book, magazine or newspaper during the course of your journey to work or college – perhaps on a bus or train? In the evening, is the TV playing 'to itself' in a corner of the room while you eat your evening meal, is it switched off, or is your meal eaten in front of the TV? Do you reject conversation with those in your home in favour of watching TV? When you work at home, do you have music playing in the background? Do you listen to music when you dress to go out for the evening?

①Ⓐ   Exercise 8.1

Think about the questions on media usage in the paragraph above. Write a list of all the media you watch/read/listen to in an average day. Write a paragraph explaining why you consume these media as you do. You could present your observations in a table like the one below.

	What did you watch/ read/listen to?	**For how much time?**	**What were your reasons for doing so?**
Monday			
Tuesday			
Wednesday			
Thursday			
Friday			
Saturday			
Sunday			

While in sociology we favour actual research over generalizations based on personal experience, which tends to be limited, it does seem that the mass media dominate our lives. They are an ever-present feature of most people's day-to-day routines. This observation has led many cultural commentators to suggest that modern life is 'media saturated' – that every aspect of our lives is swamped by flickering television images, the audio output from DVDs, CDs, the internet and so on.

Given the wide reach of all these media – a reflection of the extensive technological developments of our time – it is important that, as sociologists, we look very carefully at the media we use and ask ourselves the following questions:

- Exactly what are we consuming?
- Why are we doing so?
- What are the consequences of this consumption; what might it do to us?
- What does this say about our culture and identity?

Sociologists seem to fall into two 'camps' when thinking about the value and role of the media in society. This is also true of other popular cultural products, including clothes, food, popular forms of technology and so on. First, the pessimistic view is to see the products of popular culture as a problem for society; that they are cheap, unintellectual and have no 'artistic' value. The consumption of these products is seen as being damaging to those who do so, holding them back from thinking for themselves, denying them the pleasure to be had from looking at/reading 'great art'. In this view, popular culture has little or no value at all. Second, the optimistic view is that there is nothing wrong with, and sometimes great value to be had from, the consumption of popular culture. Simply because something is mass-produced for profit does not necessarily mean that it is unintellectual or worthless. In this view, the media audience can use popular culture in highly creative ways.

Exercise 8.2

To start you thinking about issues of popular culture and the mass media, consider which of the above two views you find most convincing. Give reasons for your choice.

BASIC DEFINITIONS

To discuss the two views given above – and the many arguments that rest between these two extremes – we must first be clear about the key terms used in what is known as 'the mass culture debate': 'culture', 'mass culture/popular culture' and 'high/low cultures'.

Culture

Though the concept of 'culture' can be thought about in many different ways (see Chapter 2), a basic distinction is drawn between 'social culture' and 'artistic culture':

- 'Culture' can refer to the 'way of life of a social group', including their values, norms, behavioural patterns, customs and rituals, and even material objects.
- The 'artistic' definition of 'culture' refers to the highest and greatest artistic and intellectual creations of an age, as defined by the society of the time. For example, we might say that a person is 'cultured' if s/he listens to opera, reads classical novels such as those of Charles Dickens or Jane Austen, or goes to the theatre frequently.

While these are quite different uses of the word 'culture', they are related. The 'artistic and intellectual' products of great worth and merit in the second definition are produced by a society and can therefore be seen as the 'material objects' of the first definition. Judgement of what is or is not 'great art' only can take place within a wider culture – a wider 'way of life', with its norms, values, customs and so on. In terms of the mass culture debate, we are more interested in the second definition – the 'artistic' one.

Mass culture/popular culture

This relates to cultural products (often but not exclusively produced by the media) that everyone has access to, and that the vast majority of the population consume. These products are often associated with the 'common person', and are easy to understand and consume.

High/low cultures

A distinction is often made between:

- 'high culture' – products that are intellectual, artistic, difficult to understand, expensive, and aimed at those with an exclusive taste not shared by 'ordinary people'; and
- 'low culture' (frequently equated with popular or mass culture) – products that are easy to understand, cheap, 'throwaway', common and so on.

Ⓤ①
Exercise 8.3

Explain in your own words what 'high culture' and 'low culture' mean, and provide around eight examples of each.

Questions concerning mass culture

The 'mass culture debate' involves the following questions:

- Are modern cultural creations less artistic and intellectual than those of the past?
- If a cultural product is 'popular', does this mean it has less value than something that is only experienced by an elite few?
- If a cultural product is mass-produced for financial gain, is it necessarily less artistic or intellectual than one produced by a 'lone artist' simply for pleasure?
- Does popular culture encourage critical thought about society, or hamper it?

Exercise 8.4

Provide a detailed answer to the above questions for each of these categories: (i) paintings (fine art); (ii) television; (iii) cinema; and (iv) podcasts. Justify your answers.

The poet T. S. Eliot (1948) saw 'high culture' as the concern and product of an educated, sophisticated, artistic and elite class grouping. The culture of the masses was seen by Eliot as less 'worthy', as having less 'value' than that of their educated 'betters'. Marxist sociologists see this highly conservative view of the popular/mass culture of the working classes as providing intellectual justification for the continuation of the class system in society; and that the working classes need the ruling class to help them 'better themselves' through ruling-class cultural products, yet at the same time only the ruling classes are able truly to appreciate such products, or deserve to have them!

THE 'MASS SOCIETY THESIS'

This pessimistic critique of mass/popular culture is often based on left-of-centre sociological theories such as Marxism. It suggests that popular culture prevents critical and revolutionary thought. It is ideological and leads to false consciousness. In this view, popular culture creates a 'mass society'; that is, a society where:

- individuals lose their sense of community;
- lose their individuality; and
- come to rely on strong authority from above.

This is seen as dangerous, since if the masses cannot think for themselves, then those who rule society can dominate the populace as they wish, for their own gain. Many mass society arguments owe a great deal to the ideas of traditional Marxism on commodification and commodity fetishism (see Chapters 3 and 11). Marx himself was concerned with the trend in capitalism towards the creation of cultural products as 'commodities' – things to be bought and sold. This process of commodification is seen as devaluing such products because their value is reduced to price, rather than reflecting their cultural, artistic and/or intellectual merit.

The process of commodification is also seen as creating false needs – making people purchase objects/products they do not really need in order to provide capitalists with profits. These false needs give rise to 'commodity fetishism', since people come to worship products and seek ownership of them, and in doing so they see the economic system as being valuable since it produces such commodities. Because capitalism 'delivers the goods' and satisfies people's desires it goes unquestioned.

Ⓐ Ⓔ
Exercise 8.5

List three strengths and three weaknesses of the traditional Marxist view of popular culture.

The Frankfurt School

Perhaps the best known and most influential version of the Marxist interpretation of mass culture and commodification was provided by Herbert Marcuse, Theodor W. Adorno and Max Horkheimer of the Frankfurt School in Germany in the period before the Second World War (see Chapters 2 and 3). Adorno and Horkheimer (1979, 1993) argued that advertising in capitalism creates and subsequently manipulates false needs and desires that are fulfilled by consumption. However, this fulfilment is only achieved by repeatedly consuming the latest, newest and 'best' products available. The consumption of cultural products – commodities – under a capitalist economy creates fetishism, which in turn safeguards the dominance of the ruling group. In this respect, consumerism is ideological.

For Marcuse (1964) commodity fetishism, this worshipping of objects through consumption, cheapens these products. Popular culture becomes only as valuable as the price paid for it. This low culture is therefore cheap, crass, vulgar and used to dominate the masses – to stop revolutionary thinking. In this way the mass consumption of mass-produced popular cultural products leads to the creation of a mass society. Free intellectual and critical thought is lost and the masses become passive victims of ideology. Marcuse referred to the masses as 'one-dimensional', since they are only able to be socialized into the dominant culture through the media. This results in a 'paralysis of criticism'.

Adorno and Horkheimer (1979) and Adorno (1991) described the media as a 'culture industry' since it does not attempt to create great pieces of art, but is simply a business – an industry – and like any other business is only concerned with making a profit. When making this claim they had in mind the early Hollywood film industry. The Frankfurt School proposed a 'hypodermic syringe' model of the effects of popular culture: the masses, living in a mass society, are passive victims of capitalist ideology – injected with false needs by the media and unable to fight, resist or think for themselves.

Evaluation of the Frankfurt School

- The Frankfurt School saw the masses as highly passive victims of ideology.
- In their discussion of commodification, they ignored the creative practices and uses to which people can put popular culture.
- They saw people as being controlled by ideology rather than as being able to manipulate and redefine it in revolutionary ways (see Chapter 9).

List three strengths of the Frankfurt School's views on popular culture.

Though criticized by some, the arguments raised by the Frankfurt School have been influential. For example, the German thinker, Walter Benjamin, writing at the same time as the members of the Frankfurt School, presented a slightly different but complementary image of the mass production of popular culture. In an essay entitled 'The Work of Art in the Age of Mechanical Reproduction', Benjamin (1970) divided the consequences of mass production and distribution into two contradictory elements:

- Mass production is in some senses anti-elitist in nature, since technology enables elite-only 'high' cultural artefacts to be copied for the masses to access and gain pleasure from.
- However, at the same time, mass production leads to consumerism, which in turn leads to the problems of commodification suggested by Marx.

Hence mass production is at the same time both liberating and dominating.

The pluralist perspective

The strongest criticisms of the Frankfurt School have come from the advocates of pluralism. This approach to sociological theorizing owes a great deal to the interactionists' concern with the active nature of human beings. It is referred to as pluralism because its exponents argue that:

- Different people perceive the media in different ways.
- Since there is a large plurality of cultural products, individuals have considerable choice over what they do and do not consume.
- By exercising their choice of what to consume, power is distributed among many different groups in society.
- Human beings are active, and as many different choices are made by these creative beings as there are creative beings themselves.

For example, Gans (1974) suggests that the mass production of popular culture does not devalue its worth, but instead offers a free and democratic choice to consumers. However, Swingewood (1977) argues that the whole idea of a 'mass culture' is a myth (see Chapter 2). Instead, it is an elitist value judgement used by some to devalue the interests, activities and pleasures of others in favour of their own.

Obtain a weekly TV guide and select one day only. Identify the eight most popular channels. How much television output is high culture and how much is low? In light of your observations, which of the above views – pluralism or Marxism – appears to be correct about the nature of popular media content? Record your thoughts in a version of the table below.

Day, date and channel	Describe the content of each channel's broadcasting on this day	How much is 'high' and how much is 'low' culture?	What types of programmes are shown at prime time viewing?	When are the more intellectual or critical programmes likely to be shown, if at all?	Which theory – Marxism or pluralism – appears correct on the basis of your evidence?

K U
I

Exercise 8.8

Summarize the Marxist and pluralist positions on mass culture in a table copied from the one below.

	Marxism	Pluralism
Key thinkers		
Key concepts		
Views on popular culture		
How do they see the consumer/audience?		

K An
E

Exercise 8.9

Write a paragraph as though you were a Marxist criticizing the pluralist view of mass culture, and then the reverse – as though you were a pluralist criticizing the Marxist view.

WHO EXACTLY ARE THE MASSES?

The mass culture debate is based on the assumption that the audience, consumers and users of popular culture are a massive 'lump' of individuals – a 'mass' – without free thought or critical awareness. This is a very difficult argument to uphold and is insulting and elitist. It seems to suggest that some sociologists can see popular culture for the 'intellectual wasteland' it is, but that everyone else – 'ordinary people' – are tricked, fooled and controlled by it.

Ang (1991) suggests that it is very difficult truly to know how people engage with the media and popular culture, since a great deal of their use occurs in the home behind closed doors, or in the individual mind, and is therefore difficult to observe. Defining the audience/consumers as simply a 'mass' is unrealistic and gets in the way of true understanding. Ang notes that despite the fact that television has become a significant aspect of society and of people's daily lives, we know little about the actual audiences of the media in general and of TV in particular. So much so that the views of 'ordinary viewers' are often ignored by TV producers, or viewers are categorized into large masses and are seen as being unthinking or fickle. This idea that the masses are 'out there' watching TV is little more than an abstraction and a gross generalization. It is not based on any real understanding of how people view TV and how they understand it.

Raising a similar argument to that of Ang, Williams (1963: 299) writes:

The masses are always the others, whom we don't know, and can't know... They are here, and we are here with them. And that we are with them is of course the whole point. To other people, we are also masses. Masses are other people... There are in fact no masses; there are only ways of seeing people as masses.

Williams is highly critical of those Marxist sociologists – such as the members of the Frankfurt School – who condemn popular culture as uncritical and therefore unworthy. To make such a claim is to devalue the culture of the working classes themselves – something that Marxists especially should not do, given their emphasis on the need to help the working classes to break free from capitalism.

How does the audience use popular culture?

A great deal of present-day discussion on popular culture is less concerned with what it might do to the audience and more with what audiences do with it. This notion that audiences have power, freedom, creativity and choice can be associated with a whole range of perspectives, including interactionism, postmodernism and some versions of neo-Marxism. Added to the image of the audience as creative and active is the idea that the definition of 'high' and 'low' culture is a matter of taste and value judgement. This position is sometimes referred to as 'cultural relativism' (see Chapter 2). In this view, all cultural products are as valuable as each other and value is ultimately in the eye of the consumer.

Some sociologists have suggested that the culture of working-class people – often based on the consumption of popular culture – is just as worthy as that of the middle and upper classes. To argue otherwise would be to adopt a position of 'cultural elitism' or 'cultural absolutism', suggesting that there exists some absolute value of artistic worth to which all products can be compared in an objective and value-free way.

The 'excorporation' of popular culture

Fiske (1989) suggests that popular culture can be used by audiences in an active and highly critical fashion. He argues that popular culture is used by subordinate subcultural groups (see Chapter 9) to resist and fight against the dominant ideology of ruling groups. This resistance by subordinate groups – including the working classes and youth subcultures – is based on a process of 'excorporation'. What this means is that the symbols and dominant meanings of a dominant culture can be changed, challenged, turned around and redefined to mean something quite different. These new meanings can then be used to create an alternative world view to that which dominates society, an alternative way of thinking that uses popular culture in an active rather than a passive way. In this view, audiences are not passive, unthinking victims of ideology in popular culture, but are highly creative actors with 'agency' (see Chapter 4).

In *Common Culture*, Willis *et al.* (1993) suggest that the culture of 'ordinary people' is by no means a reflection of passive acceptance of an uncritical low culture, but is highly creative. Willis writes of the 'symbolic creativity' of subcultures – especially of youth sub-cultures (see Chapter 9) – whereby popular cultural products, images and signs are actively manipulated. Willis notes that a massive amount of 'cultural work' is undertaken by young people in their everyday lives.

Ⓘ

Exercise 8.10

Design a questionnaire to research the ways in which people at your college, university or workplace use popular culture in creative ways.

Willis dismisses the notion that high culture is in some way better than low culture. He argues that the merit of cultural products lies not in what they are, but in how they are used. Since the use to which cultural products are put is not necessarily as originally intended, to understand the true nature of cultural consumption we need to look at what people actually do. Willis suggests that consumption cannot take place without a great amount of symbolic action, creativity and interpretation by consumers. Consumption is not passive – it is based on decoding and reading the signs and symbols of cultural products. Even cultural products that might be deemed 'throwaway' or 'profane' (unartistic) may still offer consumers pleasure, new interpretations and possibilities for free thought. In this view, there is no such thing as high or low cultures – only degrees of creativity to which all cultural products can be put, be they popular or not.

Models of the audience

To suggest that popular culture can be used in an active fashion to create identity and new cultural meanings is to give human beings a degree of agency that was denied to them by the Frankfurt School. They saw the audience of the culture industry as passive victims of media that operate like 'hypodermic syringes'. We turn here to some alternative ways of thinking about the media audience that focus on people's active attempts to construct identity and use popular culture, rather than be used by it.

Barwise and Ehrenberg (1988) describe television as 'low involvement'; in other words, the audience does not have to do much in order to consume the product. They provide two examples of this low involvement:

▨ Little effort need be made by a viewer, and s/he views TV in the same way as every other member of the wider audience.

▨ People often watch TV while waiting for something else to happen: it is used to fill 'dead time'.

Barwise and Ehrenberg therefore see the viewing of popular TV programmes as a passive activity, and not one that allows or encourages the creative cultural manipulation spoken about by writers such as Willis.

On the other hand, two models suggest that popular viewing is highly active and creative.

The first, known as the 'uses–gratifications approach', is explored in *The Uses of Mass Communication* by Blumler and Katz (1974). According to this model, the audience of popular culture – in this case popular TV – is able to use the media for specific purposes. Thus if one needs background noise, the TV is used in a different way than if one is looking out for a particular item in a news broadcast – the audience have needs that they fulfil, or gratify, through active and selective TV use.

The second model is aimed at identifying how people 'decode' (make sense of) what they see. Morley (1980) was concerned to establish how and why audiences use TV. He chose to focus on a British programme called 'Nationwide' – a magazine-style programme built around current affairs and news. Morley suggests that the audience members in his study used and interpreted the programme in different ways, depending on who they were and the backgrounds from which they came. For example, he suggests that class, gender, ethnicity, age, cultural identity, political views and personal experience served to 'filter' the messages contained in the programme.

Morley identifies three types of 'decoding' performed by audience members – that is, individual audience members 'read', interpret or pull apart (decode) the messages and images they see in different ways, with their backgrounds operating as filters through which this happens:

▨ *Oppositional.* Some audience members reject what they see and replace the intended meaning with a new one that diverges from the message intended by those who made the product.

▨ *Negotiated.* Some audience members twist the intended meaning to make it fit in with their own views of the world, and bits of each are fitted together for future use.

▨ *Dominant.* Some audience members fully accept the dominant or intended meaning of the product and go along with it.

Hence Morley suggests that popular culture produces a wide variety of responses, not just the intended or dominant ones. This idea is reflected in a study by a member of the Glasgow University Media Group (GUMG), Greg Philo (1990). Philo adopts a neo-Marxist stance, but he takes up Morley's idea that the consumers of popular culture interpret the messages of the products in different ways. He suggests that whereas some audience members are affected by ruling-class ideology (what he calls 'hegemony' – see Chapter 9), other members respond to the popular media in a more oppositional and reflexive fashion – seeing ideology for what it is and rejecting it.

Like Morley, Philo argues that our unique personal biographies, experiences and life histories act as a filter and influence our view of popular media products. The users of popular culture are seen as sophisticated, thinking beings, not necessarily taken in by the dominant ideology or unable to think critically about the world because of the influence of mass culture.

Exercise 8.11

List all the aspects of people's backgrounds – for example, class and gender – that might influence what they consume and how they interpret it.

POSTMODERNITY AND POPULAR CULTURE

Postmodernity and popular culture can be seen as fundamentally interlinked. Jameson (1983) locates the emergence of postmodernity in a change in the organization of the economy. Whereas modernity was characterized by the manufacture of products and the use of raw materials, postmodernity – seen as the 'late industrial era' – is based on consumption rather than production. Given this, postmodernity is characterized by an unprecedentedly rapid expansion in the consumption of popular culture.

Featherstone (1991) points out that in postmodernity, life-style construction and the creation/establishment of self-identity are based on the types of popular cultural products we consume, and the creative uses to which we put these products or commodities. The early development of 'modernist' mass consumerism in the West, especially in the USA, after the Second World War is seen as limited in comparison with the postmodern consumerism of today. For example, Henry Ford, the creator of the Ford motor car, is famous for his declaration that the purchasers of Fords could 'have any colour they wanted as long as it was black'. The products of mass production in the modernist era were therefore very different from the range on offer today – an almost bewildering array in terms of choice and flexibility.

The wide variety of postmodernist views on popular culture (see also Chapter 7) fall on either side of the optimistic–pessimistic divide discussed at the beginning of this chapter. For the 'postmodern optimists', popular culture has become sufficiently widespread for it to be used in many different ways – people create so many different meanings that the traditional differences between high and low cultures have been broken down. The consumption of popular culture is seen as truly liberating – offering the individual a wide choice from which to construct meaning. This optimistic postmodern interpretation is summed up well by Anderson (1996): 'No style dominates. Instead we have endless improvisations and variations on themes; parody and playfulness. Postmodern architects are unabashedly eclectic and call attention to it. People everywhere similarly combine traditions, borrow rituals and myths. All the world's cultural symbols are now in the public domain.' Popular culture is therefore seen as a vast and complex, postmodern playground where we are free to play whatever games of meaning and identity we wish.

However, writers such as Jean Baudrillard paint an altogether different, 'darker', more pessimistic and sinister picture of the playground of popular culture, one where meaning has collapsed, identity has crumbled and chaos reigns. When discussing the collapse of truth, certainty and meaning, Baudrillard (1993: 95) says:

> It has all been done. The extreme limit of these possibilities has been reached. It has destroyed itself... All that remains to be done is to play with the pieces... postmodernity is the attempt – perhaps it's desperate, I don't know – to reach a point where one can live with what is left.

For Baudrillard, all idea of what is 'real' has come to an end. There is no more certainty, no more means by which to decide what is 'truth'. He describes the experience of watching TV and the signs and images used on TV as 'hyper-real' – 'more real than real'. What he means by this is that since there is no means by which to judge the truth, individuals can turn to whatever source of knowledge they wish. No one can say what is right or wrong. Actual lived experience is no more nor or less 'true' than the 'truth' offered to audiences by TV programmes. In fact, TV images may even appear to be 'more real' than one's own life. It must be noted here that such is the ambiguity in Baudrillard's work – deliberately so, since this is also part of the 'postmodern game' – he seems to find this collapse of meaning exciting and at times even humorous.

In an even more pessimistic tone, Baudrillard (1983) warns against the rise of the 'silent majority'. He paints a picture of a postmodern future where populations return to the sort of mass society written about by the Frankfurt School. The masses become unable to be interested in, or represented by political ideas, religion, science or any other modernist view of a single absolute truth. Instead, all there is left is popular culture, which is consumed in an attempt to try to put some sort of order back into the world, but which in time becomes 'hyper-real' – more real than real. Popular culture alone remains for this silent majority to use/enjoy/think through. They turn to the flickering images on TV screens, unable to divorce the media from their 'real' world of sensation.

Exercise 8.12

Identify two strengths and two weaknesses of the postmodern view on popular culture.

TECHNOLOGICAL DEVELOPMENTS AND THEIR IMPACT ON CULTURE

The impact of technological developments characterize recent research. In particular, these developments have involved the consumer in the media in new ways. These include:

- social networking sites such as MySpace and Facebook ,which give individuals the opportunity to present the identity of their choice to their 'friends' and make connections with others they perceive to be similar;
- Twitter, which is seen by many as a social network, but is classified by Liz Pullen (2009) as an 'information network' or 'microblog' has become a form of broadcast media which is used in many different ways;

- wikis, which are produced and consumed by users with a browse and edit facility open to everyone;
- blogs – user generated online journals – have dynamic content that allows writers to express and develop their identity; and
- computer gaming has become more interactive in terms not just of playing games in a more active way, but also by playing against people globally in real time. There has been a big increase in virtual reality sites such as Second Life.

Beer and Burrows (2007) refer to the increasing sociological significance of these networked technologies 'which, popular rhetoric suggests, are reworking hierarchies, changing social divisions, creating possibilities and opportunities, informing us, and reconfiguring our relations with objects, spaces and each other.'

It is easy to consider of these new media as forming part of 'low culture'; however, the large numbers of people using them, and the variety of ways in which they can be used mean they are a valuable source of information and opportunity for theorizing for sociologists. For example, Buckley *et al.* (2010) demonstrate that students in higher education appreciated networked technologies as helping them to develop deep learning of their subjects, a high-rather than low-culture effect. Mainstream media organizations are making use of these technologies, so the work of theorists we have covered in this chapter could be applied.

The journalist Malcolm Gladwell, in *The Tipping Point* (2000), explains what factors make ideas, behaviour and trends 'tip' into epidemics. He analyses the role of context (situational factors), the 'stickiness' (memorability) of the message, and the people involved. He identifies three types of people that are significant in epidemics: the 'Connector'; the 'Maven'; and the 'Salesman'. This can explain how new ideas and new technologies impact on identity and culture. 'In a social epidemic, Mavens are data banks. They provide the message. Connectors are social glue: they spread it. But ... Salesmen ... [have] the skills to persuade us when we are unconvinced of what we are hearing'. All of these elements can be seen in users of social networks and blogs that play a part in the development of social and cultural epidemics.

Exercise 8.13

Should Twitter posts be archived by the British Library and other academic organizations? Are they of academic merit and part of 'high-culture'? What would be the viewpoints of Marxist, Neo-Marxist and pluralist theorists to this proposition?

CONCLUSION

The role of the media in society and of popular culture in general is certainly a major concern of a number of academic disciplines: sociology, media studies and cultural studies. Given that the forms and styles of popular culture vary greatly and change rapidly, it is an important area of sociological investigation. Everyone in British society is a consumer, and virtually everyone is a part of a wider media audience. Within sociological thought we have seen a move away from alarmist and pessimistic 'doomsday scenarios' of the power of the media towards a much more considered approach that looks at the content of popular culture, its producers and its audience. The audience, or consumer, is seen by many thinkers as active and creative. This is not to say that ideology does not exist, but rather that the process of 'decoding' and 'reading' is too complicated for people to be seen as 'cultural robots'. The idea of a 'decoding' individual and a creative group that uses popular culture in an active fashion will be taken up in Chapters 9 and 10.

Important concepts
Artistic culture • Commodification • Commodity fetishism • Consumption • Excorporation • High culture • Hyper-real • Ideology • Low culture • Mass culture • Mass society • Pluralism • Popular culture • Social culture

Exam focus
(a) Evaluate the idea that popular culture has limited value.
(b) Assess the claim that the media help us to create an identity.
(c) Discuss the claim that mass media output has very little direct effect on the audience.
(d) Assess the effects of the mass media on popular culture.

Critical thinking
1. 'Reality television shows such as "Big Brother" and "I'm A Celebrity" are examples of the "dumbing down" of popular culture. They have no cultural merit.' To what extent is this the case?
2. Is there a wide choice of media to cater for all consumers? Does free choice really exist?
3. 'The culture of the working class is just as worthy as that of the upper class.' Do you agree? Do individuals consume the media passively? To what extent is this the case?

Chapter 9

Youth Culture and Subculture

After studying this chapter, you should:

- be able to define the concept of 'subculture'
- have an understanding of various theoretical approaches to the study of youth culture and subcultures
- have an understanding of how theories interpret contemporary examples of youth subcultures
- understand the role played by class, capitalism and hegemony in the creation of subcultures
- be able to evaluate key theoretical interpretations of youth subcultures
- be able to reflect on the role and existence of youth subcultures in society today

INTRODUCTION

Many contemporary sociologists, especially postmodernists, are interested in the role played by popular culture in the creation of identity (see Chapters 7 and 8). 'Popular culture' – or sometimes 'mass culture' – is usually defined as media and other cultural products that are readily available, often cheap to consume and have a popular or mass appeal. Popular culture – especially fashion and music – is also seen to be a major feature of youth subcultures.

Youth subcultures, which are often perceived as 'deviant' (against the norms of society), make good 'copy' for newspapers throughout the world. We often hear of the dangers of certain 'deviant' groups of young people who are characterized as drug-taking, wild, often violent, partying all night, having casual sex, listening to unacceptable music and not facing up to the responsibilities of early adulthood. We see, hear and read about politicians criticizing single-parent families, poor discipline in schools and a decline in religious morality, and speaking of a rising tide of apathy, fatalism and hedonism among the young.

We are told by the tabloids that young people are behaving worse than ever before, and that this represents some sort of crisis that must be dealt with.

Interestingly, such fears about young people have existed in Britain and elsewhere for a very long time. For example Geoffrey Pearson (1983) notes that the idea of 'young hooligans' roaming city streets and unable to be controlled by the police can be dated as far back as 1898. Not such a modern phenomenon after all. It seems that each generation fears, blames and wishes to protect its youth in equal measure, and each older generation looks back to a time, a 'golden age', when they themselves were young and when young people respected the law and their parents – unlike the situation today. This sensationalism over the activities of the young might be described as a 'moral panic' – an exaggerated, media-provoked fear that causes members of society to perceive that a problem is much greater than it is. In some cases a problem might not exist at all until it is defined as such by the media. Such moral panics about the young have often featured in political ideologies, where young people are seen as presenting a hazard to the smooth running of society if they are not disciplined enough. While concerns have been expressed about young people back into the nineteenth century, the existence of a specific period of 'youth' with a particular way of life associated with it can be traced back to the 1950s in Western society. Young people became more affluent, a distinctive consumer group emerged, and individuals identified with music and particular forms of dress and behaviour.

Ⓤⓘ

Exercise 9.1

Write a list of recent moral panics involving young people. For each one state why you think it occurred. Present your answer in a three-column table with the following headings: 'What groups were targeted as a "problem"?'; 'What was it about the behaviour of these groups that made them a problem?'; and 'Why did this come to public/media attention?'

The young – and in particular teenagers and 'twenty-somethings' – are not targeted by the media only as a 'problem'. They are also targeted as active and discerning consumers. In other words, youth culture is big business for the 'culture industry':

- More than ever before, young people consume cultural goods, especially music and clothes.
- Youth subcultural identities are often associated with specific styles of music and/or groups.
- The life-styles of youth subcultures make interesting subjects for films, 'docu-soaps', music videos, reality television and TV commercials.

Sociologists are interested in going beyond the ways in which the media characterize youth groups and to study these people and their life-style choices. They want to explore what subcultures mean for those involved in their creation, and what this in turn means for wider structural forces.

①Ⓐ
Exercise 9.2

Consider the following examples of youth cultural style. For each one, describe the 'look' that the members of the group have, and what values are most associated with each culture:

Hip-hop • Nu-metal • Indie kids • Punk • Rave • Emo • Skater

Before we can discuss the phenomenon of youth subcultures in detail, we need to define the main terms and look briefly at the historical development of the sociological study of youth subcultures. There is an important distinction between the following key concepts:

▨ *Culture.* This usually refers to the 'way of life' of a larger group and includes the ideas, values, behaviour, ritual practices and material goods of the group.

▨ *Subculture.* This usually refers to a group that has broken away from the wider, dominant culture: a 'culture within a culture' that has its own specialist norms and values – its own way of life, shared by a smaller proportion of a population.

▨ *Deviant subculture.* While some subcultures conform for the most part to the broader norms and values of the dominant culture, other groups seek to reject these norms and values and are therefore be considered to be a 'deviant subcultures'.

According to these classifications, a group of young people might be seen as members of a subculture if, for example, they all dress similarly and follow a particular type of music; while a group of young people whose central value is committing criminal acts could be seen as members of a deviant youth subculture.

THE HISTORICAL DEVELOPMENT OF SUBCULTURAL STUDY

Robert K. Merton

An early and influential attempt to define the relationship between culture and subculture was made in the mid-1930s by Robert K. Merton (see Merton, 1989). Merton's functionalist ideas are sometimes referred to as 'strain theory', since he identified a strain or tension between what he referred to as the 'institutionalized means' and the 'culture goals' of a dominant culture:

▨ The 'cultural goals' of a society are the main desirable outcomes that the members of a society are expected to achieve. For example, in Western culture these are usually seen as getting a good job, being successful at a career, having money, owning a nice house and car, and so on.

▨ 'Institutionalized means' refers to the legitimate ways in which people seek to reach the goals of the dominant culture. For example, to achieve the dominant goals of Western culture people need to work hard at school, obtain good qualifications and work hard at a career.

Merton noted that the socialization of culture into the members of society might not lead to everyone being bonded into a state of harmony and consensus, as was believed by other functionalists such as Talcott Parsons (see Chapter 3). Instead, Merton suggested that only some of the people will be able to achieve society's cultural goals, but many others would aspire to the goals but lack the means to achieve them. According to Merton, there is a tension between the values or goals one might have, and the structural position one might hold. Those who are white, middle-class and male usually enjoy more advantages in society than those who are not. Equally, in another form of discrimination, the able-bodied are often given more opportunities than those who have disabilities.

Merton saw this tension between structural position and dominant cultural goals as a huge problem for society, and one that might provoke a range of subcultural responses. This could lead eventually to 'anomie' or 'normlessness', since great numbers of people would ultimately have a wide range of different subcultural values. They would not be bonded together, since they would be following different norms, and the possibility of conflict and social breakdown would increase.

Merton identified the following solutions to the structural problems of having a tension/strain between the goals and means in society developed by individuals who join subcultural groups:

- *Conformity*. Strictly speaking, this response is not 'deviant' or 'subcultural', since if an individual conforms s/he is following the dominant culture. However, all other responses are 'deviant' and 'subcultural', since they are not the norm. Many of the latter responses might be made by groups of young people.
- *Innovation*. This means that one accepts and pursues the goals of society, but the legitimate means of reaching them are replaced by illegitimate means – such as delinquency and crime.
- *Ritualism*. This response involves 'going through the motions' by following the means, but never achieving success. The individual loses sight of the goals.
- *Retreatism*. Here individuals 'retreat' from the wider cultural means and goals (perhaps via drugs or alcohol) and drop out of society, giving up on any form of success, be it deviant or otherwise.
- *Rebellion*. Here the goals and means of the dominant culture are totally replaced by new goals and means.

Exercise 9.3

Consider Merton's classification of deviant responses. In your own words, describe what he means by 'innovation', 'ritualism', 'retreatism' and 'rebellion', and for each one identify a subcultural group that could be classified in this way.

The Chicago School

The ideas of Merton, though based on a functionalist perspective, proved influential in American sociology. The Chicago School shared a number of common concerns with Merton, but developed their ideas differently. The Chicago School is best known for adopting the 'symbolic interactionist' approach to interpretive sociology (see Chapter 4). Robert Park (1929; Park and Burgess, 1925), a one-time student at Chicago University and by the end of his career the head of the Chicago School itself, originated the idea of 'urban ecology', an idea that was related to the more popular 'symbolic interactionism'.

With 'urban ecology', the city and its organization are depicted as a series of concentric circles, at the middle of which lies a central business district – the inner core of the city. Next to this central area is a zone referred to as a 'zone of transition', since it has a high migration rate and consequently an unsettled culture. Life in this zone mirrors, in many respects, the idea of the functionalist concept of 'anomie' or 'normlessness' since, with so many groups, many different subcultures emerge. All these have their own goals and often do not share similar values.

Theoretically speaking, Park's ideas represent the joining together of what are often seen as contradictory theoretical positions. Urban ecology incorporates the functionalist idea of the city as an organic system, but we can also see the development of symbolic interactionist sociology. Edwin Sutherland (1924) noted that individuals can more easily learn the ways of deviant or criminal subcultures in the zone of transition, since they are more exposed to such subcultures in that area. These early ideas on the development of subcultures in the city are still relevant to present-day sociology, and the chaotic life of the city is often a preoccupation of postmodern writers (see Chapters 4 and 7).

Howard Becker

Howard Becker – like Erving Goffman (see Chapter 6) – is a key interactionist figure. Becker applies the ideas of 'self' and 'self-identity' to study how deviant subcultures develop in opposition to the dominant culture. Becker's work is referred to as a 'labelling approach', since he suggests that being seen as deviant is not so much a question of what a person actually does, but more a matter of how he or she is 'labelled' by others. Others have the power to change an individual's self-image.

According to Becker (1973: 9): 'social groups create deviance by making the rules whose infraction constitutes deviance, and by applying those rules to particular people and labelling them as outsiders...the deviant is one to whom that label has successfully been applied'.

Hence, for Becker, it is not an individual's actions but the social reaction to them that creates deviance. Becker's ideas are important for the sociological study of subcultures, since they show that membership of a subculture defined by others as deviant, marks or labels the individual members also as deviant. This shows that subcultural identity can be the result of what others think about you, rather than what you think about yourself.

Ⓚ Ⓤ
Ⓐⁿ Ⓔ

Exercise 9.4

Evaluation is one of the most important skills to develop as a sociology student. It involves being able to identity both the strengths and the weaknesses of a given idea. Evaluate Becker's ideas by drawing up two lists – one consisting of what you see as the weaknesses of his ideas and the other describing the aspects of his work that you find convincing. Explain the items on both lists, using the ideas of other sociologists either to support or to critique what Becker says.

SUBCULTURAL SOLUTIONS TO THE PROBLEMS OF SOCIETY

Becker's ideas are reflected in the work of Stanley Cohen. In his classic text, *Folk Devils and Moral Panics* (1987), in order to understand how and why youth subcultural movements emerge and how they might become labelled as 'deviant' by wider society and its dominant culture. Cohen (1987) attempts to unite four factors:

- labelling;
- subcultural membership;
- structural forces; and
- action.

Cohen distinguishes between the concepts of structure and culture:

- *Structure*. This refers to those aspects of society that are beyond the control of and bear down on the individual. Cohen points to the existence of the class system in capitalism as a major structure that controls the life of groups in society.
- *Culture*. This refers to a collective response to the structures that control us. In this sense, 'culture' is meaningful to those involved in its creation and helps them to 'act out' their lives. It helps people to make sense of the world around them and is created by the people themselves. It is not an impersonal structure or force that turns people into puppets.

Cohen argues that, whereas structure creates problems, culture offers individuals potential solutions to these problems. The example that Cohen uses is the problem of being a young working-class member of a capitalist society. Such a person's life is likely, because of structural forces, to be characterized by:

- alienation;
- a poor education and few qualifications;
- low-paid, low-skilled employment or even unemployment;
- routine and repressive working conditions; and
- poverty.

Given these problems, many working-class adolescents try to act in ways that help them to 'make their own history' – to fight against structural forces through membership of a subculture that offers them the chance to gain ownership of their lives. In this respect, the term 'subculture' relates to the ways in which subordinate groups attempt to create a meaningful world to live in, by challenging their problems in a conscious way. Cohen notes that youth subcultures – since they offer resistance to wider structural forces – are frequently labelled as deviant by capitalist society, and are the subject of moral panics in the media. They represent a threat to the dominant culture of capitalism, and therefore need to be controlled.

Exercise 9.5

List the reasons why and in which way the values and actions of each of the following youth culture groups might threaten the dominant values of capitalist society:

Hippies • Skinheads • Hip-hop • Indie kids • Ravers • Nu-metal • Emo • Skaters.

In Cohen's work we can see the unification of two very different types of sociological theory: interactionism and Marxism. The synthesis of these ideas also characterizes the work conducted at the Centre for Contemporary Cultural Studies (CCCS), based at Birmingham University. The theoretical position held by the members of the CCCS is a version of neo-Marxism and is characterized by the following central beliefs:

- Both structure and action need to be studied.
- Capitalism is exploitative and creates problems for the working classes.
- Subcultures are meaningful attempts to resist the dominant capitalist culture.
- Beneath their surface 'style', youth cultures contain hidden meanings that are symbolic and enable those who follow them to evaluate society and respond to the structures into which they are born.

Subculture and resistance

A central theme of the CCCS is the idea of youth subcultures as a form of 'resistance'; that is, that all subcultures offer a challenge to the structural forces that cause problems for their members. Cohen (1987) identifies two further aspects of the notion of resistance:

- Subcultures are always fighting against a dominant culture and therefore develop only among those who are subordinate.
- The resistance offered by these subcultural groups is often not very successful. This is referred to as a 'magical' form of resistance: it does not achieve what it sets out to achieve, and contributes further to the problems of the group.

For example, working-class youths might reject education as a protest against a society that has denied them the opportunity to do well. But by giving up before obtaining qualifications their lives are even more likely to be characterized by poverty and inequality. Cohen notes that many protests by youth subcultures against the dominant culture are concerned with 'winning space'. In other words, they are trying to claim or reclaim their communities, bodies, identities, life-styles and so on by winning both the personal and the symbolic spaces needed to live a life without the problems of structure.

Popular culture as a symbolic 'battleground'

In *Reading the Popular*, John Fiske (1989) develops the idea that battles over class inequality are fought through the life-styles of youth subcultures just as much as by more traditional working-class means, such as trade unions, strikes and demonstrations. The key idea behind the notion that subcultures can fight and resist is the concept of 'excorporation'. What this means is that the cultural products, images, styles, life-styles, behavioural patterns and so on of the dominant culture are taken over by a subculture in order to challenge and change the meanings the dominant culture has given them. This fight is therefore symbolic in nature, since it is an attempt to take a dominant meaning of a symbol and change it into something else. Fiske suggests that popular culture – far from being a mass of cheap, unintellectual, throwaway and ideological media products that lack critical content – can actually contain the seeds of revolutionary struggle:

> Popular culture is made by subordinate peoples in their own interests . . . Popular culture is made from within and below, not imposed from without or above . . . Popular culture is always a culture of conflict, it always involves the struggle to make social meanings that are in the interests of the subordinate and that are not those preferred by the dominant ideology. (Ibid.: 2)

Paul Willis's ideas on the interplay between structure, action and subculture have proved to be highly influential, both within neo-Marxism and among non-Marxist sociologists. For example, by stressing the fact that individuals are born into structures that are not of their own making, and within these they create their own meaningful action, some of Willis's ideas reflect the 'structurational' sociology developed by Giddens (1984) – and this similarity is recognized by Giddens himself (see Chapter 6).

In *Learning to Labour*, Willis (1977) argues that the educational experience of working-class youths is shaped by the structure of capitalism. By this he means that schools are largely middle-class institutions that teach middle-class knowledge, are based on middle-class cultural experiences and are largely run by middle-class people – teachers. Within this environment, working-class youths often feel unvalued, alienated, bored and 'picked on' by teachers. Willis argues (as do Bowles and Gintis – see Chapter 3) that this disheartening educational experience instils in working-class youths the characteristics they will need to cope with working in factories and other routine and manual occupations. Through their boredom, they 'learn to labour'.

Willis notes, however, that many working-class youths are not passive in this process, nor are they unconscious of it; rather, they are fighting against the unequal class-based structures of capitalist society. Through the creation of a subculture based on 'having a laugh' they frequently 'bunk off' lessons, give up on homework, do not take examinations seriously and ridicule middle-class children for being 'swots' or, in Willis's study 'ear 'oles'. They refuse to be taken into the education system – they resist.

Exercise 9.6

Think about Willis's example of schooling, then write a detailed list of the ways in which young people might fight against the school system (for example, they might pass notes around the classroom in secret). For each example on your list, state why and how this might help them to define themselves as a person/individual (for example, passing notes around enables them to discuss what they wish and deny the authority of the teacher).

However, this is 'magical resistance'. It is largely ritualistic, since not only does it not get them very far, but not having qualifications further reduces their power to fight against the class-based structural forces later in life. Through their subcultural actions their worst fears about their future lives are realized.

Rethinking our definitions

Willis's ideas lead us to reconsider terms such as 'culture' and 'subculture'. Willis *et al.* (1993) makes an important distinction between the following concepts:

- *Dominant/hegemonic culture.* Western societies have a dominant culture that is based on the values of the class that rules – the capitalist class. This observation reflects the traditional or classical Marxist notion that a 'dominant ideology' (see Chapter 3) is used by one group to benefit themselves and reinforce their position of power.
- *Parent culture.* Within a dominant culture, individuals' life-styles are largely based on their social class. Thus everyone has what is called a 'parent culture' – a class-based culture from which different groups are given limited choices within the structural forces that control society. These are not 'subcultures', since this term is reserved specifically for a culture of resistance to wider dominant forces.
- *Common culture.* Whereas the dominant culture – based on the values of the ruling class (known as the 'hegemonic culture', see below for an explanation of hegemony) – structures and shapes the nature of society, some people can challenge and resist this structural force. This is 'common culture' – a place of resistance where the dominant culture cannot reach.
- *Subculture.* Each subculture (though it makes more sense to think in terms of a collection of different subcultures) is a specific example of a common culture. It is a 'counter-hegemonic' culture, since it is based on resistance to the ideas of the ruling group or groups.

GRAMSCI, THE CCCS AND HEGEMONY

The Italian thinker, Antonio Gramsci, writing in the 1930s, took the traditional Marxist accounts of 'ideology' and 'false consciousness' (see Chapter 3) further with his own concept of 'hegemony' (see Gramsci, 1971, 1977, 1978). This idea has proved to be very influential with many modern-day neo-Marxists, especially those in the CCCS. The starting point for the idea of hegemony is Gramsci's observation that ruling-class domination and control in capitalist society does not rest simply on the use of force and violence, but also operates at the level of ideas. The masses can be fooled or tricked into thinking that society is fair, when in fact it is against their true interests. This is the traditional Marxist conception of 'ideology' – that false ideas are used by ruling-class groups to hide the true nature of class inequality and exploitation.

The idea of hegemony goes further than this. It refers to the ways in which people in society consent willingly to their domination. In this way, ruling-class power is allowed to continue, without the need for physical force to maintain it. Hegemony means that culture is the result of a war of ideas between different groups, each with its own idea of what society should be like, depending on its own interests. If one side wins this struggle or battle and its ideas come to be seen as 'common sense' by groups who may not benefit from them, then this is 'hegemony'. In this way the world view of society is shaped by one specific set of ideas and the majority of cultural products will, in time, reflect and reinforce this world view without the ruling class having to maintain strict control over them. Thus people acquiesce to their domination, since their world view tells them that this is how society must be, and it simply would not make sense for it to be any other way. The CCCS sees subcultural groups as attempts to fight the dominant world view; that is, they are 'counter-hegemonic'.

However, it may be that the work of the CCCS on hegemony was appropriate for a particular time and a particular place; that is, in the United Kingdom in the 1960s–1980s. Looking at Japanese subcultures at that time, Narumi (2010) found that, while there were similarities in their appropriation of American music and dress, for example, the Japanese *zoku* (youth tribes) did not correspond exactly with their British counterparts, nor did they have the same class connection to the working class that the CCCS found in their work. Moreover, the cultural context of the equivalent subcultures also led to other differences. For example, while the hippies of the West used drugs such as marijuana and LSD, the Japanese *futen-zoku* (vagabond tribes) favoured sleeping pills and paint-thinner, with very different effects.

THE CCCS AND SEMIOLOGY

The members of the CCCS have also been influenced by 'semiology' – the study of signs (see Chapter 11). In particular, some members of the CCCS have been influenced by the ideas of the French cultural commentator and semiologist, Roland Barthes (1993). Barthes depicts ordinary life as a 'text', which, just like a poem, novel, play or painting, can be studied to find the hidden meanings that lie beneath the surface. The idea behind semiology is that day-to-day cultural activities should not simply be taken at face value. They are not 'how they appear to be', or 'just are'. Instead, Barthes and other semiologists look for the signs or symbols hidden in everyday life. What does an activity really mean? What are people really trying to say about themselves? When looking at youth subcultures, it is not simply a matter of considering their favourite music and what they wear. We need to go beyond this and ask questions such as 'What does it really mean? Why this particular style of music? What does this sort of fashion mean? Why do they use these words and not others?'

We need to 'break down' or to 'deconstruct' the hidden meanings behind youth subcultures – a theme that, combined with Gramsci's notion of hegemony, appears in Dick Hebdige's book *Subculture: The Meaning of Style* (1979). Hebdige writes about the ability of 'alternative' subcultures to create oppositional subcultures that allow the subordinate to develop counter-hegemonic life-styles, symbols and 'spaces'. These subcultures work against the ideology of the dominant cultural groups in society (the capitalist class), in the minds of the members of the subcultural groups and through the styles of dress they wear. Youth styles are 'meaningful'. They can be used to challenge, and to resist.

Exercise 9.7

To get a feel for the techniques of semiology, choose a favourite song of yours and deconstruct it, explaining what the song means and the hidden messages and references in the lyrics.

By 'style' Hebdige means the many methods of symbolic expression open to subcultural groups. For example:

- dress;
- haircuts/styles;
- behavioural patterns;
- patterns of language;
- ways of 'carrying oneself', including walking/standing, facial expressions and body language; and
- dance styles (or even the decision not to dance).

All these forms of expression are seen as being 'symbolic' – they are more than just 'being fashionable'. They can stand for oppositional values. They might attack hegemony.

Exercise 9.8

This exercise requires you to think about how youth cultural 'style' can contain hidden messages or symbols. For each of the six forms of style listed, provide an example of a youth culture that places emphasis on that style and explain what it means.

Hebdige argues that hegemony is like a 'moving equilibrium'. In this respect he shares with Gramsci the notion that hegemony is powerful, but not stable. It is not fixed, but changing. Challenges to hegemony can arise that can prove difficult for ruling groups to suppress; but other challenges can be redefined and incorporated into the dominant culture, where they pose no real threat. For example, alternative life-styles can become part of the accepted mainstream through overexposure on television, which strips them of their underground and radical qualities. These previously challenging counter-hegemonic subcultures simply become another product to consume, and to line the pockets of the capitalist media owners.

Willis *et al.* (1993) argue that though youth subcultures are popular, have mass appeal and are based on the consumption of low-culture products, they are still massive feats of creativity. This feat of creativity is indicated by the manipulation of old symbols, the invention of new ones and the redefinition of previous cultural practices:

> we insist that there is a vibrant symbolic life and symbolic creativity in everyday life, everyday activity and expression – even if it is sometimes invisible, looked down on or spurned . . . Most young people's lives are . . . actually full of expressions, signs and symbols through which individuals and groups seek creatively to establish their presence, identity and meaning. Young people are all the time expressing or attempting to express something about their actual or potential cultural significance. This is the realm of living common culture. Vulgar sometimes, perhaps. But also 'common' in being everywhere, resistant, hardy. (Ibid.: 1)

Willis *et al.* point out that though this is highly creative, it is also 'ordinary' – not in the sense that it is mundane, boring or unworthy of artistic consideration, but in the sense that it is day-to-day: it is inescapable:

> We are thinking of the extraordinary symbolic creativity of the multitude of ways in which young people use, humanize, decorate and invest with meanings their common and immediate life spaces and social practices – personal styles and choice of clothes; selective and active use of music, TV, magazines; decoration of bedrooms; the rituals of romance and subcultural styles; the style, banter and drama of friendship groups; music-making and dance. (Ibid.: 2)

As an example of such common, day-to-day yet creative uses of symbols for the purposes of identity, consider how and why young people decorate their bags, school books, folders and bedroom walls with posters, stickers, drawings and messages to and from friends. Why does this occur? What does this cultural practice mean? For Willis, this is a creative activity in which one plays with meaning and tries to establish one's identity.

Weinstein (1991) borrows the term 'bricolage' from structural anthropologist Claude Lévi-Strauss (see Chapter 10) to discuss how subcultures borrow, redefine and use styles and symbols from cultural groups other than their own. Bricoleurs are social actors who create meaningful cultural myths, stories and so on in order to think about and understand the world around them. The process of creating such myths and stories is highly creative and based on the manipulation of symbols. It borrows from traditional interpretations of symbols and reclassifies them. It uses old cultural signs and symbols in fresh ways. Though this concept was used to describe how myths are created in small-scale, non-literate cultures, the term is often used to refer to the creative symbolic interpretations made by groups in today's society. What this means is that, to establish an original place in the world, subcultural groups create a unique sense of style for themselves. To fight against the hegemony of a dominant cultural group, they borrow, redefine and re-use past and present cultural symbols in new ways. This is what is meant by 'bricolage' – the mixing of symbols by reclassifying them and actively creating new and meaningful subcultures based on resistance to dominant values.

Henry Giroux (1983, 1994, 1998) argues that, if subcultural activities by alienated youth are serious attempts at counter-hegemony, then they must be being undertaken in a conscious fashion. Giroux sees this as a paradox of youth subculture – a contradiction, but one that is almost impossible to avoid. On the one hand, many youth subcultures are attempts to reject a dominant hegemony – especially, by definition, a dominant adult hegemony. That is, they wish to separate themselves and their history from adult society. However, when rejecting the dominant adult hegemony, these youth groups eventually turn to the consumption of products largely controlled by adults, in particular the media and the music industry. Giroux, when discussing the 1970s punk movement in Britain, notes that when truly antagonistic and counter-hegemonic subcultures emerge they are quickly swallowed up by the capitalist culture industry, sometimes amid cries of 'sell-out' by the original fans.

Summarize in a copy of the chart below the theorists we covered in the above text, and include the strengths and weaknesses of their arguments to help you evaluate the ideas in this section.

Writer	Basic argument on popular culture	Strengths	Weaknesses
Stanley Cohen			
John Fiske			
Paul Willis			
Dick Hebdige			
Deena Weinstein			
Henry Giroux			

THE HISTORICAL RISE OF YOUTH CULTURE

For many commentators, the 'teenager' is a relatively recent social phenomenon. This specific age group – a symbol for young adulthood – has its origins in the rise of affluence and the emergence of a culture industry in the West in the aftermath of the Second World War. During this period there was a move away from an economy based on the production of goods from raw materials, and towards one based on the consumption of goods and the provision of services. The emerging communications industry – television, films and music – is considered to have invented the typical teenager in order to create a market for its goods. Youth music dates back to the development of rock 'n' roll in the USA, the subsequent expansion of the music industry into soul, jazz and pop music, and finally the beginnings of rock with bands such as the Beatles and the Rolling Stones. All these styles of music caused a moral panic among white (adult) society at the time. They were seen to stand for:

- rebellion by the young;
- the rejection of traditional values, especially religious and family-based ones;
- a rise in anti-authoritarianism;
- a rise in recreational drug-taking and sexual permissiveness;
- the politicization of youth and student movements; and
- the replacement of the work ethic with pleasure-seeking.

Though it seems that every generation has questioned the behaviour of its young, the Second World War is regarded as a watershed for popular culture because of the creation of a multiplicity of youth cultures.

Youth culture and television

In many youth subcultures, emphasis is placed on the consumption of popular culture. Given this, the growth of television viewing since around the early 1990s has been particularly bound up with the creation and rise of youth culture. They go hand in hand, since young people make up a significant proportion of the television audience and images of youth – especially sexual images – are used to sell numerous commodities. The media also targets the young as a subject. A great number of programmes are not just aimed at young people, but also promise to expose the true lives of the young (as is seen with the 'docu-soap' format and highly sensationalist documentaries in general), which are then used to create moral panics.

Neil Postman (1985) suggests that television is causing a 'disappearance of childhood', since very young television viewers are increasingly being exposed to images of sex, violence and other adult behaviour that children were sheltered from before the arrival of the medium. For Postman, television robs children of their innocence and causes them to grow up too quickly. Against this, without the rapid growth of television viewing, youth culture would not be as widespread or as varied as it is. TV may not strip children of their childhood; rather it may create 'youth' for the young. In an extension to Postman's argument, the role of the internet, particularly social and information networking sites, could today be argued to play a similar role to television.

Postmodern television?

In contemporary social theory and cultural criticism a great deal of attention has been paid to the rise of postmodern ideas (see Chapters 7 and 8). Given the emphasis by postmodernists on audiences' creative use of 'low' or popular culture (see Chapter 8), we should consider the relationship of youth subcultures to popular cultural forms such as TV and music.

Postmodern TV shows can be seen as sharing the characteristics of the wider postmodern culture in society. They are based on irony, self-reference and pastiche, and frequently convey ambivalent meanings that can be interpreted in many ways. For example, the US TV show 'Glee' is a combination of old and new music and pop videos, all postmodern elements, and the popular drama series 'Lost' included frequent flashbacks and a complex interweaving of plot lines.

Postmodern programmes frequently depict postmodern youth as nihilistic, hedonistic, drug-taking, interested in popular throwaway culture, and especially obsessed with TV (for example, 'Skins' and 'Misfits') and video games. Such postmodern youth are what American commentators frequently refer to as the 'MTV generation': with short attention spans, interested in cultural products that offer little substance but a great deal of style, consuming today's products now – instant gratification, over in a flash, gone tomorrow.

For example one of the characters in the animated US television show 'The Simpsons', 10 year-old Bart, has grown to love television more than his family, is totally desensitized to television violence and is interested only in 'being cool'. Though we might argue that this is only a cartoon (which it is), it is interesting to think about the image of youth presented to us in such cultural products. While programmes such as 'The Simpsons' are based on satire, they can be seen both as a representation of popular attitudes of the time, and as a massive source of meanings for the audience – meanings that might help them to construct their particular view of the world around them.

Best and Kellner (1998) suggest that another popular American cartoon series – 'Beavis and Butt-head' – offers a quite disturbing vision of the youth of tomorrow. The two central characters spend all their time as 'couch potatoes': time-killing spectators of a media-based 'reality' of which they lack the ability to be critical – the most they can manage is to say that something 'sucks' or is 'cool'. There appears to be a similarity here to the postmodern concept of the 'hyper-real' (see Chapter 7). The characters Beavis and Butt-Head are more embedded into their media world than they are into the real world, based on their own experiences. The most ironic thing of all is that while such programmes might intend their image of the postmodern young to act as a warning to society that it is losing its children to television, they are also part of the problem, since they are a part of the media-saturated world the audience is being lost to – and as such they present a 'reality' for tomorrow's postmodern children to copy.

①Ⓐ | Exercise 9.10 |

Take a popular television programme of your choice and think about the ways in which it might be an example of 'postmodern television'.

Youth culture and the music industry

Youth subcultures do not simply consume music, they are often based on a very particular form of the medium. Yet the relationship between the symbolic actions of individuals and commercial forces is not clear. When music scenes are 'underground', individuals establish and keep them alive by highly creative means – including word of mouth, the internet, via pirate radio broadcasts (as with the early development of raves and warehouse parties) and through e-mailed fanzines and blogs. However, when musical styles and scenes become more widely known they are often taken up the wider, profit-seeking music industry and hence become 'commodities' – bought for a price. Using the internet today enables individuals and groups to promote their music themselves (with relatively little cost) quite separately from the music industry. For example, the music of singer Lily Allen was promoted successfully through social networking sites before the music industry became involved; and successful bands such as Radiohead made a decision to release an album without charge on the internet, giving them freedom from record company control. They thus form 'commodities' in a different sense, with more consumer and artist control.

Though a great deal of subcultural activity is based on the consumption of cultural products made for profit by the music industry, the meanings and motives behind the choice of consumption – and the way that the music is 'used' after consumption – can still be active and creative. As Willis *et al.* (1993) note, while pop music is sometimes seen as being low-culture and throwaway, and the audience is seen as passive, this ignores the massive feats of symbolic creativity on the part of those who consume such music:

> Most musical activity... begins as and from consumption, from the process of listening to music. But consumption itself is creative... it depends too on consumer abilities to make value judgements, to talk knowledgeably and passionately about their genre tastes, to place music in their lives, to use commodities and symbols for their own imaginative purposes... For many young people the purchasing of records and tapes is an important sphere of cultural activity in itself, one that can range in intensity from

casual browsing to earnest searching for particular records. It is a process that involves clear symbolic work: complex and careful exercises of choice from the point of initial listening to seeking out, handling and scrutinizing records. (Ibid.: 61)

The consumption of music is often fundamental to youth subculture and identity. Music is often an ever-present feature of life in the home, serving as a background soundtrack to other activities. Equally, music is a source of entertainment outside the home and a topic of conversation and debate. Finally, because of home-recording it is often a personalized record of daily life – carried around from place to place via MP3 and CD players. Many of the technological developments in the world of music encourage such creative consumption. The invention of audio tapes, CDs, mini-discs, recordable CDs and MP3s can be seen as providing technological liberation from the days when music came only from a large radio in the home or from records: not portable, unable to be rerecorded and manipulated, and unable to be ever-present. Paul du Gay *et al.* (1997) consider that the use of personal stereos is a highly meaningful cultural practice. The personal stereo is 'cultural', since:

- It is a product that we can buy and consume.
- It is represented in advertising using cultural images.
- It has a cultural image of its own – as developed by advertisers.
- It is seen to have recognizable significance in everyday life – we see people using personal stereos all around us.
- The film industry often uses images of people using a personal stereo to represent certain cultural groups – often youth.
- It is used by individuals in a creative way to consume music how and where they wish.

The authors go on to argue that, as a cultural product, the use and popularity of the personal stereo raises some key issues and themes of contemporary life, based on its ability to offer 'private listening in public' (ibid.) places. It suggests:

- The lonely figure in the crowd.
- The use of media to screen out the boring, routine aspects of everyday life.
- An emphasis on mobility and choice.
- The self-sufficient individual wandering alone through the city landscape.

The authors suggest (ibid.) that the popular use of the personal stereo in everyday life is both a part of modern culture and a symbol of it. As with mobile phones, it has become an easily recognizable image for those living in the contemporary world, and enables us to understand what it means to live in such a world:

If we can conjure up a picture of what 'modernity' is like as a distinctive way of life, with an image of, say, the Manhattan skyline or some other similar urban landscape – as many television programmes and films do – we could do the same by tuning in to the typical sounds of the late-modern city. They would include not only snatches of recorded music but other familiar sounds, like the wailing siren of ambulance, fire-engine or police car, the endless murmur of traffic, the exhalations from sooty exhausts, wheezing engines and chugging juggernauts – the modern soundscape. (Ibid.: 19)

The MP3 player or mobile telephone is lightweight, small and portable – a true reflection and representation of modern technology. It is made to be 'worn' – it is part of one's identity: an extension of the body, carried wherever one goes. Finally, it is designed to be mobile – to be used by people who are on the move.

⊙Ⓐ

Exercise 9.11

What other technological objects might be seen as symbols of modern times? Listed below are five examples. Describe how each symbolizes the contemporary world and what it might say about those who use or carry it.

- Smartphone
- CD player
- Tablet
- MP3 player
- Digital watch

IS THERE A POSTMODERN YOUTH CULTURE?

We shall now discuss some recent developments in youth subcultural styles and evaluate them from the point of view of postmodernism. When sociologists describe popular culture as 'postmodern' they are referring to the hybrid, pastiche, pick-and-mix nature of the use of contemporary cultural signs and symbols in fashion, architecture, music and so on. Postmodern ideas are not just the province of academics and social theorists commenting on the young and their activities – the media have latched on to the term as a fashionable device and use it to reflect on themselves.

Variations of dance-based musical styles – such as jungle, big beat, techno, drum-and-base and garage – are often described as postmodern since they emphasize ambiguity, ironic and 'knowing' references, the borrowing of other styles and sounds, and a sometimes pessimistic, sometimes hedonistic atmosphere. These styles of music frequently blur the boundary between so-called 'high' and 'low' cultures by sampling from both and mixing the two together. Such samples might include an eclectic mixture of the spoken word, rap, chanting, snatches of famous historical speeches, news reports and film soundtracks, 'fake' distortion and feedback sound effects, and even a deliberately created 'hiss' from a record player needle – despite the fact that the recordings are digital and could be cleaned up if wished.

Pre-postmodern youth culture was traditionally seen as 'exclusive'. Membership of a movement or group involved not just liking some styles of music, but passionately disliking others. In postmodern youth culture and music there has been a blurring of musical styles as never before. For example, 'white' guitar-based rock music takes from urban 'black' music the use of drum machines, record decks and sampling to create something in between the two. Bands such as the Beatles and the Rolling Stones combined Hindi musical sounds with Hindu religious images and references, and add to these sampling and other sound effects.

Some examples of postmodern youth cultures

Slacker/grunge

According to Jonathon Epstein (1998) the members of what has become known as the 'slacker' or 'grunge' culture were 'twenty-somethings' born between 1964 and 1979 – often of 'baby-boomer' parents who grew up in the 1960s. 'Slackers' tended to be middle-class and white, and they adopted a rather nihilistic approach – seeing their future as bleak. The grunge or slacker look borrowed a great deal from some aspects of punk and in turn influenced the indie-kid look. The movement as a whole is post-punk and was taken up by American 'art school' bands, as was the case with punk in Britain in the 1970s. The musical style of the American band Green Day to some extent encapsulates this.

The members of this subculture might be described as postmodern since they are pessimistic about the future and have therefore given up on the present. Unlike punks, however, slackers were not angry about the drying up of the future – they saw this as a rational and realistic response to a changing world. Many commentators referred to them as 'Generation X', meaning affluent, middle-class people who were highly educated and could be highly successful but instead decided to drop out and take 'dead-end' jobs: what postmodern author Douglas Coupland referred to as 'McJobs' (see Lindsay 2005, Lindsay and McQuaid, 2004).

Rave and techno

Tomlinson (1998) notes that 'Chicago house music' (the forerunner of rave, techno, trance, acid house and so on in Britain) was originally based in clubs frequented by the gay community. Techno or rave thus originated from the cultural practices of a disadvantaged group. Tomlinson quotes Ross (1994), who suggests that dance music genres can be classified according to the class of those who follow them – with techno subscribed to by working-class youth, and 'ambient' followed by more middle-class devotees.

Tomlinson (1998) deconstructs rave as a genre or subculture based on the concept of 'age'. She suggests that rave culture was about reclaiming childhood: being based on primary colours and small clothes; the use of toys as props at rave events was common, especially whistles and dummies; females often put their hair into child-like pigtails; and many rave tracks included themes from TV shows aimed at children. In fact, as was claimed by the Britain media at the time, the initial popularity of the children's show 'Teletubbies' was a result of ravers coming home from clubs in the early hours of the morning and watching the programme as part of a psychedelic experience.

Rave also offered a culture of community, since the pleasure of attending a rave event is based on having physical contact with others when dancing on one's own. This is reflected in the often anonymous nature of rave musicians. Many do not seek pop-star fame and publicity, preferring to remain 'faceless'.

In *Club Cultures*, Sarah Thornton (1995) stated that the young clubbers involved in the rave and techno scenes had a highly developed sense of style and taste, and used this to judge who is an insider or outsider of the clubbing scene. Insider membership, and the sharing of common subcultural values and fellowship, is based on the possession of what Thornton calls 'subcultural capital' (developing the concept from Bourdieu): having the ability to know what is 'in' or 'hip' and what is not – ranging from styles of dress, to language, to dance steps, and even to the music itself and the DJs who play it. An important credential for an insider is a long-standing relationship with the dance-scene community (not just jumping on a fashionable bandwagon) and an understanding of the underground rave scene – not just the commercial and popular clubs. This could be seen as representing some sort of search for authenticity in the postmodern age. At a time when no claim to taste, art and identity is deemed to be more worthy than any other, are some people seeking a sense of security and membership of a scene that is perceived to have 'roots', rather than just being a cultural throwaway?

Hip-hop and rap

McRobbie (1986) and Mercer (1995) both claim that rap music – and in particular the act of 'scratching' – is a highly postmodern phenomenon and the ultimate expression of postmodern cultural values:

- The music is a pastiche of many elements.
- It is immediate and for pleasure, and lays no claim to ultimate artistic taste.
- It often mixes high and low cultures.
- It is frequently self-referential, using samples in ironic ways.

Hence the hip-hop DJ conforms to Lévi-Strauss's concept of a 'bricoleur' (someone who performs the process of 'bricolage'), since they are borrowing cultural symbols and styles, re-classifying them and using them for their own means. In the ultimate example of postmodern ironic expression, the dancing partner to hip-hop music – breakdancing, which originated in the poor ghettos of inner-city USA as a symbolic representation of gang warfare – became part of the staple diet of white, commercial dance groups and was used frequently by advertisers to sell products such as training shoes to the white, surburban, affluent middle class in Britain.

Willis *et al.* (1993) suggest that the cultural significance of rapping can be likened to the oral tradition of passing on stories in small communities. With its emphasis on the immediate environment, day-to-day life and an awareness of the political nature of class, urban and ethnic experiences, rap music represents an attempt to reflect on the nature of life and one's place in the community.

Hardcore

Locher (1998) has studied what in Britain was called 'hardcore' and in the USA was known as 'industrial' or sometimes 'industrial hardcore'. With its roots in guitar-based music such as punk, grunge and speed-metal, and its borrowing of techno-based sampling, break-beats and drum machines, this style of music can be seen as mirroring the postmodern cultural practice of picking-and-mixing from previous cultural movements. Other varia-tions combine ska (a reggae-based musical style) with speed metal or punk, and sometimes rap with heavy metal guitar work. This is often referred to under the broader heading of 'nu-metal'. Like the music of some slacker bands, hardcore music is often taken up by urban 'street-skaters' and 'boarders'.

Goth

The goth scene was studied by Hodkinson (2004). He found no specific link to class differences. Despite many members being middle class, membership was fluid and members did go to see bands outside the goth genre, so it was not an exclusive group. However, Hodkinson argues that there was 'sub-cultural substance', a distinctive set of values and a shared identity. This identity was shared with other goths globally. Many goths, when interviewed, stressed their individuality, their personal choice and style. However, Hodkinson (2004: 40) notes that there is a tendency to exaggerate their uniqueness within the subculture. There was 'a limited sort of pick 'n' mix, in which the vast majority of selections [of clothes, appearance and accessories] have to be drawn from a relatively clear subcultural range of acceptable possibilities'. The postmodern freedom of choice of cultural forms found within other youth subcultures was not present to the same extent among the goth subculture.

Ⓘ Ⓐ | **Exercise 9.12**

Select a song from a musical style of your choice and consider the ways in which it might be an example of postmodern music.

GENDER AND YOUTH CULTURE

McRobbie and Garber (1976) comment that research and theorizing on youth subcultures focused on class as a key contributory factor for their development but ignored the role of gender. Research was conducted by men into masculine subcultures. They argue that the different structural position of women (economically as well as culturally within the home and wider society), and the private, marginal nature of their subcultures, explains their absence. McRobbie (1983) found that youth subcultures for girls exist mainly in the private space of homes, as a 'bedroom culture'. This is was supported by Lincoln's (2004) research in the 1990s into Mancunian girls, and has been developed by Tonya Anderson (2010) in her research into pop idol fandom online, which she refers to as 'communal bedroom culture'. Her research looks at how being a 'fan' of groups such as Duran Duran in the 1980s or Take That in the 1990s/2000s does not stop after the teenage years. Many women continue their fandom into adulthood through fan forum communities online. What used to be a private activity has now become communal. Reddington (2003) disagreed that women were absent from subcultures before the 1990s, arguing instead that they were ignored by researchers into, for example, the punk movement, citing it as an instance of 'male hegemonic control'. Hill's (2010) research into female heavy metal fans looks at this previously neglected area, interviewing female fans and examining their letters in the fan magazine *Kerrang!*.

RETHINKING SUBCULTURE

Bennett (1999) and McRobbie (2010) have questioned whether the term subculture is relevant in current society. McRobbie argued that society has changed in the 100 years since the work of the Chicago School, that we now have a 'proliferation of taste cultures'/life-styles. People want to associate with a particular leisure activity or life-style. These leisure and interest groups are not subcultures, as there is not the association with class that existed in the work of the Chicago School. Bennett (1999) notes that coherent or fixed groups that merit the label of subculture rarely exist. He uses the term 'neo-tribes' to describe consumer groups with similar interests, who come together to express these interests but are otherwise not a single coherent group. His interpretation of youth groups as fluid echoes postmodern interpretations.

Muggleton's (2000) analysis of whether youth subcultures are best seen as modern or postmodern involves his forming 'ideal types' and interviewing more than 50 young people. He concluded that postmodern interpretations of subcultures were most appropriate because individuals expressed multiple subcultural identities or found themselves on the fringe of membership. Being a member was still important, but subcultures were more fragmented, with a focus on style.

Ⓚ Ⓤ
Ⓐ Ⓐⁿ

Exercise 9.13

Remind yourself of the differences between modern and postmodern identity and culture (see Chapter 7). Then look at the list below from Muggleton's (2000) ideal types and decide whether they refer to modern or postmodern subcultures.

Characteristic	Modern or postmodern subculture?
Homogeneous style	
Low commitment	
Low mobility in and out of the subculture	
Show political resistance	
See the media positively	
High commitment	
The subculture provides their main identity	
Fragmented identity	
Negative attitude towards the media	
Stress on beliefs and values	
They have a range of identities	
Focus on style and image	

CONCLUSION

Youth subcultures are the source of many moral panics in society, providing even more reason for sociologists to take seriously what others in society might dismiss as unimportant – as 'just a phase that young people are going through'. It is important for sociologists to understand why young people behave as they do, how they use seemingly trivial media products as a source of identity and creativity, and how such creativity is symbolic, meaningful and at times political. All this will be ignored if we dismiss such cultural groups as unimportant because they are based on fun. The early focus of young people as involved in deviant subcultures relates to only a small number of youth subcultures today.

A dominant theme in contemporary subcultural study is the idea of creativity or agency – an idea that takes us back to the action approach discussed in detail in Chapter 4. This concept is used in an interesting way by many thinkers. It is often combined with a Marxist-based approach, uniting structural and action sociologies together. Seeing recent youth culture in terms of neo-tribes or leisure interest groups reflects the fluidity of culture today as seen by postmodern theorists and the ability of consumers to participate in, and even to form, their own appreciation groups. For example, there are more than 40 British Take That fan sites online (and many more globally) which cater for a wide range of interest groups, not just for young girls, but also for boys, as well as 'Mums and Dads' who are fans. The reunion tours of both Take That and Duran Duran (bands initially popular in the 1990s and 1980s, respectively) indicates the fluidity of culture. Consumers identifying with these groups include the not-so-young, who 'revisit' the identity and interests of their youth alongside younger consumers experiencing it for the first time.

Important concepts

Anomie • Bricolage • Deviance • Excorporation • Hegemony
• Labelling • Moral panic • Neo-tribe • Strain theory
• Subculture

Exam focus

(a) Assess the sociological explanations of the rise of youth culture since the Second World War.
(b) To what extent can youth culture be seen as a popular rebellion against the powerful in society?
(c) How effective are Marxist explanations of youth subcultures?
(d) 'Postmodern explanations reflect the reality of subculture membership in society today.' Discuss.

Critical thinking

1. Do youth subcultures exist in modern society?
2. Do youth subcultures or interest groups exist around hobbies and interests other than music?
3. Are subcultures exclusive to the young? Can explanations of youth subcultures be applied to adult subcultures?

Chapter 10

Semiology, Structuralism and Poststructuralism

After studying this chapter, you should:

- understand the method of semiological analysis
- be able to apply the ideas of structuralism to culture and identity
- be able to use the semiological method to think about youth subcultures
- be able to compare structuralism with poststructuralism

INTRODUCTION

Sociology is a distinctive way of thinking about the world and it has a recognizable world view that allows us to identify issues of concern to sociologists, yet ideas, concerns, methods and theories from other social sciences and related subjects can influence the development of sociology, and vice versa. So, at one level, sociology is a distinct subject, but at another it contributes theories to a wider 'resource pool' of ideas taken from other subjects, such as psychology, philosophy, anthropology, cultural studies and so on. For example, the ideas of the postmodernists (see Chapter 7) have influenced all these subjects as well as sociology, and in this book we can see that some of the ideas of philosophers and anthropologists are of interest to sociologists. Given that this book is about culture and identity, it is necessary to look at what these other subjects have to say, since the themes of culture and identity are important to all subjects that study human life, even if they do so in different ways.

In this chapter we shall look at some of the ideas from linguistics, anthropology, media studies and philosophy that have influenced sociologists when attempting to answer the essential question of what human behaviour really means. The answer to this question can be seen as the end goal of sociological study. The business of those who 'do' sociology is not just to theorize, but to say something about what life is like and what it means. A dominant theme in sociology is the idea of a 'sociological imagination' – a term coined by the American sociologist C. Wright Mills (1959) (see Chapter 2). In our 'sociological imaginations' we aim to see and then to understand the world by detaching ourselves from 'common-sense thought' – the ideas of the culture in which we have been brought up. Though common sense enables us to be capable actors in society, it may stop us truly thinking about 'why' we do the things we do in our culture.

	Exercise 10.1

What are the problems of common-sense thought for the sociologist, and how does common-sense thought differ from sociological knowledge? Complete the table below – you might like to refer back to the ideas of C. Wright Mills discussed in Chapter 2 as well as completing some further research.

What are the features of common-sense thought?	What are the problems of common-sense thought?	What are the features of sociological knowledge?	Why is sociological knowledge better than common-sense thought?

The use of theories allows us to go beyond what common sense tells us society is like. For example, Marxists use their theories to argue that while society might appear quite fair to those involved, it is in fact highly unequal. The task – and the promise – of sociology is not just to see what humans do, but to try to understand why they do what they do – to search for the meaning behind what we see happening. For example, why might some people have their bodies pierced? What does this mean? Why doesn't everyone do it? Why has it suddenly become popular? Has this been common in other cultures in the past? One way of thinking about what things really mean, about the hidden meanings behind the action, is the method of analysis known as 'semiology' – the study of signs, originally developed for use in linguistics – the study of language.

SEMIOLOGY AND STRUCTURALISM

Thinkers who adopt a structural approach tend to believe that what we see doesn't always tell us what is really going on. Structuralists believe that we have to look beyond the surface action and study the hidden patterns that make this action meaningful. These hidden patterns are the structures that unite all the surface variations. Once we can identify the structure and understand how it works, we can better understand what human social life means. If we only observe society directly, we may see glimpses of the pattern but will never achieve a full understanding. An example of how this works can be found through the historical study of language. We may have a good understanding of the meaning of words in the English language. However, if we study Latin and Greek, as well as a con-sider how language is adapted in American English, as well as how some groups within society may use slang words, we gain a much deeper and better understanding of what the language means. We shall look at how Ferdinand de Saussure takes the study of language and meaning further than this. Structuralists want to have a deeper understanding of what human social life means by looking beyond the surface at the hidden patterns.

The philosophical ideas of structuralism are linked to semiology. Both semiology and structuralism have been influential in sociology because they have raised three key observations/concepts:

- The idea of reality being a 'structure' or pattern beneath the surface.
- The importance of symbols in human society and culture.
- The importance of the idea of 'difference' or 'otherness' in the creation of cultural meanings.

Ferdinand de Saussure

Semiology is associated with the work of Ferdinand de Saussure, a linguist lecturing at the University of Geneva at the start of the twentieth century. Saussure's *Course in General Linguistics* (1983) marked the start of a new and highly influential way of thinking about language. Before Saussure, language tended to be studied in a historical fashion. Changes in words, sounds and meanings were studied in the order they developed in the culture that spoke the language in question. Saussure proposed something very different – an idea that led to the philosophical position of 'structuralism'. Saussure drew a distinction between:

- *structure*: 'langue' – the system of differences between signs; and
- *surface*: 'parole' – the use of these signs in day-to-day speech.

Saussure thought that language should be seen as a pattern or a structure that unites all the individual acts of speech within a language into a regular whole. This is the true but unseen 'reality' of how a language exists. Acts of speech are simply the surface. The true reality of language is the rules that make all the variations in speech possible. Saussure saw all language as being made up of a collection of 'signs'; that is, collections of symbols that stand for/represent/'symbolize' something outside the language. For example, the sound we make when we utter the word 'tree' is simply a symbol for something that our particular language calls by the sign 'tree'.

Each sign has two parts to it, known as a 'dyad':

- *a signifier*: the 'sound image', the actual word itself; and
- *a signified*: the concept, in our minds, of the object that the sound image represents.

According to Saussure, the allocation of these signs to actual objects is purely arbitrary. There is no real reason why the object we call a 'tree' should actually be called 'tree' at all. This is why different societies and cultures have different ways of speaking. They have assigned different signs to objects. However, once the signs have been allocated, then those who are born into the language have no choice but to use that sign.

Why and how are signs allocated to objects in the first place? For Saussure, it does not matter what signs are used, only that there is agreement about the rules and examples. The most important thing is that signs only become 'meaningful' because they are different from other signs. Therefore, when we use the sign 'tree', because it is different from the sign 'dog' we can make sense of it. If, however, what we call 'dog' and 'tree' had the same sign, there would be no difference and thus no meaning could be established. It is important to note that while language is thus a structure – or a system – it is also abstract and communal. The rules of language make it real and allow it to shape and regulate all acts of speech, but it exists only in the minds of a collective group, and it thus unites all their individual acts of speech into a whole.

Charles Sanders Peirce

The American philosopher Charles Sanders Peirce (1991), writing at the same time as Saussure, divided 'signs' into three possible types:

- *Icon*. This type of sign is identical to what it stands for; for example, a picture of a tree.
- *Index*. This type of sign is built on a link to the senses; for example, if we were blindfolded, the feel of the bark would tell us we were touching a tree.
- *Symbol*. This is a sign that only links to an object through symbolic means. For example the written word TREE only reminds us of the object 'tree' because this is the arbitrary symbol we have learnt.

Peirce explored the link between the sign and the object it represents by suggesting that rather than a dyad, the sign is a triad: divided into three parts:

- *The sign*: the actual symbol that represents something else.
- *The object*: the 'something else' the symbol represents in the material world.
- *The interpretant*: not the person doing the thinking, as such, but the way in which we use our experience of signs and objects from the past in order to use and recognize signs more easily.

Roland Barthes

So far, we have discussed how language can be seen as being structured into a system that controls the individual examples of human speech by uniting them into a wider pattern. It is through the work of the French cultural commentator Roland Barthes (1967) that we can see the connection between these ideas of semiology and the meaning of culture (see Chapter 8). Barthes divides the process of signification – when the signifier and the signified relate together – into three 'orders' or levels:

- *First order: denotation* – the meaning of the sign that our common-sense thought gives us.
- *Second order: connotation* – the association our culture gives to each sign, which in turn links to others that are not directly 'seen' when we experience the first order. For example, if I saw a sports car, in the first order I would think to myself 'that is a car'. However, in the second order I might invoke other signs such as 'powerful', 'fast' or even 'sexy'.
- *Third order: myth* – this usually occurs at the same level as the second order, and can be seen as the chain that links together all the signs one uses. Thus, in the example above, the myth of sports cars is that they are all fast, sexy and powerful. Myths are

culturally based and tend to be well known, but this is not to say that they are 'true' – they are only true because the culture says so.

Answer the following questions, using the information presented so far in this chapter to help you.

1. Why is language important for group identity?
2. How do symbols help us to create a meaningful reality in which to live and engage with one other?
3. How might symbols bond the individual to the group?
4. How would functionalists interpret the role of language in human societies?
5. How would action sociologists interpret the role of language in human societies?
6. How would structurational sociologists interpret the role of language in human societies?

APPLYING THE SEMIOLOGICAL METHOD

In his book, *Mythologies*, Roland Barthes (1993) takes features of ordinary life and demonstrates how they can be studied in the same way as Saussure studied language. In other words, our entire culture is like a massive 'text' made up of symbols and signs that enable us to expose the meaning underlying our culture. Barthes argues that a system of signs in culture structures all meaning into a pattern that exists as a 'reality' beneath the surface of these cultural texts. Culture creates 'myths' – collections of signs that are present in the cultural products we encounter in our day-to-day lives.

As an example of myths creating meanings in society that are understood but largely hidden, Barthes looks at the significance of 'steak and chips'. Barthes says that steak and chips signify – represent – 'Frenchness' itself (we could make the same claim in terms of their 'Englishness'). He argues that 'steak' signifies heartiness, simplicity, freshness, strength and going back to nature. It is both the food of those with exotic and expensive tastes, and the simple food of the peasant. It thus unifies all French people.

Barthes provides another example by 'reading' (interpreting the signs) an advertisement for pasta produced by a company called Panzani. The advertising image used is a string bag containing some tins and some packets of Panzani pasta, together with fresh ingredients such as tomatoes, mushrooms and so on. Barthes suggests that the advertisement consists of signs denoting freshness, return from the market and Italianness – the latter because of the product's name and the Italian-flag colours of the bag's contents.

A similar use of the colours of a flag as a dress code was employed by Cape Verdean young males living in Boston in the USA. Saucier (2011) argues that the way that Cape Verdean youth has adapted 'hip-hop' styles of clothing by incorporating images of the national flag of Amílcar Cabral, the Cape Verde independence leader, is a way of constituting an identity that encompasses the local, national and global experiences of these youths and their families. The dress code that results is a 'semiotic web' that expresses their origins in Cape Verde and their new struggles in the USA. The inclusion of the pan-African colours of red, black and green in their sartorial choices adds an ethnic dimension to this reading of identity (see Chapter 13), that refers to the African struggle against colonialism but also addresses present-day identification with the black people of America.

| | Exercise 10.3 |

Summarize the ideas of Saussure, Peirce and Barthes as outlined in the table below. Try to demonstrate the similarities and differences between them.

	Time period writing in	Key ideas	How did this author extend the semiological method used by his predecessors?	Strengths of this approach	Examples of argument
Saussure					
Peirce					
Barthes					

| | Exercise 10.4 |

Conduct your own semiological 'reading' of an ordinary aspect of day-to-day life, in the same way that Barthes looked at steak and chips. Write about 200 words in all.

| | Exercise 10.5 |

While the semiological method might allow us to uncover hidden meanings, it is quite unreliable since it is highly subjective. Using this statement as a guide, list four advantages and four disadvantages of this method.

Dick Hebdige

Neo-Marxist researchers at the Centre for Contemporary Cultural Studies (CCCS) at the University of Birmingham used the semiological method extensively to analyse the meanings behind the styles adopted by youth subcultures (see Chapter 9). Dick Hebdige (1979) suggests that the styles adopted by subcultural groups – such as punk, grunge, indie, rave, hip-hop and so on – are not accidental but are highly meaningful attempts to create identity. Therefore, such styles can be 'read' as signs, which can be interpreted by sociologists.

Signs and human agency

Many structuralists refer to what is known as 'the death of the author', meaning that we have the freedom to 'read' texts in creative ways. Our interpretation or 'reading' of the signs may not be as intended by the author, hence the 'authorship' of cultural products – such as those of the media – has 'died' and the audience are free to interpret the products in any way they wish – a situation of relativism also noted by many postmodern thinkers (see Chapter 7).The idea that human beings interpret signs in different ways is reflected in the work of Stuart Hall (1993) and David Morley (1980) (see Chapter 8 for a further discussion). Hall makes a distinction between the 'encoder' and the 'decoder' of signs. The encoder is the creator/producer/author of the sign, while the decoder is the object/receiver/audience. When decoders receive signs and decode them they do not do so passively, but take one of three approaches or 'readings' (interpretations):

- dominant/intended reading;
- negotiated reading; or
- oppositional reading.

The type of decoding that takes place depends on the background and experiences of the person doing the decoding.

STRUCTURALISM AND ANTHROPOLOGY: CLAUDE LÉVI-STRAUSS

The anthropologist, Claude Lévi-Strauss (1969, 1978) takes the idea of linguistic structuralism and applies it to the study of non-Western, small-scale societies and tribal communities. In his book, *The Savage Mind* (1972), Lévi-Strauss differentiates between societies at two different stages of historical development. There are 'hot societies' – literate societies – where rapid social change has been experienced and massive, complex social hierarchies have emerged; and there are 'cold societies' – pre-literate societies – where social change has either been resisted or is happening at a slower rate. The latter maintain their social systems in a state of unchanging equilibrium or balance. For Lévi-Strauss, cold societies offer an excellent opportunity to investigate how human social life is shaped, regulated or structured by the cultural system.

Lévi-Strauss is highly critical of the functionalist anthropology of writers such as Malinowski (1922, 1954) and Durkheim (1982) (see Chapter 3). In *The Elementary Forms of the Religious Life* (1982), Durkheim suggests that Western thought is superior to that of tribal societies, because Western knowledge is based on rational scientific knowledge. However, Lévi-Strauss argues that while 'hot' and 'cold' societies do use different forms of knowledge they are only different at the level of surface variation, and that there is a deeper structure that unites these two ways of thinking.

The 'savage mind'

At a deep structural level the thoughts of the 'savage mind' are not that different from ways of thinking in the Western world. This 'savage mind', despite how it might appear to functionalist thinkers, is not inferior, less organized or more open to irrationality. Rather, it is based on a 'science of the concrete'; that is, it uses analogies to think about the world and to develop massive and complex systems of classification – just as Western science does. For example, the 'organic analogy' (see Chapter 3) used by functionalists is no different, as a mechanism to aid thinking, from a myth or legend in a tribal culture.

Therefore all human thought, while appearing different on the surface, can be seen to be united by the deep structure that runs through all human thinking: the mechanisms of organizing, classifying and thinking about differences or opposites. An excellent example of the way in which human thought classifies the world around it is provided by kinship patterns in tribal societies. Many such communities have complex rules on who can and cannot marry whom, and who is related to whom and how. These kinship patterns are found in many different types of society and are an indication of an underlying logical structure in the way that all humans classify the world, their relationships with each other, and therefore their own identities. Kinship tells you who you are, and who you are not. Like Barthes and Saussure, Lévi-Strauss uses the concept of 'difference' to explain how cultural myths and patterns of kinship work. Myths tend to be based on stories or legends that categorize, group and organize systems of knowledge by indicating what is the same and what is different, or 'other'.

Exercise 10.6

It is often useful for the sociologist to step back from his or her own culture and think about what other cultures are like. Use anthropological textbooks, the internet and any other sources available to you to find out about the cultures of two societies other than your own. Using the guide below, note the obvious differences between these cultures in respect of each of the key social features listed.

	Your own society	**Society 1**	**Society 2**
Kinship			
Religious practice			
Knowledge			
Entertainment			

Bricolage

When describing how culture and cultural signs are created and given meaning, Lévi-Strauss uses the term 'bricolage'. This concept is used to discuss the role played by humans in the creation of cultural meaning. 'Bricoleurs' – individuals or group of individuals who perform the act of 'bricolage' – can be seen as working in the manner of artists or handymen. They collect many different elements of cultural meaning and fuse them together to create new meaning; that is, they take a whole collection of signs and work on them as though they are materials and tools to create new cultural meanings. As with objects of art or other material objects, these cultural meanings have form and texture – they are multilayered, sign upon sign, forged together in an ad hoc fashion.

Bricoleurs create new cultural meanings from the vantage point of existing meanings within the cultural system, from which they borrow their raw materials. Accepted cultural meaning is 'played with' and changed, but from within the structure. Meaning cannot come from 'nothingness'. It has to use what is already there, but in different forms and combinations. This process of bricolage – the creation of symbolic cultural meanings – is the same for a work of art as it is for a tribal cultural myth, a sociological theory or even a Western scientific law.

STRUCTURALISM AND MARXISM: LOUIS ALTHUSSER

Althusser (1971, 1976) takes the principles of structuralism and uses them to update or reassess the original ideas of Marx (see Chapter 3). However, this is a very different update from that offered by the 'humanist' neo-Marxist, Antonio Gramsci (1971, 1977, 1978). Gramsci argues that the class system of capitalism can be resisted and actively combated through the self-conscious and self-aware cultural activities of ordinary people. The dominance of the ruling class is the result of a 'war of ideas' in which their ideas take precedence over all others and shape how people see reality around them. This is known as 'hegemony'. The hegemony of the ruling class can be fought through the 'agency' of the working classes.

Althusser (1968) argues that a distinctive break or rupture can be observed in the ideas of Marx if they are read in a structuralist fashion. The 'early Marx' was preoccupied with the humanistic concerns of ideology and alienation (see Chapter 3), while the 'late Marx' was concerned with the way in which production structures and shapes the inner logical workings of society. Althusser refers to this difference as an 'epistemological break' (epistemology refers to the way in which people gain knowledge – Althusser argues that Marx changed the way he perceived the world around him during his career) and he adopts the second position, which he sees as a scientific version of 'mature Marxism' produced by a 'sympathetic rereading' of the economic determinism in Marx's book *Das Kapital*.

In *For Marx*, Althusser (1969) stresses the role of class conflict in the shaping of human history. Gramsci locates class conflict in individual consciousness, but according to Althusser we should look instead at the structure of the wider class system, which is made up of numerous groups of people, not just individuals. The true determining or structural force in human social history is economic production. This is the force that directs society and social change – it makes society what it is, and what it is likely to become. Althusser does not adopt a simplistic view of the economy, where class forces alone shape society. Instead, he argues that eventually the economy does shape society, but at most times the social system is determined by many different forces – not just economic but also cultural. Ultimately, however, it is the conflicts caused by the way in which production is organized that lead to change in the structure of the system.

Althusser suggests that there are three structural levels in a class-based society: economic, political and ideological. While the political and ideological levels have a degree of autonomy from the economic, in the end it is still the economic structure that is dominant. In the same way, the class system can be seen as layered, and while all the layers are interconnected they also have some autonomy. Collectively they constitute the 'structure' into which humans are born, and by which they are shaped.

Unlike Gramsci, who attributes some free will ('agency') to individuals, Althusser believes that individual self-identity is not independent of the structure of the system.

Since we are born into a society that pre-dates us, its structure makes us its subject. The structure of society moulds us, and allows us to 'know ourselves' only from within it. Althusser refers to the simultaneous existence of an 'ideological state apparatus' and a 'repressive state apparatus', which shape us into who we think we are. The state can use ideology to control us – we can be socialized by institutions such as the family, religion and the media into thinking that our society is 'normal' and accepting it as it is. However, if ideology fails, the state can control us physically through the use of force and violence. For example, the police have the legal right to use force against us, and we can be locked up in a prison or an asylum.

Exercise 10.7

List six similarities and six differences between the ideas of Gramsci and Althusser.

Exercise 10.8

This exercise requires you to consider the key arguments and ideas of Lévi-Strauss, Hebdige and Althusser, as discussed in the text. Record your findings in an extended version of the table below.

	What hidden structures do they look at?	Basic ideas	Strengths	Weaknesses	How useful do you find their ideas? Explain your answer.
Lévi-Strauss					
Hebdige					
Althusser					

STRUCTURAL FEMINISM

As we have seen, writers such as Althusser use structuralist ideas to update Marxism. Other writers have applied similar ideas to feminist sociology. These writers argue that a particular structure controls and unites society – the structure of gender.

Hélène Cixous

Hélène Cixous (1980; Cixous and Clement, 1986) observes how culture often designates a gender to objects, words, attitudes and other concepts through the use of language. For example, being strong is seen as an attribute of masculinity, whereas being irrational is seen as feminine. Cixous takes up the idea of the 'birth of difference' from the work of

Saussure and Lévi-Strauss. She notes that cultures often contain pairs of opposites – one of which is seen as male, the other female. For example:

Masculine	Feminine
Strong	Weak
Rational	Irrational
Economically productive	Sexually reproductive
Emotionally 'hard'	Caring and nurturing
Emotionally detached	Over-emotional

Though humans are controlled by such 'differences' by being socialized into common-sense thought, they can and do fight against it. This means that inequality is not natural, but the product of learned and cultural behaviour (see Chapters 2 and 12). In her essay 'Sorties', Cixous (1980) lists, among others, the following examples of binary opposites frequently found in Western cultures: culture/nature, head/heart, form/matter, speaking/writing. As a feminist, for her the most powerful binary opposite is the male/female one, and she suggests that this division structures – or patterns – everything else in society. Though one of the two has more power – in this case 'male' – both need each other in order to exist. They are defined as much by what they are not as by what they are.

Luce Irigaray

Luce Irigaray (1985, 1992, 1993), who originally trained and worked as a psychiatrist, suggests that schizophrenic patients are not biologically sick, they are merely defined as being 'ill' by the cultures in which they live. Irigaray is particularly interested in how language structures and defines reality for humans within their culture and governs their sense of self-identity. Some people become 'overwhelmed' by language – they become the subject of language and are controlled by it, rather than being able to use it in a reflexive and active fashion. Such people, frequently women, are unable to create a stable sense of self-identity and as a consequence are defined as schizophrenic. Irigaray argues that women in particular find it difficult to create a sense of self, because language has a masculine bias that dominates them and what they see as reality.

Julia Kristeva

Julia Kristeva (1981, 1986) – also a psychiatrist – criticizes Saussure's structural linguistics for treating language as a structure that controls humans, rather than being open to human creative manipulation. Her work is based on a reworking of Freudian psychoanalytic theory (see Chapters 2 and 3), combining this with some aspects of symbolic interactionism (see Chapter 4) and structural linguistics.

Kristeva draws a distinction between the semiotic (the informal, pre-verbal language developed in infancy and based on the uncertainty surrounding our biological desires and drives) and the symbolic (the adult verbal language, based on rules and a common structure). Kristeva states that both types of thought and communication exist within us when we interact in everyday life, and that when we do so we manipulate signs both consciously and unconsciously. Self-identity is established and reinforced by the transition from semiotic to symbolic communication. It is vital for their self-identity that children learn the concept 'I' and therefore develop a sense of their 'difference' from others – they come to see themselves as a separate being. In adult life these two aspects of humanity – the culturally created structure of language, and early preverbal biological drives – exist in tension with one another, and the conflict between the two – the cultural structure and the biological – can result in mental illness and identity problems.

Kimberle Crenshaw

Crenshaw (1991) posits a theory of identity that she calls 'intersectionality'. Her interest in ideas about identity stems from her legal background and the ways in which women experience 'interlocking oppressions' according to their gender, class and ethnicity. Her argument was that black women's experience of domestic violence and rape in the USA was different from that of white women, because the identity of black women was forged at the intersection between gender and ethnicity. This has consequences for the way that black women are treated in the criminal justice system. Prins (2006) argued against this formulation of the intersectionality of identity because it reduced the role of individuals in negotiating that intersection in various ways, allowing them to create an identity rather than having one thrust upon them.

(K)(U)

Exercise 10.9

List the key concepts used by each of the structural feminists discussed above (Hélène Cixous, Lucie Irigaray, Julia Kristeva and Kimberle Crenshaw) and the key features of their arguments.

(An)(E)

Exercise 10.10

Consider structural feminism as a whole. Identify two strengths and two weaknesses of this approach.

POSTMODERNISM AND SIGNS

Jean Baudrillard

Baudrillard (1981) takes some ideas from Marxism and uses them to further his argument about the new role that signs have taken on in postmodernity. Marx (see Chapter 3) saw the production of objects for consumption as being controlled by those who own the means of production. This 'economic determinism' – where the nature of production influences and determines everything else in society – is reflected in the general Marxist idea that the ruling class rule because they control the productive forces, and this gives them power over everything in society.

For Baudrillard, capitalism continues to rule society because it has created false desires that are fulfilled by consumption. While many Marxists would agree with this statement, Baudrillard goes one step further and suggests that it is the manipulation of signs that makes us think that we need these objects in the first place. Baudrillard argues that objects that are commodities – such as televisions, washing machines, videos, trainers, mobile phones and so on – have both a 'use value' and an 'exchange value' associated with them as part of their sign:

- Use value is the purpose ('utility') to which we put objects – in other words, why we might need something, and what we would do with it.
- Exchange value is how much something is worth in terms of how much we are prepared to pay for it – also referred to as 'commodity value'.

Baudrillard states that the use value of the sign or object hides its exchange value. Capitalism tells us to buy this or that product because it is the 'best' or the 'newest', or even the 'smallest', and this use value is seen to relate to a human need and desire for the object. Baudrillard says that this is really the other way round: use values are ideological. We do not really need the commodities we buy. In fact we only want them because we are told by advertisers that we do need them. We think that use and need come first and then a commodity is created to meet that need – but actually it is the other way round. We only need that commodity because it has been made. Therefore the ideological illusion of the so-called use value of the sign hides the fact that such objects only exist because of their exchange value – because they make a profit for capitalists.

Writing from the postmodern perspective, Baudrillard argues that, in the present age, symbols or signs have become commodities. They have taken on a reality of their own, over and above the objects they represent (see Chapter 8). For example, when purchasing an item of designer clothing, we are not buying the object for what it is, rather we are buying the sign – we are consuming signs and images, and trying to represent ourselves with them.

The hyper-reality of signs

Baudrillard suggests that if we separate the signifier from the signified (if we separate the sign from the object) we soon see that signs create culture, not the other way round. Signs give us meaning; they are not given meaning by culture. All we have left to consume, in postmodernity, are signs, since there is no reality, no absolute truth, no way of seeing the world in such a way that we can create a dominant meaning. Signs not only become real – because this is all there is – they become 'more real than real' – 'hyper-real'. Since we have no means to get at the truth, we simply accept the signs given to us by the media and use these to create meaning.

Jacques Derrida

Baudrillard's ideas have been greatly influenced by Jacques Derrida's idea of 'deconstruction'. Derrida (1973, 1977, 1978) argues that we need to pull signs apart to see what they are hiding from us, to separate the sign from the object in order to see more clearly what is the real truth of the matter. This is what he calls 'deconstruction'. We must deconstruct ideology and illusion. Derrida wishes to move beyond the structuralist idea that structures control human action and give meaning to human life. In Derrida's view, structures have no meaning apart from that given to them by humans through the use of language, and that it is the use of words by some people to create meaning that leads to the lack of power of others. Derrida suggests that we should study how words – in speech, writing and sets of communication-based interactions, known as 'discourse' – limit those whose identity is controlled by them. This idea has been highly influential in the creation of the perspective known as 'poststructuralism'.

(An)(E)

Exercise 10.11

Identify two strengths and two weaknesses of the postmodern approach to the study of signs.

POSTSTRUCTURALISM

The term 'poststructuralism' originally referred to the work of a collection of French philosophers writing in the wake of structuralists such as Althusser, Lévi-Strauss and Barthes. These poststructuralists include Jacques Derrida and Michel Foucault, though the term 'post-structural' is sometimes rejected by these writers themselves. In many respects the views of poststructuralists represent a blending together of ideas already covered in this chapter: ideas from some structuralist thinking and some postmodernist thinking.

Poststructuralism argues that:

- Language is the key feature of power in society and it shapes and controls human action.
- Signs have become detached from the objects they represent, and have become 'real' themselves through language.
- Since signs are detached from reality we are no longer able to speak of a single 'truth', since we have no basis upon which to establish this. We are simply left with many different interpretations.
- Human beings are not controlled by invisible structures, but are defined and given identity by 'discourses' – sets of languages – with which they can fight, resist and seek self-identity.
- What we consider to be 'reality' is created for us by language, and is based on the construction of 'difference'. In other words, for something to be seen or defined as real or true, its opposite has to be defined as untrue or unreal, at the same moment of definition.

Within these claims we can see elements of a wide range of ideas from other sources:

- Saussure's emphasis on 'difference' as the basis of meaning.
- Baudrillard's view that signs have become detached from reality.

- The general postmodernist view that there is no truth – only relativism.
- The structuralist idea of the 'death of the author'.
- Derrida's view that language controls humankind.

According to post-structuralism, the signifier has priority over the signified; that is, the signifier controls and shapes the signified by giving it meaning and identity. In addition, there are more signifiers than signified in culture, and thus signifiers take on a reality of their own. This means that truth is relative, since the languages we use are not linked in any concrete way to the objects of the material world. Power is the ability to control and use sets of languages – called 'discourses' – to define others. This idea is associated with the work of the French historian and philosopher, Michel Foucault.

Michel Foucault

Foucault (1984) is influenced both by the structuralist notion of 'difference' and by Derrida's idea of 'deconstruction' and the role of 'discourses' in society. Foucault takes as his starting point a critique of the ideas of a French intellectual, wartime resistance fighter and political campaigner: Jean-Paul Sartre.

Sartre's particular version of philosophical thought – known as 'existentialism' – was in turn based on Husserl's phenomenology (see Chapter 4) and it suggests that the 'essence' of humans follows only from the 'being' of humans. In other words, unlike objects, we cannot say much about the nature of a particular person before that person has been born and grown up. If we consider an object – say, a chair – we can be sure of a number of things about the 'essence' of this object even before it is made, before its 'being'. The chair will have a seat and a back, and it will be raised from the ground in some way. We cannot do the same with humans. We cannot say that a 'yet to be born' person will be kind, or clever or good at mathematics. Therefore, for Sartre, 'being' precedes 'essence' for humans.

Sartre goes on to suggest that humans only become the people that they do – individuals with an identity – because they make it happen themselves. We have free will to decide who we are, so if we feel unhappy with our life and our being – our identity – we are living in a state of 'bad faith' if we blame anything or anyone other than ourselves for this. We have the power to be whoever we wish. We have agency (see Chapters 4 and 5). Foucault disagrees with this. He suggests that identity is formed by the combination of languages that are used to observe and define us. These languages are referred to as 'discourses'.

Discourses and power

We can see discourses as sets of ways of thinking about, knowing about, classifying and speaking about a subject that takes priority in being used to control and observe people involved in different aspects of social life. They are sets of specialist or technical languages that define, control and observe – or, as Foucault says, 'gaze'. For example, medicine is a discourse that is used to control the body in our society, and it is seen to have specialist knowledge with which to think about the body. The knowledge associated with this way of thinking and speaking is powerful as it can be used to limit and to control. If you are defined as being unwell by the 'gaze' of your doctor, you might not be allowed, legally, to go to work until you are redefined as being well or healthy again.

Other discourses include:

- *Pedagogy*: thinking and speaking about how children (or other learners) learn.
- *Penology*: thinking and speaking about how we should control prisoners.
- *Criminology*: thinking and speaking about how we should stop crime.
- *Economics*: thinking and speaking about how we should organize production in society.
- *Psychiatry*: thinking and speaking about how we should treat mentally ill people.

The structure of society, then, is seen as a complex and vast web of many different discourses. Power is thus multi-layered, and each individual might be under the gaze of many different discourses at any one time.

Truth and power

Like postmodernists such as Baudrillard, Foucault does not believe in a single, identifiable and absolute truth. Knowledge is simply a way of thinking that allows the exercise of one's will against others. This idea is based on the ideas of the German philosopher, Friedrich Nietzsche, who spoke of a 'will to power' whereas Foucault speaks of a 'will to truth'. For Foucault, different discourses present different truths and different ways of thinking about, speaking about and knowing the truth. The truth thus becomes a site or battleground over which different discourses exercise their will – their desire to take control, to have power. In Foucault's words: 'There is a battle "for truth", or at least "around truth" – it's a matter not of a battle "on behalf" of the truth, but of a battle about the status of truth and the economic and political role it plays' (Foucault, 1984).

What he means by this is that powerful groups have the opportunity to define the particular sets of ideas and ways of thinking that come to be seen as the truth. This must mean that 'the truth' rather depends on where you stand. Discourses create the truth – they provide ways of seeing, thinking and speaking about the world and our experiences of and in it. Culture is thus made up of a variety of discourses and our identities are the result of them defining who we are. Foucault reserves the term 'power-knowledge' for the particular way in which truth is a feature of those who have knowledge.

Discourses and the birth of difference

Foucault adopts a historical method drawn from the ideas of Nietzsche – a method known as 'genealogy'. This is based on the idea of 'the birth of difference'. Whenever a discourse invents or creates – gives birth to – a new way of thinking about the world, it does so through the creation of binary opposites. For example, when we have sanity we also have insanity. The same goes for healthy/unhealthy, normal/deviant, decent/perverted.

In his historical studies, *Madness and Civilization* (1989a) and *The Birth of the Clinic* (1989c), Foucault notes that the introduction of the mental asylum, which promised to help and to cure 'sick' people, was actually responsible for defining and controlling both the insane and the sane, since each was defined within the discourse by its opposite. The job of the historian should be to identify the historical break or rupture that causes the birth of difference. This is often referred to by Foucault (1989c) as an 'archaeological' method, and he is critical of historical accounts that ignore the birth of difference since he sees this as contributing to the sort of discourses that try to define 'how things are' and in doing so gain power – that is, knowledge.

Foucault seeks to develop a history of the hidden and the silent in historical studies: to understand those who are on the 'forgotten', 'silent' and 'powerless' side of these differences – to try to see how they have their identities created for them by the complex fields of discourse into which they are born. Foucault sees the structure of discourses as both enabling and constraining, and in this respect his ideas echo those of Anthony Giddens on structurational sociology (see Chapter 6). Though one's identity is created and defined by the multi-layered structure of the discourses that hold individuals under their gaze, one can nevertheless resist and subvert. But one can only fight this structure within the structure itself, since no one can live outside it.

Poststructuralism and fluid identities

One trend in poststructuralism approaches to identity is to reject all formulations that rely on the idea that our identities are 'fixed' in any way. Rather, identity is fluid, both in time and space, and is constituted by 'assemblages' (Deleuze and Guattari, 1987). Puar (2005) offers a picture of identity that draws on dispersed networks, which may be made up of people (bodies), institutions, ideas or emotional connections, to assemble a particular 'node of connection' for a specific moment that makes up an individual's identity for a time. Assemblages are therefore inherently unstable as the various networks may be called upon in different combinations, at different speeds, for different purposes, at different times. Identity is seen here as a process rather than a state, constantly being constructed and reconstructed by the individual and always in motion. Discourses, power relations and social structures all play a part in this fluid assembling and disassembling of our identity, but they play no privileged part, and are merely networks that can be called upon in the process of construction or deconstruction.

Zingsheim (2011) offers a 'mutational' theory of identity, in which the fluid processes of identity formation are influenced by four characteristics, usually associated with mutants in popular culture. First, there is evolution, in which identity is affected by slow evolutionary processes such as ageing or in swift evolutionary changes such as the loss of a loved one. Second, there is multiplicity, that identity formation and dissolution occurs on many levels and employs both internal and external resources, including the power that exists moment to moment outside of the individual and the power that resides within. Third, there is embodiment, that the process of identity is associated with a physical manifestation that has both a material and a discursive reality. The connection between the two is dialectical; that is, the physical body will intersect with discourses about the body (for example, how body image is idealized), and discourses about bodies will influence the emergence of an identity at any moment in time. Finally, there is agency. Zingsheim accepts that there is a limit to the agency that an individual can have in relation to identity. For example, even where an individual has a great deal of control in assembling the components of an identity, s/he has little control over how that identity will be received and perceived by others in the networks that constitute the specific context of identity.

Match each statement below to the author(s) most likely to make that statement.

Statement	Who would say this?
(a) Clothes act as signs to other people	Dick Hebdige
(b) People who are schizophrenic have become 'overwhelmed' by language	
(c) Signs have become hyper-real	
(d) Language is like a set of rules that enable us fit into a group	
(e) Some groups can gain power since they control knowledge	
(f) We can uncover the hidden meaning behind everyday images and objects	
(g) Western science and tribal religions are united by a common, hidden, structure	
(h) There is no truth separate from what we decide is the truth	
(i) We are what we buy	
(j) Symbols can be manipulated in a creative way to create new identities – an act of bricolage	
(k) Discourses control us – they label and define us	
(l) Class forces are the underlying structure of all societies	
(m) Language contains symbols that are used to perpetuate female subordination	
(n) The media audience is free to interpret signs as they choose	

CONCLUSION

Structuralist and poststructuralist ideas raise important issues about how people think about the world around them, about how people create reality, and about the role of power in the creation of what we regard as 'truth'. These ideas allow us to think about identity as an issue of 'difference' and power in a similar way to Marxist ideas, as explained in Chapters 3, 8 and 9. The role of power in culture, identity and language is a theme that dominates the work of Michel Foucault, and his ideas have influenced a great many sociologists. His ideas are being taken up by other branches of sociology, such as Marxism, some feminisms and postmodernism, and in this way sociology is moving forward – new and interesting ideas are being developed from previous ideas.

Important concepts
Bricolage • Deconstruction • Discourse • Semiology • Sign • Signifier • Structuralism

Exam focus
(a) How useful are the ideas of structuralism in helping us to think about how identity is created in society?   (b) To what extent can we say that in the contemporary age 'signs' have changed as sources of identity?

Critical thinking
1. 'Knowledge is power.' To what extent is this true?   2. Understanding language is essential to understanding culture and identity. Do you agree?

Chapter 11

Class and Consumption

After studying this chapter, you should:

- understand the relationship between class and identity
- have knowledge of the changing nature of class identity in contemporary times
- be able to evaluate the idea of class identities from New Right and postmodern perspectives
- understand the idea of a consumer culture
- be able to relate the idea of a consumer culture to postmodern views on identity
- understand how class and consumption relate to patterns of life-style choice
- understand the role played by new social movements in identity formation
- reflect on the underclass and the role of 'chav' culture

INTRODUCTION

For many sociologists, the concept of class is the idea 'par excellence' of sociology: it is seen by many as the major contribution sociology has made to academic thought on the nature of society and social relations, and it is one of the most powerful tools at the sociologist's disposal. Discussions of the nature of class – and of class culture and identity – are often vehicles with which the key themes of sociology – power, inequality, domination, social control and ideology – are presented in a clear way. Class itself is most associated with the insights made by Marxist sociology and the great variety of theories that have been influenced by Marxist ideas.

In more recent times, the idea of class has undergone a quite profound reassessment. Many sociologists have substituted the concept with 'consumption' and/or 'life-style'. This is seen as reflecting changes in sociology since the Second World War, based on observations of actual changes to the class structure in Western societies. Operationalizing and researching class, consumption and life-style patterns are not straightforward. Assigning individuals to classes or socio-economic groups is commonly done using occupation as an indicator; however, some theorists argue that the indicators have changed, that lifestyle and culture as well as factors such as geographical region should be considered. However, there is a direct link between occupation and income, and the lifestyle or cultural commodities one can consume.

Ken Roberts (2001) identifies that the debates around class culture and identity centre around two issues:

- that class is no longer a central concept in identity formation; and
- that indicators of class have changed (for example, the types of occupation and forms of work are more important; a wider range of classes exist, such as an 'underclass' and an 'overclass'; and consumption, not occupation, is central).

We shall explore both traditional and contemporary views on class culture and identity, but first we review some theoretical interpretations of the role of class in society.

A THEORETICAL REVIEW OF CLASS IDENTITY

Exercise 11.1

Using a range of other sociological sources, look up the concept of class and write your own definition.

Exercise 11.2

Using your own definition of class, in what way and why do you think the concept is important in today's society? To answer this question, consider whether class matters in each of the following areas of social life. Justify your answer for each.

- Voting
- Consumption
- Life-style
- Identity
- Politics

Exercise 11.3

1. For each of the following statements, tick whether you have similar attitudes or behaviour patterns as your parents.

Attitude or behaviour	Tick if similar to your parents
The political party you vote for	
Whether you recycle your rubbish	
Hobbies and interests	
Do you save money regularly (if you can afford to!)?	

Support (or not) of the monarchy	
Similar occupation	
Support (or not) of charities	
Religious beliefs	
Attitude to taking time off of work for illness	
Musical taste	
Similar leisure activities	
Level of education achieved (post-16, post-18, graduate, post-graduate, other professional)	
That trade unions are beneficial for workers	
That you should try to own your own home if possible	
How you feel about unemployment and receiving benefits	
Public (fee-paying) education is preferable if you can afford it	
The newspaper you read regularly	
Marriage is an outdated institution	

2. Do you place yourself in a class? If you do, which class, and why do you identify yourself in this way? Make a note of your responses, and after reading this chapter, reflect on your answers. Which theoretical position best reflects your attitude to and experience of class?

Traditional sociological theories focus on the attitude and role allocation of social class and how social class is involved in cultural reproduction. If you have identified that many of the above attitudes and behaviours are similar to those of your parents and close family members this could be a result of cultural reproduction. We shall be reviewing sociological research on identity and culture and considering whether class-based attitudes, beliefs and behaviour exist in modern society.

Traditional theoretical interpretations

Functionalists (see Chapter 3) see class division as being natural to the smooth running of society. Distinct class cultures create clear class identities, since those in a similar class position are similar people with similar values and life-styles. Equally, class allows individuals to 'know their place' in the pecking order – the 'best people' occupy the highest positions and have the most 'refined' cultural backgrounds.

Traditional Marxists see class culture and identity as tools of ideological domination. For example, Frankfurt School members Adorno and Horkheimer (1979) argue that the working classes, being deprived of education and therefore of critical thought, are subjected to a stable diet of popular/low culture that serves to perpetuate their class position over time (see Chapters 3 and 8). This is known as 'cultural reproduction' – the way that culture helps to reproduce the class structure with each succeeding generation.

Neo-Marxists, such as those working at the CCCS, are interested in how subcultures – which are oppositional to the dominant culture of the ruling classes – develop as pockets of resistance. A class identity is created that enables the development of true class consciousness, through struggles with the hegemony of those who rule (see Chapters 8 and 9).

①Ⓐ

Exercise 11.4

The traditional Marxist interpretation of political action in society would be to claim that class is the basis of all political action – such as strikes, demonstrations, protests and so on – and that this is because of the importance of class in defining our sense of group identity. Conduct some research to see whether this is still true today. You will need to use online sources and newspapers to obtain the most up-to-date information.

Theoretical reassessments of class

The New Right claims that, in modern society, class identity and culture are fragmenting or decomposing. For example, Peter Saunders (1990) suggests that class is irrelevant to people's lives, and it is no longer a meaningful factor in their life-styles. Saunders cites home ownership as a more important factor in both inequality and identity formation today. These ideas are reflected in the claim by the former Conservative prime minister, John Major, that Britain had become a 'classless' society.

Equally, some New Right thinkers argue that people who work hard can be any class they wish, and those in the 'underclass' deserve to be there since they are lazy and ill-motivated. In this view, class is not important, since those who work hard will move upwards in an open or meritocratic society. Those who do not work hard and are in the underclass present a significant problem, but one that can be solved by the withdrawal of state benefit. This solution was proposed by the 2011 UK Coalition government to deal with an underclass on long-term unemployment benefit. Many feminists argue that the overemphasis on class within sociology has led to the creation of a 'malestream' sociology that ignores, and renders invisible, women and gender as a source of identity and inequality. In 'malestream' sociology, men are central in the research process, as researchers and participants, and the conclusions of this research are then generalized to the population as a whole, making the assumption that the findings can also be applied to women. Abbott and Wallace (1997: 2) argue that: 'the feminist challenge to malestream sociology is one that requires a radical rethinking of the content and methodology of the whole enterprise, one that recognizes the need to see society from the position of women as well as from the standpoint of men'.

Finally, postmodernists such as Crook *et al.* (1992) suggest that present-day identities are much more fluid and ambivalent than they were under the rigid constraints within class identity in the past. Now individuals are free to become whomever they wish, through consumption and the creative adaptation of life-styles (see Chapter 7).

We shall use these basic theoretical approaches to consider the ways in which class, life-style and consumption shape identity. However, before we do this we need to conduct a brief historical review of how class culture and identity have been treated within sociology.

THE HISTORICAL TREATMENT OF CLASS CULTURE AND IDENTITY

The traditional working class

Paul Willis (1990) sees culture as the routines and patterns of everyday life. Culture in this sense exists everywhere, and it orders or makes sense of every aspect of social reality:

> Culture is not artifice and manners, the preserve of Sunday best, rainy afternoons, and concert halls. It is the very material of our daily lives, the bricks and mortar of our most commonplace understandings, feelings, and responses. We rely on cultural patterns and symbols for the minute, and unconscious, social reflexes that make us social and collective beings: we are therefore most deeply embedded in our culture when we are at our most natural and spontaneous: if you like, at our most work-a-day. (Ibid.: 183)

Given the emphasis on work as a defining feature of one's life and identity, the nature of our culture is most evident in our work: how we organize, interpret, make sense of and cope with our daily routine. Willis associates traditional working-class culture (that may have changed today) with the following values, which were meaningful responses to life in a factory:

- Mental and physical bravery (when working in hostile workplace conditions).
- Physical strength.
- Masculinity.
- Skills obtained through experience, not education.

Willis (1977, 1990) suggests that a key feature of working-class culture in everyday life is the use of humour – 'having a laugh' –to get through the day and to bring meaning to the long periods of relentless boredom, whether on the factory floor or at the work site. Many commentators suggest that, in postmodern or post-industrial society, this traditional working-class culture is in decline.

Exercise 11.5

Does class still matter? Drawing on all that you have read and investigated so far, explain the position taken on this question by each of the following theoretical branches:

- Functionalism • Traditional Marxism • Neo-Marxism • The New Right • Feminism
- Postmodernism

Miller (1962) suggests that working-class culture is made up of a number of 'focal concerns': masculinity; immediate gratification (instant pleasure seeking); excitement; and a willingness to leave one's life open to chance, not to plan ahead. Some sociologists suggest that such focal concerns create a 'culture of dependency' that prevents the working class from being upwardly mobile. These focal concerns hold back the working classes by placing no real value on education. Opportunities are thrown away in favour of immediate pleasure seeking. They encourage poverty and being 'happy with one's lot' rather than trying to 'better oneself'. Finally, reliance on these focal concerns may encourage rule breaking, which may lead on to delinquent and criminal behaviour.

Exercise 11.6

Compare the ideas of Willis and Miller. Identify and list five similarities and five differences between what they have to say about working-class culture and identity.

The main criticism of Miller's ideas is that he is very judgemental about working-class life. He seems to see working-class life-styles and tastes as being inferior to those of the middle classes. Such attitudes tend to 'pathologize' the working classes. They make the working classes seem different from other people and dysfunctional, which holds them back. The association of working-class people with crime is also highly suspect. If crime statistics do show a preponderance of working-class criminality it might be a result of selective policing practices and the more visible nature of their crimes, rather than because they are more prone to criminal activities than anyone else.

Other sociologists, such as Willis (1977) and Cohen (1987), see working-class culture as containing a great deal of creativity, given that the society individuals live in is highly exploitative of them. John Lea and Jock Young (1993), adopting a position they describe as 'New Left Realism', warn against the tendency of writers such as Cohen and Willis to romanticize the criminal and delinquent activities of working-class youths by portraying them as 'Robin Hood' figures, engaged in a symbolic and creative fight against capitalism. Such portrayals provide little comfort to the victims of nasty and ignorant crimes, victims who themselves are often working-class people living in inner city areas.

Some of Miller's ideas, especially his claim that the culture of the working class is responsible for their position in society, are reflected in the thinking of the New Right and the New Left (in society today these are no longer 'new' ways of thinking – consider 'new' as meaning a break from previous thinking in this area). For example, US New Right thinker Charles Murray (1984) is highly critical of the 'underclass' – the long-term unemployed – whom he regards as lazy, intellectually inferior, criminal and responsible for their own position because of their dependence on state welfare. Such ideas caused the British Conservative governments between 1979 and 1997 to reduce state spending on welfare amid moral panics over 'social security scroungers'. New Labour, in power from 1997, adopted a very similar policy towards the underclass in the welfare reform referred to as 'welfare to work', as has the 2010 Coalition government in the UK. According to one Marxist-based interpretation of this, the underlying assumption is that the majority of the unemployed are simply too idle to look for work and therefore should only be given benefits if they start to do so.

Using the internet and newspapers, collect information on the present government's views on poverty, class and welfare. What do you think this information suggests about how class is seen by politicians today?

The fracturing of class identity

Since the Second World War, and especially during the 1960s, there has been a sociological debate about the changes the traditional class structure has undergone, and what the consequences of restructuring might be for work, inequality, culture and identity. An early contribution that shaped ideas on the 'death' of class identity was the work of Zweig (1961). Zweig argued that, as a result of a process of 'embourgeoisement', there had been a reduction in the size of the traditional working class and the growth of a 'new', more affluent, service-based middle class.

In opposition to this idea, Goldthorpe *et al.* (1968) claimed that, rather than a new middle class, a new working class had emerged. This new working class had rejected the class-based Labour politics of their forefathers and adopted what was described as a more 'instrumental orientation' to both work and politics. This class would readily vote Conservative (described at the time as 'deviant voting') if they thought that doing so would bring them financial benefits. This new working class adopted a life-style that was home-centred, and thus the family became an important site for consumerism. This was an early sign of the rise of a 'consumer society' and the decline of class identity in postmodern times.

Savage *et al.* (1992) point to the 'fracturing' or decomposition of the middle class into a number of middle classes with different life-styles and identities. First, there are new consumer identities based on life-styles and a concern with the body as source of and object for such life-styles. Second, there are identities based on 'cultural capital' – the highly educated who work in the service sector of the economy or in the caring professions and who possess high cultural tastes. Finally, there are the more 'traditional' middle-class life-styles based on the family, home ownership and foreign holidays.

The rapid expansion of non-class identities has been explored by Bradley (1996). Bradley suggests that class does still exist – something that many postmodernists and members of the New Right might challenge. However, she notes that it is no longer regarded as important by people themselves. It is frequently rejected by those very people who could objectively be classified as working class but have chosen to adopt a consumer orientation towards the world that is more reminiscent of the middle classes.

To conclude our discussion of the relevance of class identity today, and to support the Marxist position against the postmodern views described above, look up the current statistics on poverty and inequality in your country. Do you think that class is still important?

Kerr *et al.* (1973) and Bell (1973) suggest that the post-war rise in affluence, the creation of the welfare system, the growth of consumerism and the decline of traditional class identities signalled a profound change in society: the dawn of the 'post-industrial society'. Such a society is characterized by:

- increased affluence;
- increased consumption;
- the decline of primary industry;
- the rise of a service-based economy;
- the rise of knowledge as a commodity to be used as a basis for status and power; and
- the rise of new managerial and professional classes.

Exercise 11.9

How might increased affluence lead to changes in life-style and identity? Copy out and complete the following table. A few examples are provided to get you started.

Feature of affluence	How might this lead to changes in life-style and identity?
1. Having more money to spend	1.
2. Credit cards	2.
3. Increase in affordable domestic appliances	3.
4.	4.
5.	5.
6.	6.
7.	7.

The optimism inherent in this image of Western capitalist nations is based primarily on the belief that capitalism has 'delivered the goods'. This claim has influenced a diverse range of writers, including writers from the New Right and postmodernists. For example, New Right thinker, Francis Fukuyama (1992), suggests that capitalist societies in the 'late', 'advanced' or 'mature' stages of development have seen the erosion of class and the fracturing of traditional class cultures and identities. Similarly, many postmodernists suggest that, with the shift towards a service economy and mass consumption, society has become very different.

Exercise 11.10

The following thinkers claim that class has 'declined' or 'fragmented'. Summarize their views in an extended version of the following table.

Name of thinker	According to this thinker, what change has occurred in society?	What, in this thinker's opinion, has this done to class?
Zweig		
Goldthorpe		
Savage		
Bradley		
Kerr		
Fukuyama		

FROM PRODUCTION TO CONSUMPTION

The alleged decline or death of class as a factor in identity formation has been traced back to the decades after the Second World War, and to three key developments:

- The rise of a much more affluent new working class/new middle class.
- The expansion of popular cultural products.
- The shift from an economy based on production to one based on consumption.

These three developments have been important for a wide range of theories with very different ideas, such as the New Right, the theory of 'post-industrial society' and postmodernism.

Exercise 11.11

1. List ten products you would like to own in the next ten years, or that would be on your 'to buy' list if you won the lottery.
2. Review your list. What do the products say about your identity? Do they indicate anything about your social class and background or lifestyle?

The origin of mass consumption lies in the mass production that took place during the USA's 'wonder years' of the 1950s: the mass production of popular Ford motorcars for the 'average man', television sets, washing machines and so on – and the rapid growth of the advertising industry as well as the media as a whole. With the rise in affluence, those previously denied the opportunity to consume could now also become consumers.

Two other historical developments took place that went hand in hand with the three identified above:

- The creation of large multinational companies that developed brand-name products and invested massively in advertising.
- The rapid expansion of the music industry and the development of 'youth' as a distinct cultural group (see Chapter 9).

This was a time of massive expansion in the availability of popular culture and popular products, many of which we take for granted today: fashion, pop music, consumer durables, the home entertainment provided by stereos and MP3 players and so on. This early consumption was still structured by the class system. While many working-class people were more affluent than ever and more products were available, there were distinct differences between the tastes and desires of the different classes. These tastes were both structured and played upon by the advertising industry, which marketed their customers' products according to market research based on class categories. Today we have a 'consumer culture' – detached from traditional class identification.

In his book, *Keywords*, Raymond Williams (1983: 78) observes that the word 'consume', which has been present in the English language since the fourteenth century, originally meant 'to destroy' or 'to use up'. The word 'consumer', which dates from the eighteenth century, was also associated with 'waste', in the sense that a consumer was someone who used something up. The word is now used to denote the purchase and use of cultural products. Implicit in the term is the idea that once a product is used up, once it is 'spent', then it no longer has any value and is thus thrown away.

Therefore a consumer culture is one where people regularly purchase and use a wide variety of cultural products as a matter of everyday life. The consumer culture has the following elements:

- Consumption is bound up with a capitalist economy based on the production of commodities.
- The commodities consumed come from popular cultural sources.
- Consumption is immediate, based on the instant gratification of needs.
- Advertising plays a large role in the creation of wants and desires.
- Once products are consumed they are thrown away and rapidly replaced by the next – the 'newest' and the 'best'.

With the arrival of postmodern ideas in sociology, we can add the following to the list of characteristics of a consumer culture:

- We are consuming not just the material products themselves but also what they stand for. We are consuming 'signs'.
- The process of globalization has led to an increase in the types and range of products available to be consumed.
- The act of consumption involves the manipulation of symbolic meaning in a creative fashion.
- What we consume is a source of our identity: we are what we buy.
- Consumption plays a part in life-style formation.

Exercise 11.12

Provide an example of each of the five points listed immediately above.

According to many sociologists, consumption patterns have changed dramatically since the 1950s and 1960s. Consumption has become a 'reality' in its own right, not structured by class but superseding class as a way of defining who we are. As Willis *et al.* (1993) observe:

> The early history of marketing was precisely about separating consumer groups into socio-economic categories so that products could be aimed at them more exactly. Modern marketing, however, has moved on from delineating socio-economic groupings to exploring 'new' categories of life style, life stage, and shared denominations of interest and aspiration.

Many sociologists insist that it makes little sense to speak of distinct class cultures or tastes. This is not to deny the importance of financial and economic structures in consumption, but to illustrate that traditional class differences are no longer as clearly identifiable as they once were. As Bocock (1993) observes, for many, identity is in a state of 'flux' whereas before it was stable and fixed as a result of the importance of class in society. Individuals can develop their own identities, or add to their identities through consumption. They can buy fashionable or designer label goods that symbolize something about them, the view that 'we are what we own'. However, Bocock stresses that the freedom to consume and create an identity still rests on the amount of money available to individuals. In which case, is the significance of class really dead?

The traditional Marxist view of consumerism is based on Marx's idea of 'commodity fetishism'. Marx (1989) believed that the money we pay for the commodities our economy creates – their 'exchange value' – is based on a false conception of our need for such things/objects/commodities. We do not really need many of these things, but this is obscured by the fact that they are perceived to have a 'use', and their cost is a reflection of their perceived usefulness. This simply hides the true nature of production – working-class people are the ones whose labour creates these commodities, yet they do not own them and have to pay for things that they themselves made in the first place. This money is paid to the ruling class, who have contributed no labour at all. Marx referred to this 'isolation' of workers from the products of their labour as 'alienation'.

Marx saw commodities as 'false idols' that are worshipped by the very people who produce them with their labour power, but do not own them. According to the traditional Marxist view of consumption, consumers are tricked by the ideologies of the capitalist economy into buying things they do not really need and, when they do so, they feel happy about the society that is exploiting them. Though consumption may be open to ideological manipulation, this view depicts the consumer as a passive robot, and advertising/marketing as an all-powerful, manipulative tool.

With the rise of postmodernist ideas (see Chapter 7) the nature of consumption has been reassessed. It is no longer seen as a 'trick', but as the result of human agency. Consumption is seen as a highly creative act, involving the active manipulation of symbols. Advertising is a highly important aspect of popular culture. It may be true that advertising manipulates and creates 'false needs' – that is its purpose – but it is also a real source of popular images. It creates, but it uses others and taps into the popular cultural ideas of the times.

Exercise 11.13

Draw up a copy of the following table and in it summarize the ideas of Willis, Bocock, traditional Marxism and postmodernism on the role of consumption in society.

	Key ideas on consumption	Is consumption creative or is it a 'trick'?
Willis		
Bocock		
Traditional Marxism		
Postmodernism		

Types of consumer culture

There are many types of consumption in the postmodern age, and many types of consumer, for example:

- The *passive cultural robot* 'duped' by the power of advertising.
- The *creative actor*, constructing his or her life-style and identity from consumption, exercising free choice.
- The *deviant consumer*, manipulating dominant popular cultural messages, signs and commodities to create a new life-style meaning based on the rejection of popular, consumption-based capitalism; still fighting the class struggle, still resisting the dominant hegemony, using consumption as a political act.
- The *postmodern consumer*, playing with meanings and styles, picking and mixing, creating throwaway identities, forever recreating him/herself, concerned only with outer image and style, not inner substance.

Ⓤ Ⓘ
ⒶⓃ Ⓔ

Exercise 11.14

In your own words, define each of the four types of consumer listed above, and state how realistic you find each of the four interpretations of consumption.

In *The Consumerist Manifesto*, Martin Davidson (1992) notes that both the politically oriented deviant consumerism and the playful, pick-and-mix postmodern consumerism have been held up by some feminists as offering female liberation from traditional gender roles. For example, when discussing the image of (post) modern femininity presented in contemporary women's magazines, feminist Stuart (1990) argues that the magazine *Elle* is targeted at liberated female readers who take pleasure from consumption and are able actively to manipulate their own identities. The contents of *Elle* indicate that its readers have postmodern 'fractured identities' – liberated, sexually ambiguous and racially varied. The 'fracturing' of identity refers to the breaking up of class, ethnicity, age and gender as single coherent characteristics of identity and then interweaving them into a more complex relationship including other factors such as religion. These 'new women' may have confused identities but these are 'played with' in order to construct meaning.

Davidson (1992) himself seems doubtful about the claim that consumerism within the capitalist system can lead to freedom from it. He sees this as 'having your cake and eating it'. It is an excuse to have fun and not worry about the politics of identity and life-style formation, while at the same time feeling that one is not a 'cultural dupe' – that one is still in charge. Many Marxists would also be sceptical about this claim. They would insist that such 'playing' with consumption means that the capitalist economy is still being supported, and inequalities in wealth and power will continue. Any pleasure from such consumption is merely a state of false pleasure created by ideology.

Featherstone and Hepworth (1991) have identified three aspects of postmodern culture in which consumption plays an important role:

- The pursuit of pleasure.
- The rise of a throwaway culture: the 'playful' use of throwaway popular and low cultural products and venues such as theme parks are pleasurable simply because they are throwaway. They are not of sufficient value to be permanent aspects of our culture but are consumed and then disposed of, ignored or forgotten.
- The emergence of an important role for new social movements in identity construction.

Featherstone (1991) also notes that political action, life-style creation and consumption are frequently focused on the body as an object to be moulded, shaped and redefined as the individual wishes. Body images are everywhere in popular culture, and many symbols for identity are based on doing things to or with one's body, such as so-called 'deviant sexual practices', body piercing and tattooing, which have become increasingly common since the early 1990s. These are called 'body practices', and those who manipulate their bodies in this fashion are seen as being active and creative. The body has become politicized within these life-styles, since body practices are often used to symbolize alternative life-styles or counter-cultures against dominant hegemonic values (see Chapter 9).

①Ⓐ

Exercise 11.15

List the things that people can do to/with their bodies to express their individuality. How might each of the items on your list contribute to identity formation?

'DIY' postmodern politics

Postmodern politics can be seen as having less to do with traditional political parties and voting, and more with how one lives one's life at the more local, everyday level. In this sense, politics can be seen as making creative choices about style, sexuality and the body, and such politics operate through informal networks, gatherings and subcultures. In this sense, people 'do' postmodern politics themselves, and to themselves.

While not a postmodernist, Giddens (1991) writes about 'life-style politics' as the basis for 'projects on the self': moulding one's identity and trying to deal with the insecurities inherent in having to take responsibility for oneself. This is further reflected in Ulrich Beck's (1992) idea of a 'risk society' (see Chapter 7). Because of the 'manufactured uncertainties' of the present age, largely caused by the involvement of science, we are prompted to adopt life-style practices that help us to avoid harm – such as harm from environmental pollution and so on. These practices in the risk society are focused on the body; for example ,wearing sun-block to avoid skin cancer, practising safe sex to avoid AIDS, and eating non-genetically-modified (GM) and organic food to avoid harmful effects and damage to the environment. These body practices are political since they are based on criticizing the world, and seeking to improve one's life and protect oneself.

①Ⓐ
Exercise 11.16

Listed below are a number of items that threaten to cause us harm. Consider each one and suggest how it can be avoided by a change in lifestyle.

- HIV/AIDS • Pollution • Crime • Genetically modified food • Skin cancer • Heart disease

New social movements

As Hetherington (1998) shows, new social movements frequently incorporate the above observations. These movements are life-style politics based on the body, and are localized and identity-forming. New social movements are non-class-based, and are frequently formed by those on the margin who feel that they, their life-styles and identities are not represented by the traditional politics of the ballot box. New social movements develop around issues such as:

- sexuality;
- ethnic identity;
- gender; and
- environmental concerns.

The rapid rise of such movements since the 1970s is seen as further evidence of the death of class and the rise of post-class formations in society. Heller and Feher (1988), however, argue that modernist, class-based politics coexist with the more postmodern variations based on the body, life-styles and new social movements. The decision to embrace postmodern politics comes from a willingness on the part of individuals to accept society and their place in it as being pluralistic and fragmented. In other words, postmodern politics are about the awareness of others, the understanding that one's body and life are political, and the realization that political struggles can exist at both the local (community-based) and the national level. Politics can be about freeing one's street from traffic, protesting about the building of roads through woodlands, exploring one's sexuality in new ways, and even engaging in body practices such as tattooing and body piercing. Postmodern politics are therefore about fighting for who you are. Identity is a key political issue in the postmodern age.

McAllister-Groves (1995) uses Goffman's idea of 'framing' to explain why people join new social movements and how they might help in the process of identity formation. These movements are seen as providing 'frames' or 'frameworks' – sources of meaning – with which to make sense of personal, emotional and intimate feelings. The life-styles and views associated with each new social movement allow individuals to think about their feelings and make sense of them. Thus vegetarians might join groups or movements against GM foods or animal testing, since they provide a set of ideas with which to express their feelings.

In *Beyond Left and Right*, Giddens (1994) argues that the rise of new social movements represents a move towards the further democratization of society and identity, since more views, life-styles and people are being 'included' in the processes of power and decision-making. They have created new 'spaces' – arenas or areas – for debate on political issues. These new political spaces include intimacy, identity and life-style. Giddens calls this 'life politics'.

Exercise 11.17

In a table similar to the one below, summarize the theoretical ideas on new social movements (NSMs) covered in this chapter.

	Beck	Hetherington	Heller and Feher	McAllister-Groves	Giddens
Basic beliefs about the rise of NSMs					
Key concepts					
Any examples of NSMs given?					

RECENT ANALYSIS OF CLASS CULTURE AND IDENTITY

Is class relevant to culture and identity in modern society?

The concept of class and its link to culture and identity is much more complex in modern society. Postmodern theorists argue that identity has become individualized, and that choice, diversity and fluidity does exist, that individuals can 'play' with their identities. However, Heath *et al.* (2008: 4) found that people were just as likely to have a class identity now as they were in the 1960s, and that there is still a link to occupation. But, significantly, class does not appear to have a lot of social significance:

> for neither men or women does social class seem to be an especially salient group identity. People who feel a sense of belonging to their class differ little in their attitudes, values and voting behaviour from those who have only a nominal sense of class identity or indeed no class identity at all.

However:

> while class may not be especially important as a source of values and collective action, it does seem to retain importance in structuring people's social lives ... class has become

'depoliticized' and has declined in salience in the public sphere whilst retaining salience in the more private sphere of face-to-face social relations.

So, interestingly, Heath *et al.* found that people might identify with a class, but this does not mean that it is an important part of their identity.

In contrast to this, Pedrozo (2010) explores the links between social class and consumption in developing countries and, in particular, Brazil. For Brazilian young people, the main determinant of access to the consumer society is their class of origin. While education forms a ladder of mobility for some working-class children, the education system itself is heavily framed by social class interests. The result is that large numbers of the working-class and poor are excluded from the consumer society, while the rich and privileged engage in conspicuous consumption. This leads to resentment among the poor and the lower classes, whose desire to be 'cool' through the consumption of particular goods and services is thwarted by their inability to resource appropriate life-styles. This social exclusion is fuelled by global forces that emphasize consumption as the defining characteristic of identity formation, while increasing the unemployment and underemployment that cuts large sections of poor Brazilians off from 'realizing the dream' and forging a 'cool' identity.

Is class reasserting itself, but in a different form? Sarah Womack, drawing on research by Curtice and Heath (quoted in Smith, 2007) refers to the current class confusion as 'the muddle classes'. Research studies over the decade of the 2000s have produced mixed findings in relation to the continued existence of class and its relevance to culture and identity. Charlsworth (2000) found distinctive working-class identities in Rotherham. However, Savage *et al.* (2001) found that in Manchester the majority of people were ambivalent about having a class identity; they 'disidentified' with class.

Geoff Payne and Clare Grew's (2005) study of two rural areas in England found that many still talked in class terms. They are critical of the findings of Savage *et al.*, arguing that the methodology used impacted on their findings, and that people might not be as 'ambivalent' as Savage *et al.* have concluded.

Some theorists point towards an 'upper, upper class' comprising a super-rich elite, which results from the widening gap between the rich and poor, linked to the life-style that the super-rich can consume. Tyler and Bennett (2010) argued that class was still important in contemporary societies, and that the 'cult of celebrity' fostered by the media was grounded in social class and gender identity. By this, they mean that claims that the rise of celebrity culture represents a weakening of social class as a way of expressing social identity were wrong. On the contrary, 'celebrity chavs' (high-profile members of the working class who engage in anti-social behaviour; we shall look at the term 'chav' and who it represents in more detail later), especially women, were portrayed by the media as 'offensive', 'trash' and 'repellent' and this representation stood for the more general moral panic surrounding working-class young women who did not conform to middle-class norms of femininity. The treatment of 'celebrity chavs' by the media can therefore be read as a warning for working-class girls who seek to 'get above themselves', and celebrity serves to reinforce class identity rather than undermine it.

There is an increasing acceptance of the importance of looking at economic factors in combination with cultural factors to gain a full understanding of class identity. Postmodern theorists look to the hybrid and flexible nature of identities in a global culture, but many class theorists argue that identities are only flexible for those who have the resources and power to choose.

According to Skeggs (2005), culture has been commodified and is of growing importance in capitalist societies. Culture is a central part of advertising. Working-class culture is portrayed in two very different ways. On one side, working-class culture is portrayed as of low worth and moral value, and on the other side it is seen as being 'authentic'.

Throughout this context of change, Heath *et al.* (2009) reported in Muir and Wetherell (2010: 6) 'find that British people remain almost as able to allocate themselves into middle or working class categories as they were in the 1960s... at the level of simple class recognition... we seem to be as class conscious a society as we were 50 years ago'.

The existence of an 'underclass' or 'chav' culture indicates that forms of class are used as a form of derision and inequality. Do all groups within society have genuine choice? Giddens and Diamond (2005), in *The New Egalitarianism*, argue that, in the twenty-first century, social class is no longer the main source of inequality in the UK, but that 'social exclusion' is.

The underclass and 'chav' culture

In the first decade of the twenty-first century the term 'chav' has entered popular culture. The term itself has a number of potential origins, a slang term used in Kent, from the Romany word 'chavi', meaning 'child' or 'chavo', meaning 'boy', or 'chavvy', meaning 'youth', or could have entered the English language through the Geordie dialect word 'charva', meaning a rough child. The term has been applied to certain young people in the UK. The stereotypical 'chav' is seen as an aggressive teenager, typically unemployed or from a working-class background, who repeatedly engages in anti-social behaviour, such as street drinking, drug abuse and rowdiness. Stereotypically, they wear tracksuits and hoodies, often counterfeit versions of clothing made by 'named' brands such as Nike, Reebok and Burberry. The widespread use of the 'chav' stereotype has attracted some criticism. Some argue that it is snobbery and elitism, that serious social problems such as anti-social behaviour, teenage pregnancy, delinquency and underage drinking in low-income areas are not subjects for derision.

Stephanie Lawler (2005) notes how the term 'chav' refers to a group of people blamed for their lack of taste, and seen as morally inferior and with restricted opportunities. However, Skeggs (2005), in her study of working-class culture and its presentation in popular culture, notes that culture has become commodified, with 'signs' and 'experiences', not products, being sold (see Chapter 10 for more on structuralism and poststructuralism). Interestingly, she argues that working-class culture is not always seen negatively in terms of its signs and experiences. It can be argued that 'chav' culture has become distinct from the wider working class and does not receive any of the positive publicity reserved for the rest of the working class.

Hayward and Yar (2006) argue that the term 'chav' is a successor to the term 'underclass'. Where the underclass referred to the position of people in terms of production (or lack of economic production, generally being long-term unemployed and/or relying on benefits), the term 'chav' refers to the same group of people in terms of their consumption patterns. 'Chav' culture, as noted above, is portrayed in the popular media as consuming specific products that form their identity.

Greg Martin (2009) links the development of 'chav' culture to subcultural theories (see Chapter 9):

> In their subcultural style (e.g. the donning of designer brands) chavs attempt to realize, but in an imaginary way, their consumerist aspirations. All of this, however, is strangely familiar. Chavs' subcultural response to the contradictory signals sent out by a society that simultaneously excludes them materially yet includes them commercially is similar to the subcultural solutions sought by the working-class youth subcultures studied by the CCCS in the 1970s.

Exercise 11.18

Review the concept map (see Figure 1.1) on class and consumption and create your own copy. Add further theorists, issues, strengths and weaknesses you have read about in this chapter.

CONCLUSION

The concept of class (along with gender and ethnicity – see Chapters 12 and 13) has shaped today's sociology, and sociology would be very different without it. However, while class has been seen as a major source of identity, this is now being questioned. Postmodernists, feminists and reflexive modernists question the role of class identity in contemporary society, and therefore its role in sociology. With the rise of consumption, new social movements and globalization (see Chapter 14), the centrality of class is questioned. As a tool, it does enable sociologists to think about the key features of capitalist societies, but it is also vital for sociologists constantly to question and re-evaluate older but strongly held ideas.

Important concepts

Class • Consumption • Cultural capital • Embourgeoisement • Fragmentation

Exam focus

(a) Assess the view that different classes develop different subcultures.
(b) How has class identity changed in contemporary society?
(c) Has postmodern theory resulted in the end of a class-based analysis of identity?

Critical thinking

1. 'We cannot consider identity in society today without considering the role of class.' To what extent do you agree with this statement?
2. Is class too complex to operationalize (to make measurable when conducting research) to be a significant factor in individual identity?
3. 'Class used to be ascribed at birth, now it is a matter of choice and achievement.' Discuss.
4. Is there a class comprising the super rich (exceeding the majority of the upper class), with a distinct lifestyle and identity?

Chapter 12

Sex and Gender: Femininity and Masculinity

After studying this chapter, you should:

- understand the role played by gender in the construction of identity
- understand how gender roles have changed in recent years
- understand the process of gender-role socialization
- understand a variety of feminist theories
- be able to evaluate feminist ideas
- be able to reflect on masculine identity in modern society
- be able to relate feminist ideas and queer theory to the sociologies of gender, sexuality and the body

INTRODUCTION

There has been a shift since the 1980s away from seeing studies of 'gender' as meaning purely a 'feminist' critique. Recent theory and research includes an analysis of both feminine and masculine cultures and identities. Feminism has had a big impact on sociology and the study of gender relations, and has resulted in a broadening of focus to include sexuality and masculinity. This chapter will address the feminist critique and approach to researching culture and identity as well as research into masculinity and male identity and culture, which could be argued to have been neglected since the 1970s. It will consider recent criticisms of feminism and reflect on where recent research and theorizing will take us. Sociologists and cultural theorists have not just based their study on the masculine/feminine divide. There has been a recognition of the fluidity of identity, to see gender as much more than the simple difference between men and women. Research includes consideration of transgender individuals, and the social and individual construction of these terms and diverse forms of sexuality.

Feminist sociology is an example of 'critical sociology'. What this means is that feminism seeks to re-evaluate the way we understand society. Unlike functionalist theory, it does not seek to protect the status quo – the way things are – but rather to challenge and change society. The ideas of feminism often complement those of Marxism, since both are critical of the way society is ordered. Feminist ideas also complement action sociology, since feminists often use micro or ethnographic methods in their research.

For many feminists, the relatively recent (1960s and 1970s) introduction of feminist ideas into sociology and their widespread adoption in textbooks and syllabuses is evidence of the past invisibility of women contributors to sociology – mirrored by the devaluation of 'female knowledge' in other academic areas, especially science. Many feminists feel that feminism has been ignored for too long. The invisibility of female writers is reflected in the fact that sociology often talks about 'the founding fathers', but never about 'founding mothers' (for example, the work of Harriet Martineau discussed in Chapter 3). This mainstream or traditional sociology is referred to as 'malestream' (see Chapter 11), since it is dominated by male sociologists and the male world view. It is, in the words of Abbott and Wallace (1997), 'by men, for men and about men'. This applies in particular to positivist methodology, since its scientific nature is seen to represent – through the experimental method – patriarchal ideology. It devalues female knowledge and treats the social actors involved in its research as 'objects' to be thrown away after use. This mirrors the way that men treat women in society.

Feminist thinkers such as Mackinnon (1982) and Callaway (1984) note that priority is given to the male world view over the female one and the gathering of female knowledge. This is a position of power that male sociologists enjoy over their female colleagues – the power to define the key issues to be discussed within the subject; the power to say what are and what are not acceptable avenues for sociological investigation.

As well as a recognition of the need to study masculinity, 'queer theory' attempts to redress the heterosexual bias of the founding fathers. This chapter will also consider the role of sexuality and its part in culture and identity.

Exercise 12.1

1. Why do you think sociology started as a male-dominated discipline? List your reasons.
2. What evidence can you find for this still being the case today? Look at an older sociology textbook (ideally pre-1970s) and write a list of the ways in which such a book might (if at all) disadvantage women and feminism.

Through the criticism of malestream sociology, a number of feminist thinkers have come to advocate a whole range of feminist viewpoints. It is important to recognize that there is no such thing as a unified feminism; rather, there are many feminisms. We shall discuss these varieties of feminist sociology first.

FEMINIST THEORY AND RESEARCH INTO FEMININITY

Varieties of feminism

While there are many different types of feminism, they have a number of assumptions in common. This is the feminist 'world view'. First, society is seen as male dominated, and this domination is based on ideological and coercive forms of social control. Second, the aim of sociology is to highlight social injustice against women, and to try to challenge and change this. Such a male-dominated society is often described as 'patriarchal'. This means 'rule of the father', but is frequently taken by feminists to mean male dominated. Finally, it is considered that women have been ignored within sociological discussion until recently, both as thinkers and as topics of study. As Abbott and Wallace (1997: 5) note: 'sociology has been at best sex-blind and at worst sexist'.

Oakley (1982) argues that sociology is founded on sexist assumptions, and that these were a fundamental part of the origin of the subject in the nineteenth century. This means that, unlike other theories, feminism has twice as much to do. It not only wishes to challenge the nature of society, but it must first fight an internal battle within sociology. This is not the case with theories based on male knowledge, such as Marxism. The major contribution made by feminism to modern sociological thought is to encourage an awareness of the positions of inequality of a whole range of previously 'invisible' groups. Many aspects of feminist theory discuss a wide range of issues, not just those relating to sex, gender and sexuality. For example, many feminists have raised awareness of issues of race and ethnicity, and issues relevant to people with disabilities. Some feminist research has encouraged a focus on the role of men in modern society, the development of masculinity and explanations of male disadvantage.

In discussions of the history of the various types of feminism, a distinction is usually drawn between two 'waves' of feminism – two historical stages in the development of feminist thought and feminist campaigns in society. The first wave of feminism started at the end of the nineteenth century but was almost totally ignored by the founders of sociology. At that time, feminism was concerned with the establishment of equal rights for women – political and legal rights in particular. Feminist groups included the Women's Social and Political Union (WSPU), which aimed to reverse women's standing in society as 'second class' citizens. The early feminists were often part of the suffragette movement and were focused on fighting for women's right to vote. It was not until 1928 that the vote was granted to all adults (men and women) over the age of 21 in Britain.

Ⓘ | Exercise 12.2

With the help of additional reading and research, make some further notes on the aims and campaigns of the suffragette movement.

The second wave of feminism began in the mid- to late 1960s with the rise of the consciousness-raising movement known as 'women's liberation'. During this second wave, feminists began to be characterized in a number of derogatory ways in the popular imagination, fuelled by media moral panics about 'lesbian bra-burners'. Such insulting, sexist, patronizing and incorrect stereotypes still exist today and are a barrier against which feminists fight to gain respectability and popularity. Feminists claim that this is as true of the social scientific community as it is of society as a whole. Maynard (1998) notes that, in this second wave, feminist views were categorized narrowly into what she calls the 'big three': liberal feminism, Marxist feminism and radical feminism. The concentration on these three views at the expense of other versions of feminism has led to almost all feminists being categorized in this way, with the rich variety of other feminist ideas being ignored.

①Ⓐ
Ⓔ

Exercise 12.3

For the duration of your study of this topic, compile a folder of newspaper cuttings that discuss feminist ideas and issues of female liberation as well as concerns relating to masculinity and male disadvantage. To what extent do these stories and reports categorize feminist ideas, and to what extent are they based on the use of sexist and homophobic assumptions?

Liberal feminists seek to resolve female inequality through the legal system. They wish to bring about Acts of Parliament that improve the lives of women in every sphere of society, but especially in the world of work – Acts such as the Equal Pay Act of 1970. Liberal feminists study a wide range of explanations for gender inequality and consider the role of men and masculinity. The liberal nature of this perspective is usually contrasted with what is described as 'radical feminism', which is often associated with the ideas of Firestone (1979). This view is 'radical', since it argues that power and domination are inherent aspects of all males. The system of patriarchy reproduces and sanctions this domination and exists in all societies. All men are viewed as being prone to violent and physical domination of all women. Heterosexuality is seen as further exploiting and oppressing women, since men are able to dominate women's bodies through the act of reproduction. Men benefit from the fact that women give birth and men do not. Women are also oppressed through acts of violence, daily interaction and non-verbal communication, and norms of feminine appearance and behaviour promoted through the media.

Finally, Marxist feminism suggests that capitalism and patriarchy are interlinked. Patriarchy serves the interests of a capitalist economy. For example, female housework benefits capitalism, since those who undertake it represent an unpaid workforce doing an essential – yet undervalued – job. This unpaid work provides the economy with men ready and able to work for the benefit of the bourgeoisie. Power is retained by a small group of men who pass wealth to other men through inheritance of private property (ideas initially developed by Friedrich Engels; see Chapter 3). The solution to male domination and female subordination is seen by Marxist feminists to lie in the overthrow of capitalism – without capitalism there would be no need for patriarchy to continue in society. This is why they are 'Marxist feminists' and not 'feminist Marxists'.

As Maynard (1998) notes, while these three versions of feminism are important – and have made a great contribution to sociology – they are just the beginning of the feminist story, not the end of it. Heidi Hartmann (1981) has described Marxist feminism as an 'unhappy marriage', as in this particular form of theorizing, class is given priority over gender. In other words, Marxism takes the lead and feminism follows. Hartmann argues that this is the sort of malestream thinking that feminism should be criticizing, not supporting. Instead, Hartmann and others offer a 'dual systems' theory, where both capitalist exploitation and patriarchy are seen as symbiotic, feeding off each other. They are interlinked and in some historical situations one might take precedence over or even contradict the other, but it should not be assumed that in every case the class system takes priority over gender inequality. This is very similar to a point made by Abbott and Wallace (1997), who argue that even if class is more important than gender, this has yet to be proved adequately by malestream sociologists.

The idea of interconnected forms of inequality is reflected in the development of what Walby (1989, 1990) describes as a 'triple systems' approach. In this view, patriarchy and capitalism intersect and sometimes overlap, and they also intertwine with racism. All three forms of power combine to shape society and make it as it is. Black feminism and Third-World feminism also seek to understand the relationships between patriarchy and racism in society. Many black feminists claim that just as day-to-day life in society is experienced differently depending on whether you are a man or a woman, it is also experienced differently by different ethnic groupings. Collins (1990), arguing from the standpoint of a black woman, discusses not just the economic oppression but also the cultural oppression of black women. Mama (1989) suggests that discussions of the experiences of ethnic groups should not just be 'tacked on' to feminism, but should be seen as an opportunity to reassess the whole theory. In a similar fashion, James and Busia (1993) argue that the concepts of class, patriarchy and racism do not exist separately in a person's life and therefore simply cannot and should not be separated in sociological study. All three operate simultaneously and therefore should be studied as a single, integrated concept.

ⓀⓊ
ⒾⒶⁿ

Exercise 12.4

Summarize the main types of feminist theory in an extended version of the table below.

	Key thinkers	Why did this theory develop?	Basic beliefs	How can inequality be challenged and changed?
Liberal feminism				
Radical feminism				
Marxist feminism				
Dual systems theory				
Triple systems theory				

Black feminism				
Third-World feminism				

Identify two strengths and two weakness of each of the feminisms discussed so far in this chapter:

- Liberal feminism
- Dual systems theory
- Black feminism
- Radical feminism
- Triple systems theory
- Third-World feminism
- Marxist feminism

Postmodern feminists seek to give a voice to a whole range of marginal and previously 'silenced' groups in society. They believe there is no single identity shared by all women; women experience plural identities. Like other postmodernists, they argue that definitions of 'truth' are merely the result of power struggles that some groups have won over others. Postmodern feminists emphasize plurality and ambiguity in society. That is, they believe that gender – what it is to be 'masculine' or 'feminine' – has been 'deconstructed'. The binary opposition of the two terms reflects the unequal power balance between men and women (see the discussion of structural feminism in Chapter 10 and on postmodernism in Chapter 7). Its definition as a fixed, either/or category of 'truth' has changed and been replaced by a whole variety of femininities and masculinities. Male language should be deconstructed so that the world is not seen in terms only of masculine and feminine. This means that what it is to be a man or a woman in society is more plural and ambiguous than ever before, and such definitions are still changing rapidly. They are identities or masks to be played with, rather than absolute, fixed biological facts.

The strength of postmodern feminism is that it moves beyond simplistic notions of identity based on distinctions between opposites – such as being either male or female, or black or white. It suggests that identity is more pluralistic. For many feminists, this strength is also the main weakness of postmodern feminism. For example, Bordo (1990) notes that postmodern feminism rests on the assumption that there are no more absolutes in society, no definite ways of getting at a single 'truth'. This means that, if identity has become fragmented or 'fractured' into a plurality of identities, it will be difficult, if not impossible, for women to unite under a collective feminist banner to change society. Increasing fragmentation of identity means that women are less likely to feel close to other women, and the whole project of feminism might therefore be in danger of collapse.

Exercise 12.6

Complete the following table.

Statement	Associated with which type(s) of feminist theory?
(a) All men are rapists	
(b) Class and gender are as important as each other	
(c) All men as a global class dominate all women, because of the global expansion of capitalism	
(d) If the problems of capitalism are solved, sexual discrimination will also be solved	
(e) Marxist feminism is an 'unhappy marriage'	
(f) By nature, all men wish to dominate all women	
(g) Patriarchy serves capitalism	
(h) Ethnic identity may lessen the problems of patriarchy for some women	
(i) Western women enjoy greater equality than women elsewhere in the world	
(j) Gender identity is no longer fixed: women can be who they wish to be	
(k) Changes to the law can bring about equality for women	
(l) Class, gender and ethnicity overlap as forms of inequality	
(m) Society is male-dominated	

Exercise 12.7

Re-read the descriptions of the varieties of feminism above and list six similarities and six differences between the different forms.

Exercise 12.8

Which version of feminism do you find most convincing? Explain your view in 150 words.

GENDER SOCIALIZATION

Traditionally, sociologists are more interested in studying 'gender' than 'sex'. The distinction here is that sex refers to the biological features that differentiate men from women, while gender refers to the culturally learnt characteristics of what it means to be masculine or feminine. Feminists argue that, since gender is a product of society and not of biology, matters of gender are not fixed. Hence, discrimination against women is a cultural creation and can therefore be changed.

The 'normal' way to act as a man or as a woman has nothing to do with one's reproductive organs but rather with how one is taught to act. We are socialized into learning how to behave in a masculine or feminine way through the instilling of 'gender roles'. The process of gender role socialization starts in the early years in the family home and continues through the education system and into the world of work, reinforced by media representations (see Chapters 5 and 8).

Those who adopt a sociobiological approach (see Chapter 2) claim that how men and women behave is a matter of their genetic codes and natural urges rather than the result of the way they are brought up. According to this approach, men and women have different roles in society as a result of their reproductive organs, and so from birth they are pre-programmed to behave in different ways. In this sense, inequality and difference between men and women is a natural feature of all human societies. A similar claim has been made by the functionalist Parsons (1951, 1971), who suggests that men and women are predisposed to behave in different ways and to learn different sets of roles, based on their natural instincts. Parsons makes a distinction between the 'expressive roles' taken on by women in society and males' 'instrumental roles'. What he means by this is that cultural roles differ between men and women because women are naturally more expressive and emotional and men are more task-orientated. Parsons therefore concludes that women are more suited than men to caring roles. Many feminists view Parsons' ideas as patriarchal ideology – his views justify male oppression and excuse inequality and discrimination in society.

As a result of the devaluing of many early feminist ideas in academic thought, some feminists have turned to the work of the early Marxist thinker, Engels, as a source of feminist ideas. Engels considered female roles and their general subordination to be the result of nurture (upbringing) rather than nature. He argued that the traditional view of women as best suited to a domestic, caring role had only existed since the introduction into society of private property. This is an example of the Marxist idea of 'economic determinism': changes in the economy determine or cause cultural changes. Before property became private, Engels claimed, there were no 'families' in the modern sense, or monogamous marriage. However, with the increase of property ownership, a system of inheritance was needed and therefore marriage – in the present-day sense – was invented to control the sexual behaviour of women and give power to men. If women's sexuality was controlled, it was easier to identify who the father of a child was, and therefore easier to say who should inherit property. In support of this argument, feminists point to anthropological evidence that in earlier societies 'women's work' was defined differently from our present understanding of it. They therefore conclude that gender roles must be social and not biological.

Feminists note that discrimination in society is often the result of society equating sex with gender when in fact they are not the same. For example, just because women can bear children it does not mean they have to wear skirts. Equally, just because men have a penis it does not make them good drivers. These examples are rather obvious ones, and the links between sex and gender are not always so straightforward. For example, just because women give birth does not necessarily mean that they are naturally more suited than men to the work of looking after children. What happens, argue many feminists, is that biological sex differences become confused with learnt cultural differences. Such an argument is found in the work of Ann Oakley (1972), who notes that in other societies women perform heavy manual work and men engage in child care – the opposite of the so-called 'natural' way described by Parsons and those who adopt the sociobiological view.

Walby (1990) recognizes that traditionally the status of women was constrained within the private and limiting sphere of the home and family, but as women entered other spheres of public life since the early nineteenth century inequality is being experienced publicly (in law, the media, the workplace and so on).

Hochschild's (1983) work on emotional labour (not just the caring and supporting role within the home, but the emotional component of some occupations) highlights the additional work, the double or triple shift that women face. Occupations requiring emotional labour are strongly linked to women (as in Hochschild's work on airline flight attendants). Some roles require the exhibition of specific emotions, which she argues is more costly to the individual; women make up the majority of employees in these fields.

①Ⓐ
Exercise 12.9

List ten stereotypical sexist assumptions in society about the differences between men and women (for example, men are thought to be better drivers than women; women are thought to be more suited to child care than men).

In *Different for Girls*, feminist writer Joan Smith (1997) argues that culture makes females different from males – it treats them as separate simply because they have different reproductive organs. Like many other feminists, she is critical of this and does not consider that there is any real link between sex and gender other than that created by culture itself. It is a 'social construction', a product of society.

Smith makes five propositions about the nature of femininity in society and the relationship between sex, gender and identity:

- Men and women become different because they are treated differently.
- Religious values and other theories about male and female difference, such as those from science and medicine, are used in society as evidence or proof of the difference between men and women.
- The difference between men and women is believed by many in society to be a natural phenomenon, yet the evidence suggests this is not the case – that nurture is more important than nature.

Being defined as a 'woman' by society is not simply a matter of biology but also involves restrictive moral judgements about how one should behave as a woman.

  Because of the emphasis on sex or biology in common-sense patriarchal thought, all women are seen as being fundamentally different from all men, yet similar to all other women. In other words, sex differences are seen in society as a vital source of difference.

Kirby (1999) points to a growing body of evidence that the concept of 'sex' is not a fixed biological reality but a product of social creation. For example, Hood-Williams (1996) notes that the biological determination of whether an individual is a male or a female is not always clear cut, and a choice sometimes has to be made by adults of the sex of a child. For example, some males have more female chromosomes than the scientific definition of 'being male' prescribes (one male and one female chromosome), yet because they look male at birth they become categorized as male – not a very scientific basis upon which to make a judgement. This is supported by Anne Fausto-Sterling (2000), who argues that transgendered people (including hermaphrodites, individuals with hormone imbalances and those with chromosome abnormalities) indicate that we shouldn't look at sex and gender in terms of being only male and female. Gender is a result of social and biological processes. Being assigned a gender involves both. Seeing gender dualistically can result in surgery and potential psychological harm for those not falling neatly into a category. This issue is well illustrated by the Olympic Games. In the Beijing Games in 2010, Caster Semenya, an athlete from South Africa, underwent gender testing because of her 'masculine' appearance. This is not a new issue. Gender determination tests were introduced in the Olympics in 1968 after concerns were raised that some female athletes looked too masculine and had an unfair advantage. The tests include reviewing appearance as well as blood tests to review the competitors' genetic make-up, sex hormones and chromosomes. These tests have been widely criticized as humiliating and have shown a number of athletes to have chromosomal abnormalities.

Exercise 12.10

List the arguments that feminists would use to criticise the claim that inequality between men and women is natural.

Understanding 'motherhood'

For O'Hara (1996) there is no such thing as an essential, biological female 'reality'. Rather, this depends on how those in power decide, in a particular historical time period, to use females. For example, during the Second World War, women performed heavy physical work that had traditionally been associated with men. However, with the end of the war and the arrival of men returning from the armed forces, the 'reality' of what a women was reverted to what O'Hara describes as the 'cult of motherhood' – the view that the best place for women was in the family home engaging in child care. This means that categories of feminine and masculine behaviour are not absolutes, since they change with the cultural and economic circumstances of societal change. This view is influenced by postmodern ideas in that O'Hara claims that the 'truth' of being a woman is defined by those in power rather than by objective, absolute criteria. The truth is therefore a site for power struggles.

This view is reflected in the work of Woodward (1997), who suggests that while motherhood as a source of identity might appear fixed, stable and rooted in natural biology, it is in fact a social construction. Woodward notes that everyone can relate to the idea of motherhood and knows what this means in society – even those of us who are not and cannot be mothers still have mothers and can therefore understand what this concept means. To be a mother is seen first and foremost as a biological act since it is based on the ability to reproduce. It is seen as natural. However, in today's society, bearing children is not necessarily the 'natural biological act' it was once considered. There is artificial insemination, there are surrogate mothers and there are lesbian mothers – all of which suggest that motherhood is not a single, absolute, 'natural' concept. Motherhood also implies child care as well as childbirth, yet this can vary considerably within and between cultures. Finally, there are 'good' mothers and 'bad' mothers, and many of the latter are blamed by the media for causing delinquency in society by failing to exercise discipline in the home. If motherhood is natural, why is it so difficult to get right?

Woodward (1997) points out that feminists adopt different positions on the nature and role of motherhood as a source of identity. On the one hand, motherhood might be seen as serving to control the female body and female sexuality, whereas on the other it could be seen as a liberating way for women to embrace who they are, to understand their bodies, and to distinguish themselves from men. For example Millet (1970) and Firestone (1979) see the family – and the woman's role within it as a child bearer and a child carer – as the prime source of gender inequality and female oppression. The physical act of bearing children limits what women can do and are allowed to do, and their role within the home limits their day-to-day actions. This consideration has informed a great deal of the recent feminist criticisms of the New Right's view of the role of women in society. For example, during the time in office of Conservative prime minister Margaret Thatcher in the UK women were seen as being essential to the provision of care in society and such care was located in the family home – the 'natural' place for women to be. This policy – called 'care in the community' – echoed the ideas of sociobiology and the views of functionalists such as Parsons. In this way, ideological images of 'motherhood' are used by society to define what women should be like, and are often used by women themselves to define who they are.

Woodward (1997) suggests that Western society uses 'myths of motherhood' to socialize and control the activities of women by defining what and who women are and should be. Such myths include the view that being a mother involves giving up one's personal identity/independence for the good of one's offspring – to be self-sacrificing. Or, in other words, a woman is defined as a woman not by who she is, but by who she looks after. Many feminists see this as a distorted and false view of motherhood in particular, and womanhood in general, a view that operates to control women in a male-dominated society. See the masculinity section later in this chapter for a discussion of fatherhood and male identity.

Femininity and popular culture

A great deal of feminist discussion on popular culture concerns the way in which women and girls are represented to the audience. Such representations are seen as highly ideological and as serving to reinforce patriarchy. For example, women are considered to take on a limited number of roles – usually as sex object, mother and housewife.

A great deal of feminist research into representations of femininity has concerned the nature of teenage girls' magazines and women's magazines. For example, Ferguson (1983) and McRobbie (1983) have identified an ideology of femininity in media products aimed at women. Such products depict female gender identity as being based on romantic love, finding and keeping a man, marriage, being a good wife, being a good mother and so on.

Early feminists saw media audiences as being largely passive (see Chapter 8). Men and women were thought to 'soak up' ideological images and to see these as a true picture of society. While many feminists still suggest that representations of femininity are ideological, there is a tendency within sociology to recognize that media audiences are more active. For example Ballaster *et al.* (1991) have argued that, while women's magazines might portray women in limited ways, women themselves get pleasure from them and 'read' or 'decode' them in a variety of ways. Having said this, Ballaster *et al.* note that magazines – and popular cultural products in general – allow both men and women to make sense of the world around them, and do so using highly ideological images.

Is feminism dead? Has it gone too far?

In *Backlash*, Susan Faludi (1992) argues that there has been an anti-feminist retaliation against the rise of the female voice in society. Women have made considerable and significant inroads into the dismantling of an unequal society, but many men feel that their masculinity and male identity are being threatened by such social change. This suggests that there is still a patriarchal struggle in society, and gender is still a source of difference between men and women and an important source of identity.

Within sociology, perhaps as part of this anti-feminist backlash, there has been a rise in 'post-feminist' ideas and rational-choice theory. This movement is often associated with the ideas of Catherine Hakim (1996), who suggests that women's lives have been improved significantly and hence there is no longer a need for feminism. Its job is done. Hakim suggests that women are totally free to make whatever choices they wish, and are not held back in any way by their status as women. They can be mothers, have full-time careers, or even combine the two. She suggests that women are not disadvantaged in the labour market but choose to engage in poorly paid, part-time employment – it is a conscious decision. Not as many women have entered the labour force as might be thought, but this is because they have chosen not to. Women wish to get married, have children and look after them in the family home. If they do not, then there are opportunities in society for them to do whatever they wish. This view has come under attack by other feminists, who still see patriarchy as putting a powerful structural constraint on women.

Andrea Stuart (1990) also questions whether feminism is alive or dead, but her answer is different from that of Hakim. Stuart notes that many women still feel strongly about feminist issues, many see gender as an important source of identity, and many feel that society is still unequal. Yet they feel that feminism as a movement is irrelevant. It does nothing to actually help them. She suggests that the feeling of togetherness that accompanied previous waves of feminism has been all but lost in modern-day society. Women do not feel part of a wider whole, united by their common experiences and gender. A gulf has developed between 'feminism the profession' – in universities – and the popular feminism that is found in many women's magazines – advocating anti-sexist legislation, giving advice on sexual pleasure, presenting the male body as an object for the female gaze (rather than the other way round) and providing images of strong, career-oriented, independent women. Women are still finding strength in such messages and still understand what it means to be a woman in society, yet these identities are transmitted through popular media rather than a clearly defined feminist movement. Stuart sees this as a product of the increasing postmodernization of society – an increasing plurality of identities for women to adopt.

Imelda Whelehan's (2000) studies of gender in the media and in popular culture led her to propose that through 'lad culture', patriarchy and sexism still exist. Some men's magazines portray sexist male behaviour (see the later section on masculinity in this chapter). There is an increased hostility towards feminism in popular culture. The existence of 'girl power' (illustrated by Whelehan through the Spice Girls and Madonna) gives the appearance of equality, but Whelehan queries whether this has resulted in greater choice and empowerment for individual women. They are isolated cases of empowerment. Single women are portrayed as being desperate for a husband (in the 'singleton' of *Bridget Jones' Diary* and the women in *Sex and the City*) and not as powerful women making their own choices. This is supported by Greer (2000), who notes that patriarchy is still very much in existence. Men have achieved greater sexual freedom than women, and women are still expected to focus on their appearance, a limiting factor perpetuated by patriarchy. Caitlin Moran, in her partly autobiographical *How To Be a Woman* (2011), argues that women need to 'reclaim the word "feminism"'. The political liberation of women is, according to Moran, still necessary, and is beneficial for men as well as women. Therefore, reflections on the culture and identity of women are still significant within both feminism and wider social and cultural theory.

POSTMODERN THEORY AND GENDER

Along with class and ethnicity, gender has traditionally been seen within sociological thought as a structural constraint on the individual and a major source of personal identity. All three sources of identity are now being challenged by the postmodern idea that class, gender and ethnicity are being pluralized and are no longer the rigid structural constraints they once were. The importance of the postmodern feminist view in modern-day sociology has led some to describe it as a 'third wave of feminism'.

Some thinkers from the postmodern perspective have taken the sex–gender distinction further. For example, Butler (1990) suggests that it is impossible to talk in any meaningful way about femininity or masculinity. These are such plural terms as to be meaningless. All that exist are biological sex differences and the many different ways that people choose to live their lives. As soon as we speak of femininity we are attaching, by definition, a narrow set of characteristics to women, and suggesting that such characteristics are much more woman-like than they are man-like. By using the concept 'gender' we are shaping the world around us, and in doing so are creating female oppression by limiting women's opportunities. This means not only that the question 'What does it mean to be a woman?' is impossible to answer, but also in asking the question we are drawing a distinction between men and women that is oppressive and restrictive.

The influence of postmodern ideas has led to the observation that gender identity is a matter of active creation and at times liberation. A similar theme is explored in *The Company She Keeps* by Valerie Hey (1997). Hey's ethnographic fieldwork was influenced by post-structuralist ideas (see Chapter 10) and in particular the idea that, to establish one's sense of identity, one thinks about others and their 'differences'. While conducting a 'participant observation' study (where the sociologist becomes involved with the group of individuals being studied, in an attempt to see the world through their eyes and thus gain a richer understanding of the norms, values and attitudes held by the group) of school-girls in a secondary school, Hey reflected on the meaning of note-passing during lessons. She argues that the writing and circulation of such notes is a symbolic activity in which young teenage girls reflect on the nature of friendship, intimacy, sexuality and their own self – their personal identity. By writing these notes, which are like ongoing conversations between a number of parties, girls create for themselves a private 'space' in which they consider what it means to be a young female in today's world. This is seen as an active and creative process of gender identity formation rather than something that is handed down ready-made from culture as a structure of constraint.

Exercise 12.11

During her research, Hey (1997) used the technique of participant observation. This exercise requires you to assess the usefulness of this technique by answering the following questions. Refer to research methods texts for additional guidance if needed.

1. Define what participant observation means.
2. What is the difference between covert and overt observation?
3. List five advantages of observation.
4. List five disadvantages of observation.
5. When applied to the study of girls' friendship patterns, what are the problems with observation?
6. When applied to the study of girls' friendship patterns, what are the strengths of observation?

Nicholson (1999) suggests that the concepts of 'sex' and 'gender' hold a contradictory place in feminist thought. For example, whereas feminists are critical of 'biological determinism', they advocate a form of it themselves. For sociobiologists, biology (nature) determines how one behaves – it makes us who we are. Human beings are seen as little more than the product of biological urges. This biologically determinist view is rejected by those feminists who claim that we are who we learn to be. Culture places norms and values on us, and in doing so it moulds who we become. Therefore, so the argument goes, women and men might behave differently, but this does not mean that by nature they are any more different than the simple difference in reproductive organs. However, Nicholson notes that many feminists go on to express the views they claim to have rejected. Such feminists suggest that, while women might act differently in different cultures, underneath they are all female and therefore have common bonds of womanhood between them. Such arguments, for Nicholson, are not really about gender – they are actually about sex, since they do not recognize that people of the same gender might none the less have many differences. This emphasis on differences within gender illustrates the influence of postmodern ideas on Nicholson's argument.

MASCULINITY

Masculinity and popular culture

Perhaps one of the most noticeable changes in popular culture in recent years has been the growth of male life-style magazines (such as *FHM* or *Loaded*) and the new 'lad' culture that many seemed to be advocating in the 1990s. Such magazines frequently included highly sexist stories and sexualized images of women. New 'lad' culture refers to a view of young men as being dominated by the desire for entertainment, as pleasure-oriented, insensitive, and exhibiting some elements of the culture of the traditional working class (for example, the consumption of alcohol for leisure, and the desire for immediate gratification). This is exemplified in 'lad'-oriented ads on television, such as those for Pepsi Max, WKD and Lynx. However, at roughly the same time there has also been an increased sexualization of the male body for female audiences. This can be been in TV ads, films and between the covers of teenage girls' magazines offering sexual tips and independence to 'modern young women'. This phenomenon has led many sociologists to consider not just images of femininity but also images of masculinity.

McRobbie (1994) argues that while the male body – like its female counterpart – has become sexualized, this does not mean that sexual equality has been achieved. In fact, it is far from being the case. Gender inequality and oppression continue, but now both men and women are portrayed in limited roles and are oppressed by ideological representations. Theorists draw attention to the limiting images of men in the media and popular culture. Michael Kimmell's (2005, quoted in Dillon, 2010) research on masculinity in the USA found a predominantly macho identity that suppressed any signs of femininity and exhibited a form of disguised homophobia.

It could be argued that researching masculinity and masculine identity can be traced to liberal feminists as well as 'New Right' theorists such as Charles Murray (1984). Murray expressed concern for family life, with the absence of fathers following relationship break-up. He argued that family life was becoming dysfunctional without male role models as fathers, leading to educational underachievement, crime and disorder. Critics of Murray question whether the family in modern society is dysfunctional, arguing that being in a happy single-parent family rather than an unhappy dual-parent family is better for both children and society. This concern for men and masculinity is reflected in media concerns, and subsequent research about male underachievement in education and the overrepresentation of young men in the criminal justice system. The UK campaign group 'Fathers for Justice' promote equal rights for fathers and mothers following relationship break-up, though much of the media coverage of the group has been negative and contemptuous in tone. Is this a reflection of structural and cultural inequality for fathers? Do men increasingly view fatherhood as a major part of their identity?

Collect copies of so-called 'lad' magazines aimed at teenage males, and magazines aimed at teenage girls and young women. How do they portray femininity and masculinity? Compare one new 'lad' magazine to one young women's and one teenage girls' magazine. How are sexualized images used, and what do these magazines say about what it is to be male or female in modern society? Is this similar or different from the ideas of Ferguson (1983) above? Discuss your findings in 200 words.

Research into masculine culture and identity

Victor Seidler

Seidler (1989) identified that masculinity in Western societies is associated with ideas from the modern period, specifically rationality and the rejection of emotion. There is a clear link from here to patriarchal power, based on logical arguments being superior. Critics of Seidler focus on the abstract nature of his argument and the lack of empirical evidence.

David Gilmore

The anthropologist David Gilmore's (1990) *Manhood in the Making: Cultural Concepts of Masculinity* identified three main features of masculinity: the impregnator, the provider and the protector. He highlights the evolutionary nature of these roles, fulfilling a need for survival and reproduction. Gilmore identified that biological and cultural factors are important in masculine identity formation, but also that these three features are not universal in all cultures.

Máirtín Mac an Ghaill

In *The Making of Men* (1994), Mac an Ghaill, in his study of a British secondary school, examined how heterosexual masculinity was formed through education. He identified four types of masculinity, in addition to homosexual male students:

1. Macho lads.
2. Academic achievers.
3. New enterprisers.
4. Real Englishmen.

Though a stereotype of the heterosexual male definitely existed, Mac an Ghaill's research identifies some diversity in male roles. This opens up the possibility for fluidity and choice among young men, with a wider range of options open to them than has been expressed in some research.

Raewyn Connell

Raewyn Connell (1987, 2001, 2005) sees gender relations as dynamic, a product of everyday interaction. Her research has been influential, seeing biology and culture combined to form our identity. Connell looks at the different forms masculinity can take, and makes a distinction between hegemonic masculinity (maintaining dominance over social life) and other types of masculinity. Connell's research into four groups of Australian men indicated that there were some elements of a crisis of masculine identity. Hegemonic masculinity is being questioned increasingly, resulting in men being unsure about what it means to be masculine. Connell highlighted that there were different masculinities regardless of the background from which people came. Overall, according to Connell, men still benefit from hegemonic masculinity but their dominance is no longer taken for granted.

Connell's four masculinities include:

1. Those who 'live fast and die young', characterized by material disadvantage and exaggerated heterosexuality and displays of toughness.
2. Those who have distanced themselves from the hegemonic masculinity that influenced their youth. One group of men Connell studied had a particular interest in the environmental movement. Men in this group tended to be raised in female-headed single-parent families who nurtured their environmental interests.
3. 'Very straight gays' who were homosexual but with conventional definitions of masculinity.
4. Heterosexual professional men identifying with reason, hostile to unconventional masculinities.

Diane Richardson

Drawing on the ideas of Connell (1987, 2001, 2005) and Robinson (2008), Richardson (2010) starts from the position that there is no single form of masculinity. Rather, there are many different masculinities that are, in themselves, not fixed, but fluid and changing, contextual and localized, depending on the intersections of class, race and gender that apply to particular individuals and groups. She explored the lives of some working-class young men in close-knit North East communities, with a particular focus on their definitions of masculinity and its relationship to heterosexuality. For these young men, rather than 'compulsory heterosexuality' (see later) being the dominant force, Richardson argued for 'compelling heterosexuality'. By this she meant that young men (but not so much women) felt that they had to express their masculinity through a repudiation of 'being gay', whatever their feelings about homosexual behaviour, and through heterosexual intercourse, regardless of whether they felt ready do so. The peer pressure to 'perform heterosexually' led many of these young men to engage in heterosexual activity because they 'just *have* to' (2010:737–56) and despite their fears of sexually transmitted diseases or the young woman getting pregnant. She concludes that, while there may be alternative models of 'being male' around, there are compelling forces that privilege a particular form of heterosexual identity formation.

Eric Anderson

An alternative view is put forward by Anderson (2009), who argues for a theory of 'inclusive masculinity'. Here, hegemonic masculinity thrives in times of intense homophobia, which is used to police the borders of heterosexual identity. Where homophobia has declined, alternative views of what it is to be male can coexist – one that is more anti-gay and another that is gay-friendly – but neither view attains hegemonic dominance. The existence of models of inclusive masculinity in particular contexts and times thus counter-acts the effects of traditional heterosexual hegemony. McCormack and Anderson (2010) build on this theory to argue that heterosexual boundaries are maintained in situations of inclusive masculinity through 'heterosexual recuperation'; that is, the reassertion of a mas-culine heterosexual identity through boasting of heterosexual desires, or ironically taking on board a 'gay' identity to reassert their heterosexuality. In the latter case, McCormack and Anderson found that hugging among hetereosexual boys at a firmly anti-homophobic school was used in an ironic way to express their heterosexual identities.

A crisis of masculinity?

Mac an Ghaill (1994) referred to a crisis of masculinity where men no longer have a clear masculine identity. Many theorists have linked this to changes in the labour mar-ket and the reduction of traditional working-class occupations. McDowell's (2003) study of employment change and white working-class youth in Sheffield and Cambridge shows how the low-paid occupations they found resulted in them being dependent on family members for a long period. Consumerism as a component of identity was thus not avail-able to these young men. This is at odds with the traditional view of man as provider. Many of the occupations available to them were in the feminized service sector, poten-tially causing contradictions for their masculine identity. However, McDowell found they were able to adjust their working-class norms and values to retain a sense of masculinity. The boys displayed traditional views of the role of women and many engaged in anti-social behaviour.

The boys in McDowell's study were 15–16 years old. Frosh *et al.* (2001) studied a slightly younger sample of 11–14-year-olds in London schools. Their longitudinal research focused on how the boys created a sense of identity. They found masculinity to comprise a separation from femininity and being 'hard' (shown through an interest in sport, 'tough-ness', bad language and a lack of interest in school). Many were emotionally insecure. This research is particularly interesting in that it shows how these masculine identities are formed by a young age.

Connell (1987, 2001, 2005) found some tendencies towards a crisis of masculinity in her research, whereas other research has shown masculine identity to change and adapt to the needs of men and society today (see King, 2010). King's research into the com-memoration of soldiers killed in Helmand, Afghanistan, illustrates changes in the way soldiers are honoured. King notes that soldiers are not just seen as individual, almost anonymous members of the armed forces as they were in twentieth-century conflicts. Obit-uaries now give details of their domestic lives, including their status as family members. 'In acts of remembrance today, soldiers are personalized and domesticated, remembered as fathers, husbands, wives, sons and daughters' (ibid.: 1). This indicates an adaptation in the portrayal of masculine identity in the public sphere, not just by profession but also by 'domestic relations'. King (ibid.: 18–19, 20) argues that, through globalization:

> British people are beginning to understand themselves and their social relations in quite different ways. In commemoration, personality and family have become the primary

spheres of definition, debate and action while others (the nation, state, class or trade unions) have receded... The dead soldier is no longer identified in the first instance with the nation and its armed forces. The dead are remembered for their individual professionalism but they are primarily defined by their personalities and their domestic relations.

Research has been undertaken with older males to gain a broader picture of masculinity. Jenny Hockey et al.'s (2007) 'masculinities in transition' research in South Yorkshire looked at men in three occupations: firefighters, estate agents and hairdressers. They were studied while at work and in their home environments, to look at masculinity in both the public and private spheres. Hockey et al. conclude:

> Our data show a proliferation of challenges to traditional forms of masculine identity rather than a "crisis of masculinity"... Arguably, the shifting economic and social conditions of late modernity have brought scope for individual choice and innovation. Yet our data showed standardisation and chronologisation persisting within young people's perceptions of their lives – though in complex ways. While young men and women described clear age-based milestones marking the transition to successful adulthood, individualised and *gendered* modes of thought were also being brought to bear upon lifecourse chronologies. (Ibid.: 1)

The crisis in masculinity is having a global impact and is affected by the forces of globalization. Yang's (2010) research in China showed that the changes in the economy brought about by globalization meant that many male workers were made redundant from large-scale industries. This led to feelings of emasculation among many working-class males, who were left with contradictory messages about what it meant to be a man in post-Mao China. The government stressed the need for redundant workers to continue to be the main provider for their families, as was traditional, while at the same time taking away the means to do so. The net effect of this 'kindly power' exercised by the state was to encourage men to take up work positions usually associated with female workers, at reduced wages, thus establishing a more flexible labour market as required by the needs of a globally connected economy.

Extensive research into masculine identity has been undertaken since Mac an Ghaill (1994) referred to a crisis of masculinity. Much of this research does indicate changes in the perception of masculinity within the workplace and home environments. Research among younger men, particularly those with a working-class background, indicates the persistence of more 'traditional' attitudes that are characteristic of hegemonic masculinity.

SEXUALITY

Whereas 'sex' refers to the biological – often reproductive – differences between being male and being female, 'sexuality' refers to an individual's sexual desires and participation in the sex act. Billington et al. (1998) suggest that while sexuality might at first seem natural, it is still shaped by culture: 'If sexuality is something deeply rooted in our 'nature' how is it that we need to learn how to do it and develop a variety of religious, moral and even legal rules and regulations about who it is appropriate to do it with, when, where and how?'

They note that the idea of 'sex' is in fact highly problematic – even the word itself is confusing. It can be an act, a biological type or a gender. Given that the sex act is regulated so much, and that some means of sexual gratification are defined as acceptable and others as deviant (and that this changes over time), sexuality must be understood as a cultural process. For Billington *et al.*, the question 'Is sex and sexuality natural or cultural?' is a false question. It is impossible to answer. That is because sex, sexuality and sexual identity are often seen as 'either/or': coming from either nature or nurture. This is not the case, they argue. Sexuality is a complex interplay between culture and biology, plus there is an element of free choice in the types of sexual act people engage in and the life-style they adopt. Billington and her colleagues see sexuality as a prime source of power. Those who have power are able to proclaim the 'truth' of sexuality that everyone else must follow.

Segal (1997) notes that academic interest in sex and sexuality moved from a biomedical model based on scientific studies of why and how sexual pleasure occurs, through psycho-analytic theories that looked at male and female sexual activity, to feminist interpretations that either sought to encourage women to achieve sexual pleasure for themselves and to embrace their sexuality and sexual desires, and to feminist theories that advocated non-penetrative sex and lesbianism as a way to challenge male sexual power. Today, sociologists tend to discuss sexualities – a wide range or diversity of sexual acts, pleasures, meanings and behaviours. There is also, as a result of the influence of postmodern ideas in sociology, the observation that many people develop life-styles that 'play' with sexuality and traditional images of masculinity, femininity, heterosexuality and homosexuality. This is further reflected in recent popular cultural images and representations that use highly ambiguous masculine/feminine images.

Exercise 12.13

1. Write a list of advertisements you have seen that 'play with sexuality' – presenting ambiguous images of sexuality and gender that break away from the more traditional understanding of how males and females should behave and look like physically.
2. Why do you think advertisers use such images? (One paragraph.)
3. What effect do you think such images might have on audiences? (One paragraph.)

Segal observes that discussions of sexuality – both popular (in the media) and academic (within sociology) – are 'complex' and 'contested'. Young children are sexualized in themselves and for adult audiences, and male bodies have become sexualized for the viewing pleasure of a female audience.

There has been a large number of moral panics over sexuality and the risks of sex, especially for young people and children. The position of 'child sexuality' in these moral panics is especially problematic. On the one hand we have witnessed the widespread use of sexualized images of young teenage girls in the fashion industry, in beauty advertisements and in advertising in general, yet on the other hand the newspapers have expressed great concern about single mothers, underage sex, illegitimacy, child pornography and child sexual abuse.

Adolescent and sometimes prepubescent girls are often presented in a sexualized way in the media by the advertising industry. Such girls are portrayed as figures of adult male fantasy, as objects of the 'male gaze'. Many feminists are concerned that such representations provide role models for the young girls who make up the media audience. These images suggest that certain forms of sexual behaviour are the norm for young adolescents, and that certain body shapes are more desirable than others.

The argument that representations of women are designed to fulfil male sexual fantasies is a familiar theme in feminist media and cultural studies. For example, Mulvey (1975) suggests that the female body is characterized in media representations in a very narrow way. Females are often depicted as sexual toys for men – as objects to be used – and, as with adolescents, certain body types are held up as the 'ideal' to which women should strive.

In discussions of sexuality, many feminists identify what they call a 'compulsory heterosexuality' within the wider patriarchal picture of the nature of society. For example, Richardson (1993) notes that heterosexuality is seen as being biologically 'natural' – a 'normal' state to be in – and therefore every other type of sexual behaviour is deemed to be 'unnatural'. It was only recently that sexuality came to be seen as a choice, as a basis for life-style creation rather than something that is fixed at birth. Simon (1996) suggests that, in the postmodern age, gender and sexual identity are important to each individual and are not handed down by society 'ready-made'. Instead, they are a product of negotiation between the individual and the wider culture in which s/he lives. There are many different and changing identities from which to draw. For some this might lead to confusion, personal anxiety and uncertainty, but for others it might be liberating. Simon makes a similar claim for sexuality as a source of identity. He argues that sexuality is increasingly becoming less a matter of biology and 'normality' and more one of life-style and choice.

In *The Transformation of Intimacy*, Giddens (1992) argues that contemporary sexuality is very different from earlier forms. He describes the emergence of what he terms 'plastic sexuality', where sexual pleasure is separated from the act of reproduction. Instead, sexual desire is a source of personal pleasure, liberation and a significant feature of one's life-style. In this way, sexuality has become a matter of identity – it tells people about who they are and who they wish to be. Giddens notes that plastic sexuality is an outcome of, and in turn has led to an increase in, women's liberation in society. Unlike in earlier times, women's sexual pleasure is not seen as a deviant act, but as a natural and important part of a healthy relationship. Such changes in sexuality have led to a move towards a 'pure relationship' for many 'ordinary women' – an emotional and intimate relationship based on equality between the partners, without violence or domination. Sexuality is no longer something to be hidden or denied, especially for women – it is based on increased democratization between men and women in the intimate sphere of private life. It is bound up with human identity, and who we wish to become. Giddens calls this 'life politics': matters of personal identity over which humans have active control.

Sexual identity and 'sabotage'

As Segal (1997) notes, cultural identities – including gender and sexual identity – are more open and fluid in today's society, which for some writers is evidence of the postmodernization of social life. Such identities can also be seen as political acts. For example, many gay and lesbian life-styles are based on 'gender sabotage' – redefining what it means to be 'straight' or 'gay', using and playing with images and cultural identities from one gender and sexuality from the viewpoint of another. Such political life-styles based on sexuality and gender identity seek to push back the boundaries of what is considered the norm in modern society. They seek to redefine what is considered 'deviant', and in doing so to create new meanings and identities.

Foucault, sexuality and identity

These acts of gender redefinition are based on the political ideas of Michel Foucault (see also Chapter 10) and the idea that invisible or silenced identities can fight back against their invisibility by changing the existing structures from within. Foucault recognizes that sexuality is a social concept, created by those in power. Social institutions have exerted increasing control since the nineteenth century. Classifications through the government census and other institutional processes control our identity and sexuality; we have to classify ourselves as married or not, with or without children. Fertility rates and number and status of household members are recorded. Foucault highlights the increased surveillance, regulation and control of the body, which in turn controls sexuality. Claudia Malacrida and Jacqueline Low (2008), in *Sociology of the Body*, show how gender inequality is continued through control of the body.

Queer theory

As feminism focused on women's issues, queer theory, as developed by Seidman (1997) and others, puts the focus on to sexuality, attempting to redress the heterosexual bias in sociological analysis (as well as in other academic disciplines). Legal and social changes (such as civil partnerships in the UK) are making some inroads into discrimination on the grounds of sexuality, but there is still stigma and prejudice impacting on identity. As Seidman (1997: 131) argues, 'sexual identity management ... [is] still part of the lives of lesbians and gay men in America. Today lesbians and gay men find themselves in a very different situation. Their standpoint is that of an elaborated culture founded upon an affirmative identity. Many individuals who are self-identified as lesbians and gay men have built coherent and meaningful lives around this identity.'

Foucault was a key influence in the development of queer theory, as were the growing movements for gay and lesbian rights from the 1970s and 1980s onwards. There are two distinct approaches to sexuality, reflecting the biological and cultural debate within gender identity as a whole. On the one hand, sexuality can be seen to be biological in origin, ascribed at birth, or it can be seen as socially constructed, an identity choice. Queer theory, echoing postmodernism, argues that there is not a clear distinction between heterosexual and homosexual; there is a degree of fluidity between the two. They argue that sociologists should revisit all areas of society to reflect diverse forms of sexuality.

However, queer theory is not just about lesbian and gay identities, but, as Gauntlett (1998) highlights in his analysis of Judith Butler's contribution in *Gender Trouble* (1990), ' "queer" refers to what is different, and unexpected'. Butler was critical of the limiting focus of feminism on both males and females. Queer theory highlighted the fluidity of identity, that gender is a 'performance' (see Chapter 6). In a range of countries there are well-established gay and lesbian subcultures and communities. Queer theory has not yet had an impact on sociology in the same way as feminism has. However, it has encouraged sociologists to revisit the language they use, and to include a consideration of sexuality as well as gender.

The emphasis in traditional queer theory is on culture as the key dimension of forging a queer identity. The construction of gay-friendly discourse is seen as an important process in the construction of gay sexualities and identities. However, some theorists (known as 'material queer theorists', are critical of the dismissal of socio-economic forces, especially class analysis, in influencing the trajectory of gay lives. Heaphy (2011), for example, argues that there are significant social class effects on gay people as they struggle to establish their identities in a social world that is occasionally hostile to and often ignorant of their sexual behaviours. He found, in his exploration of the personal narratives of 48 gay men, that there were different processes at work, from the 'exceptional embracing' of a class as well as a gay identity, through an ambivalent attitude to the importance of class in their lives, to the rejection of class as a factor in the conscious construction of a gay identity. Heaphy (2008) maintains that the reflexivity of lesbian and gay identity is closely intertwined with power relationships. Structural factors are still important.

Other queer theorists have called on the concept of 'intersectionality' (see earlier) to explore the experience of gay men and women in at the crossroads between hierarchies of oppression. Rahman (2010) looked at the lives of gay Muslim men in the USA at the intersection between political and cultural Islamophobia and homophobia in the dominant discourses of the USA. However, Rahman goes further than just describing the problems of Muslim gay men in terms of racist and homophobic discourse, but, drawing on the work of Habib (2010) argues that Western notions of 'egalitarian' homosexual experience are not useful for exploring the lives of gay Muslim men in both the Western and Islamic worlds. The position of gay Muslims at the intersection of religion and sexuality means that their very existence challenges the notion of both what it is to be a Muslim and what it is to be gay.

Moore (2010) argues, in her analysis of lesbian and gay identities, that while sociology has placed increasing focus in recent years on the reflexivity of identity in an uncertain and unpredictable society, it is still important to consider the impact of collective identities. She refers to the work of Elias (1970) to argue that individuals do not exist in isolation. Individual identity is therefore dependent on others.

Ruspini (2007) argues that transexualism and transgenderism show how personal identity has multiple meanings in society today, and highlights the importance of identity for individuals. 'It is not the renouncing of an identity, but the search for a fluid and, at the same time authentic identity' (ibid.: 9). Ruspini links the development of masculinity and femininity to historical and culturally specific processes that involve constant redefinition. This echoes the focus of Moore (2010) on the collective as well as the individual in identity formation.

THE 'KNOWING CONSTRUCTION OF IDENTITY'

Gauntlett (2002), in his review of gender identity in the media, refers to the 'knowing construction of identity'. He concludes that, in Western society, we are well aware that our identity is something we construct, and this involves our choosing from an array of possibilities in the social world. This recognition of the role of the 'actor' and of individual choice (with an awareness that some have more choice as a result of structural factors than others) is central.

> The traditional view of a woman as a housewife or low-status worker has been kick-boxed out of the picture by the feisty, successful "girl power" icons. Meanwhile the masculine ideals of absolute toughness, stubborn self-reliance and emotional silence have been shaken by a new emphasis on men's emotions, need for advice, and the problems of masculinity. Although gender categories have not been shattered, these alternative ideas and images have at least created space for a greater diversity of identities. (Ibid.: 248)

CONCLUSION

The sociology of sexuality and gender is a complex field, with a number of contributing areas and an interplay between identity, politics and power. A number of dominant themes can be identified in modern-day feminist sociology, despite the wide range of approaches. These are based on observations that the feminist movement has come a long way from its early origins; that women's lives in society are very different today than in the past; that feminist sociology is beginning to receive the recognition it deserves, though a great deal of 'malestream' sociology still exists; and that gender remains a massive source of personal identity. Contemporary feminists have also noted that the nature of gender identity is changing for both women and men. Women are still disadvantaged in a patriarchal society, but they are no longer totally passive victims – they are creative users of popular culture even though they are portrayed in a sexist way by this same culture. In terms of disadvantage and identity, there has been a growing awareness of transgender, lesbian and gay identity and inequality. Gender is still a central issue in terms of identity, but is recognized as being more fluid and fragmented than earlier sociological analysis reflects. It is a significant field of study in its own right within sociology and other academic disciplines; however, some feminists argue that in many areas gender is 'tacked on' and in others (such as politics) research is very limited.

The field has expanded to include the study of masculinity, male identity and inequality. The development of research and theory into masculinity will be interesting to follow into the second decade of the twenty-first century, particularly the interaction between feminist sociology and the study of male identity, culture and equality. Many theorists argue that gender is still one of the primary aspects of an individual's identity, and it is a field that is changing as we write.

Important concepts
Hegemonic masculinity • Femininity • Feminism • Masculinity • Patriarchal • Queer theory

Exam focus

(a) To what extent do the media construct masculine and feminine identities differently?
(b) How useful are the insights of feminism for a sociological understanding of identity?
(c) Discuss the role and development of traditional masculinities in modern society.

Critical thinking

1. Has feminism resulted in the promotion of the diverse identity and rights of women at the expense of the diverse identity and equality of men?

Chapter 13

Ethnicity and Identity

After studying this chapter, you should:

- understand the problems involved in the definition and use of terms such as 'race', 'ethnicity', 'black' and 'white'
- understand the role played by ethnicity in identity creation
- understand the arguments for increased ethnic hybridity in modern society
- understand the debate surrounding multiculturalism
- reflect on the impact of globalization and recent social change on ethnic culture and identity

INTRODUCTION

When asked to tick a box reflecting your ethnic background on forms, do you find it difficult to decide which box to tick, or is it a straightforward question to answer? Do the options available on forms reflect your identity accurately, or do you want to opt for more than one category? Would you prefer to be asked to identify your ethnicity or race? Are they the same, or different? Do you object to being asked the above questions? Your answers to the questions above highlight the personal as well as the political sensitivity of ethnicity, race and identity. Sociological analysis of ethnic identity and culture reflects social change and is itself a reflection of, and a product of, its time.

Early sociological discussions of ethnic identity tended to portray ethnicity as a problem. Immigration after the Second World War was discussed in terms of the 'assimilationist model', which argued that, in the interest of order and harmony, it was important for ethnic groups to fit or blend into the wider 'host' culture. It was assumed that the immigrant culture would fade as individuals took on the values, beliefs and traditions of the host culture. However, with the growing awareness of racism in society and race riots in urban areas, ethnicity came to be treated as more of a problem. The early sociological study of race relations aimed at solving the problems of a multicultural society, rather than valuing difference (see research from the Chicago School and theorists such as Robert Park (1950)). Studies of US society refer to US culture as a 'melting pot', a 'blended' culture, multicultural, or a cultural 'mosaic', depending on the time period and context in which they are written. This is reflected in research in other societies around the world.

The sociological study of ethnicity and ethnic identity today is very different. For a start, 'ethnicity' is something everyone has, not just 'others', and difference is seen as being important to the creation of who we are. Ethnographic research has been conducted with a variety of minority and majority ethnic groups to understand what culture and identity means to them, and the contribution of their ethnicity and other factors to their identity.

When studying ethnicity it is important to be aware of the country and culture being studied as well as the time that the research was conducted. The context is important. Consideration needs to be given to whether research and theories from one culture can correlate with another.

The study of ethnicity, race and identity has been given greater significance since the 11 September 2001 (9/11) attack on the World Trade Center in New York and subsequent terrorist attacks in Europe. Terrorist activity has led to an increased awareness of difference. The impact of communications technology and globalization on ethnic identity and culture is significant, as is a consideration of how ethnic identities are influenced by both global and local factors. A number of key issues in society today (as portrayed by the news media) are about identity. Ethnicity features in many of these – terrorism, religious fundamentalism, conflict, inequality and extremism, which gives a great deal of scope for researchers to apply sociological analysis to current events.

DEFINING 'ETHNICITY'

Put rather simplistically, 'ethnicity' refers to cultural characteristics, whereas the term 'race' emphasizes biological difference.

According to Yinger (1976), ethnicity has three defining characteristics:

- The perception by others that the group in question is different.
- The perception by those in the group itself that they are different from others.
- The fact that those defined as being in the same group – with the same identity – share activities based on their 'sameness', whether real or imagined.

What this means is that ethnicity is about awareness, identity, belonging, culture and difference. Membership of an ethnic group suggests that there are others who are not similar. There is a significant focus on culture, and self-identification. This approach sees ethnicity as a central concept in terms of culture and identity. We shall consider whether this is the case, or whether other aspects, such as class, gender and nationality, are more significant.

Yinger goes on to identify four general characteristics of a multicultural or multi-ethnic society:

- The society might be based on a collection of different ethnic groups who are equal.
- The society might have a majority 'national' group alongside a number of smaller ethnic groups.
- The self-identity of some ethnic groups might be based on a 'mother' society outside the host society.
- Some ethnic groups might be disadvantaged in relation to other groups in the same society.

Matters of ethnicity – especially its definition – are open and subject to change. This is a key theme in the definition of ethnicity. Eriksen (2002) recognizes that ethnicities do not exist in isolation. However, there are distinctive elements that can be used to define an ethnic group. An important factor is the self-defining nature of ethnicity: members of the group will feel that they share a common origin, and the focus is on how individuals characterize themselves. Eriksen argues that, in this sense, ethnicity is a more useful term to use than race. Richardson (1990) argues that ethnicity may be a more useful term than 'race', but it can be difficult to distinguish between different ethnic groups. There is diversity and overlap between ethnic groups, which could be based on regional, language or religious differences. When studying ethnicity, keep these other factors in mind. There is debate about the extent to which society can be multicultural, to which we shall return shortly.

Exercise 13.1

Reflect on your (and your friends' and colleagues') use of social networking sites. Is ethnicity significant in terms of how people portray their identity? Is it a part of how people define themselves in their profile? If ethnicity is not a factor, which other aspects of identity feature prominently? How might you interpret your findings with regard to ethnic identity and culture?

Sociologists often disagree about which key terms should be used to describe a given aspect of social reality, and the meaning of the same term often varies between theories and theorists. This is especially true of the terms associated with the study of ethnic identity, including the following:

- race
- ethnicity
- coloured
- white
- black

Paul Gilroy (1997: 302) provides a good example of the problem of definition:

Think, for example, of 'black' as a shared identity. Does it refer to the notion of genetic differences between people or to the colour of their skins? Is it a descriptive term or a political one? Can you be 'black' and 'British'? Identity has clearly become a core component in the scholarly vocabulary designed to promote critical reflection upon who we are and what we want. Above all, identity can help us to comprehend the formation of that fateful pronoun 'we' and to reckon with the patterns of inclusion and exclusion that it cannot but help to create. This may be one of the most troubling aspects of all: the fact that the formation of every 'we' must leave out or exclude a 'they', that identities depend on the marking of difference.

Exercise 13.2

Reread the above extract from Gilroy (1997) and then answer the following questions. Explain your answers.

1. Does 'black' refer to the notion of genetic differences between people or to the colour of their skins?
2. Is 'black' a descriptive term or a political one?
3. Can you be both 'black' and 'British'?

Exercise 13.3

What does Gilroy mean by 'that fateful pronoun "we"'? Answer this question in approximately 100 words.

Gilroy's analysis highlights how culture and identity can relate to power. The notion of 'us' and 'them', of those that comprise the 'we', reflects how some ethnic groups hold and retain power while others experience inequality and isolation. Particular ethnic identities are a form of capital.

Pierre Bourdieu's theory and the concepts of social, cultural and economic capital are relevant here, as is wider Marxist debate. We shall return to the issue of power, identity and culture later in the chapter.

Race versus ethnicity

Traditionally, the concept of 'race' is biological whereas 'ethnicity' is cultural – much the same distinction as that made in Chapter 12 between sex and gender. However, the term race has become problematic in modern-day sociology. Classifications of race according to different biological types often ignore the vast diversity of human life. Such classifications have sometimes conformed to racist views themselves, since these biological types are seen as all-powerful fixed biological realities. Many have rejected the term ethnicity on similar grounds. Ethnic differences are seen as being as fixed in cultural differences as races are fixed in biological differences. Gilroy (1987) describes this situation as 'cultural racism', while Barker (1981) uses the term 'new racism' to describe the same problem – that cultural differences are treated as 'essentialist'. They are used to reduce the diverse and multiple features of varied and changing groups to a limiting set of characteristics that account for every aspect of behaviour and identity. This leaves no room for the idea that ethnic identities are readjusted constantly as society changes. Anagnostou (2009) links ethnicity to an individual's ancestors, arguing that there is a biological component when using the term 'ethnicity' as well as when using the term 'race'.

Many sociologists attempt to define groups by using the terms and labels those groups themselves use. In the 1970s and early 1980s the term 'coloured' was rejected by many in favour of 'black'. The argument put forward was that everyone was coloured, that white was as much a colour as black. By calling people who were black coloured, you were denying their true colour – hiding it as if it was something to be ashamed of. At that time, 'black power' movements were fighting a conscious battle against white racism.

The term black, however, has had a problematic history. As Tariq Modood (1988, 1992) notes, the word black might have been adopted by some people of African descent but it has been rejected by many of Asian descent. Modood argues that 'black' – as was argued above in the case of 'coloured' – denies the existence of ethnic diversity and difference, and instead lumps all non-white peoples together. It is often the case that differences of identity within and between ethnic groups make the use of a single term unacceptable. This is because it sets up a very simplistic distinction between black and white, causing many identities to be ignored, lost or silenced. Similarly Brah (1992) suggests that while Afro-Caribbean and Asian people might all experience racism and inequality in Britain, they experience different types of racism based on different racist assumptions, stereotypes and ideologies. We should therefore use different terms, because their experiences and the causes of those experiences are different.

Twine (2010) studied the role and perception of 'whiteness' in interracial families. Her research showed that 'whiteness' and 'black', despite being fluid concepts, are still significant. Twine refers to research by Ruth Frankenberg (1993) which 'shifted the lens away from ethnic minorities to white people and whiteness'. Twine's research looks at how black family members see themselves as being different from those classified as 'white', and how they view interracial family members: 'Black family members may perceive whiteness as an asset, a cultural disadvantage, a liability or a harbinger of ethnic erasure.' She notes that it is important to look at how white members of interracial families conceptualize race, as well as the black members, and that views of race and ethnicity are complex and multifaceted. The terms 'blackness' and 'whiteness' are not straightforward, but are still socially significant. We have seen that, as well as ethnicity, 'white' and 'black' are terms that are socially constructed. Caroline Knowles (2003, quoted in Twine, 2010), argues that 'In geopolitical terms, whiteness is insignificant. But if we are trying to understand the power geometries of globalization and in the operation of racism, then whiteness needs closer analysis'. For example, Hughey (2011) argues that overt discourses of racism have disappeared from many public spaces, but that the reproduction of white identity has moved to 'backstage spaces', where the construction of white masculinity is accomplished through an emphasis on the difference between non-white masculinities and an idealized form of what it is to be a white male. This is not to say that all white men share these backstage discourses, but that different groups of white males may draw upon implicitly racist cultural scripts among themselves. In doing so, white males do not merely adopt these traditional cultural scripts wholesale but are creative actors in formulating changing identities about whiteness and maleness that are related to wider political and social events in society.

Exercise 13.4

List the problems associated with each of the following terms:

• Race • Ethnicity • Coloured • White • Black

As we can see, definitions of ethnicity in particular and identity in general are the result of political acts, both when such definitions are imposed by dominant cultures on to minority groups and when they are adopted by the members of ethnic groups themselves. As Jeffrey Weeks (1990: 89) notes: 'Identities are not neutral. Behind the quest for identity are different, and often conflicting values. By saying who we are, we are also striving to express what we are, what we believe and what we desire.'

Ethnic hybridity

Ethnic hybridity is sometimes referred to as 'new ethnicity' – an awareness that notions of difference do not simply limit and characterize, but that difference can also be positive and powerful. Hybridity refers to the combination of more than one form of identity. Such notions can be used by ethnic groups themselves in order to be whom they wish to be, and to have valued about their cultures what they wish to have valued. For Stuart Hall (cited in Woodward, 1997) ethnic identities can be 'located' within the lines of the past and the future. In other words, ethnic identity is a matter of finding a 'real' or 'authentic' past – a sense of history and tradition – but also a sense of future. The history, or past, of ethnic groups will vary, as will the experiences of individuals. Individuals may be first-generation immigrants, or second- or third-generation immigrants, born in their country of residence, or products of mixed race or ethnicity parents. In the words of Woodward (1997), ethnic identities are about both 'being' and 'becoming'. Gilroy (1993) suggests that ethnic identities are constantly undergoing change. There is no such thing as a 'pure' ethnic identity; rather, groups create their own sense of identity in relation to social structure, their sense of history (real or imagined) and what they envisage for the future. As Gilroy (1993: 304, in Woodward 1997) notes, 'The "raw materials" from which identity is produced may be inherited from the past but they are also worked on, creatively or positively, reluctantly or bitterly, in the present.' The study of ethnic identity and culture should reflect this dynamic. This introduces the element of choice for individuals and groups: which ethnic identities will they stress or choose? However, it can be questioned whether all individuals and groups have choice.

Peter Aspinall *et al.* (2008) looked at how people classify themselves when completing the UK census form, after the 2001 census showed an increase in the numbers of people classifying themselves as 'mixed race'. Aspinall *et al.* found that many of the 'mixed race' group would tick multiple boxes when given the opportunity. This can be seen as evidence of hybridity and increased complexity of ethnic identities. Aspinall *et al.* (2008: 1) say 'research on the "mixed group" has revealed the importance of fluidity, shifting boundaries, and multiplicity with respect to how its members identify'. However, many in the groups didn't think that ethnicity or race was the most important element of their identities. Age, family background and occupation were cited as being more important. This research highlights the complexity of measuring ethnicity. Grosfoguel (2004) stresses the importance of looking at the history of a group and its past as a colonial power, or colonial subject; its relationship with the host culture; and the resulting power it has. He calls for the use of 'racial/ethnic identity' as a preferred form of categorization which takes the past into account. Ethnic group identity is a reflection of past power hierarchies, which are still influential on a global scale.

Explain what is meant by 'ethnic hybridity' in 100 words. Use examples. Why is this a significant area of study for sociologists today?

Migration patterns and the historical and social context

The context and sense of 'history' is therefore a part of constructing ethnic identities. Trends of migration will have an impact. There are significant differences in terms of identity and culture between first-generation immigrants to a country and third- or fourth-generation immigrants, for whom it will be their only country of residence.

There are very few places in the world unaffected by migration. European and American societies reflect centuries of movement of people for personal, social, political and economic reasons. See Table 13.1 for some examples. So, when studying ethnicity and identity, the background and context are significant.

There have been a number of Acts in the UK since 1999 that aim to reduce opportunities for people to seek asylum. These have strengthened border controls and isolated asylum seekers in centres dispersed around Britain. This has led to limited contact with the

Table 13.1 Immigration and emigration, Britain and the USA, 1907–2011

UK	USA
Pre-1914 Jews seeking asylum from parts of Europe.	**1907** Peak of European immigrants
During Second World War Jews seeking refuge.	**1930s** Great Depression. Decline in immigration, increase in emigration
Post Second World War Immigrants actively recruited to solve labour shortages, many from the West Indies	**1965** Immigration and Nationality Act Amendments; more non-EU immigration
1960s Immigrants from South East Asia (particularly Pakistan and India)	**2000–2010** nearly 14 million immigrants, 'a record-setting decade of immigration' (Camarota 2011).
1967 East African Asians from Kenya; immigrants from Eastern Europe, Poland	Over the years, a range of different immigrant groups:
1990s Asylum seekers and East Africans	• Irish
1999 Immigration Act, increase in illegal immigrants	• Italian • The Philippines
Since 2000 Immigrants from a wide range of countries	• Latin America • Korea
2011 Number of asylum applications decreased	• Mexico • India
2011 Cap on non-EU immigrants	

wider community and identities developing in resistance to this experience. The Coalition government in 2011 aimed to put a cap on the number of non-European Union (EU) immigrants to Britain, including those entering the country as students, and to track the numbers of people leaving the country as well as those entering.

The extensive debate about definition and context may result in one wondering where this leaves us in the study of ethnicity and identity. Eriksen (2002) argues that ethnicity serves a purpose, as it is an active creation, shaped by socialization. However, according to Eriksen, ethnic identity tends not to be a choice (though individuals may choose to hide it, or to play it down) – we are generally born into our ethnic group. Fenton (1999) makes the useful observation that ethnicity has different levels of intensity. Some individuals will feel strongly about their ethnic identity and it will be a significant part of their lives, whereas others will not consider it a central part of their self-concept (as many respondents indicated in research by Aspinall *et al.* (2008) by favouring age, family background and occupation as indicators of identity). Later in the chapter we shall consider the role of power and inequality in ethnic identity and culture. Do some ethnic groups have more power than others? If so, does this power give them greater opportunities to choose their identity? Some ethnic identities are highlighted by individuals and used to their advantage, whereas others are played down. If people have a choice, which do they choose? Gilroy's (1993) point above is particularly useful. Ethnicity is constantly changing and evolving – but it is something 'real' in terms of how people experience it on a daily basis. Maintaining an abstract level of scrutiny is not helpful (as postmodernism is not always helpful in terms of further analysis). Keep these issues in mind as you read further.

Exercise 13.6

Why are notions of difference important to the establishment of who we are – to establishing our identity? Answer this question in approximately 100 words.

Exercise 13.7

Fenton's (1999) observation that ethnic identity is not an important part of an individual's self-concept is an interesting one. Identify people in the public eye who embrace their ethnicity, and note down a second group of people who play down their ethnicity. Reflect why this might be the case.

Classification of ethnicity

As we have seen, defining ethnicity is not straightforward. Self-identification is commonly used in research. When ethnicity is measured quantitatively, this limits the opportunity for individuals to elaborate. An increasing number of people would class themselves as of 'mixed' race or ethnicity. Peter Aspinall *et al.* (2008) researched 'how "mixed race" people perceived their range of identity options and how they made decisions about these options'. Aspinall *et al.* (2008: 1) write that:

research on the "mixed group" [those who categorised themselves as of mixed racial heritage] has revealed the importance of fluidity, shifting boundaries, and multiplicity with respect to how its members identify. This has challenged official bodies such as census agencies with respect to how they capture this group in the decennial enumerations and, indeed, of the sustainability of using single category options as opposed to multi-ticking across categories... research in the UK and USA has increasingly demonstrated that the children of inter-ethnic unions and those with more complex heritages do exercise identity options in terms of their desire to embrace one or more of their origins, thereby creating a complex range of racial/ethnic identifications.

When asked during interviews what their ethnic/racial group was, the majority of individuals responded with a description. Their research highlights the need for the design of survey and census questions to allow greater variety and depth of responses.

Exercise 13.8

1. If you were conducting quantitative research on ethnic identity, how would you word a question asking for participants' ethnic identity?
2. What issues do sociologists face when operationalizing ethnicity? Write approximately 200 words.

ETHNICITY, INEQUALITY AND POWER

Identity and resistance

The diversity of ethnic groups in many societies results in differing experiences of inequality. Groups that experience inequality often experience their identity in opposition to others.

Gilroy (1997) argues that while black people are disadvantaged in society they should not simply be characterized as helpless victims – black cultures often involve political resistance against racism. As Hebdige (1979) (see Chapter 9) notes, subcultural styles and the creation of identity through group membership are symbolic means of resisting oppressive dominant values and ideologies in society. Forms of music, styles of dress and even ways of speaking can be used as symbolic tools to fight against powerlessness and alienation. In this sense, 'style' is counter-hegemonic. It can be used to resist dominant ideologies and to maintain a sense of difference, which in turn allows the members of a group to think about who they are and who they wish to become.

This idea of cultural resistance through style was taken up by Mercer (1995), who notes that ethnic groups use style as a political tool. Establishing one's membership of an ethnic cultural group can be a liberating and political act. Mercer takes as an example of such identity politics the part played by hairstyles in black culture. The 'Afro' of the Black Power Movement in the 1960s and 1970s and the 'dreadlocks' of Rastafarians are examples of identity construction through the use of symbols and resistance to a racist and oppressive society through symbolic style. Both hairstyles symbolize pride, unity and difference from an essentially racist society. They are forms of resistance to dominant ideological values. However, consumerism and the symbols of consumption can also be used to establish within-community economic hierarchies, such as those found by Pattillo-McCoy (1999) in the USA, and to help construct social rather than merely individual identities, such as the process whereby 'green' consumer goods are deployed to indicate a social dimension to consumption (see Deutsch and Theodorou, 2010).

Claire Alexander's (2000) research, *The Asian Gang*, suggests that in the 1990s Britain experienced a moral panic about Asian youth. Alexander identifies a number of factors that led the Asian community to be portrayed negatively in the media at that time. Her research identifies racism in terms of misrepresentation in the media, in particular the reference to gang membership. In terms of ethnic identity the boys saw themselves as predominantly Muslim or Bengali, not as British Asians. This led to a distinct subcultural identity being created among their peer group, in opposition to the negative perception of them in wider society. Their identity was a form of resistance. Alexander's research indicates the creative and dynamic nature of identity creation for ethnic minority groups (see Chapter 9 for a more detailed discussion of youth subcultures). One impact that inequality and lack of power can have is to result in a stronger subcultural identity, and for resistance to become part of that identity.

①Ⓐ

Exercise 13.9

Consider the symbols used by black hip-hop artists and black reggae artists. For each group, list the ways in which style is used as a form of resistance and to create a sense of identity.

Do some identities have more power?

As discussed earlier, some ethnic identities have more power than others, and some ethnic groups are make use of their identity as a form of resistance. There are structural factors involved here. Ethnic groups are more likely to be concentrated in the lower social classes. However, this is not the case for all groups. Archer (2011) made an exploratory investigation into ethnic-minority, 'middle-class' individuals. They were a mixed group of 36 wealthy ethnic-minority individuals, who conformed to objective criteria of 'middle-classness', such as financial well-being and high occupational status. However, their identity was not uniformly constructed as middle class; rather, many resisted a personal identification with being middle-class, partly because the identity was organized around 'whiteness', with which they did not identify, and partly because they were originally from working-class backgrounds and therefore were the 'embarrassed' middle class, if they identified with the middle class at all. The ethnic minority individuals in this study were therefore at the intersection between race and class (and, for the female respondents in particular, gender). This social location is open to differing social constructions of identity, depending, for example, on feelings of exclusion or inclusion, influenced by specific circumstances. Archer concluded that histories of migration played an important part in the development of these feelings, and therefore with any identification or non-identification with 'middle-classness'.

In *Orientalism* (1978), Edward Said argued that those in the West, and specifically Europe, have created a vision of what the 'East' – the 'Orient' – is. This view is flawed, and contributed to the oppression of the East by the West. There is no recognition of the diversity of identities within the 'East'. In a later edition (Said, 1995) he included a discussion of Islam, arguing that Islam was portrayed in the media (particularly in the USA and the UK) with 'highly exaggerated stereotyping and belligerent hostility'. Islamic identity is an example of the link between ethnicity and religion. Recent research and theorists have looked at how the media have contributed to anti-Islamic attitudes following the global terrorist attacks in New York, London and Madrid, and the effect this has had on identity. Allen (2005) believes Islamophobia has increased and that divisions are growing between Muslim communities and wider society.

Ron Geaves (2005) sees the Muslim and non-Muslim communities joining together for the first time in protests against the Iraq War as being significant because it 'challenge[s] essentialist thinking regarding ethnicity by exemplifying the creation of hybrid or flexible identities' (Kwale 2003, in Geaves 2005: 74). This is a more optimistic view about Muslim identities in the UK. We shall go on to discuss these more 'flexible' or hybrid identities and the impact of globalization on ethnic identity.

DIASPORA, HYBRIDITY, MULTICULTURALISM AND GLOBALIZATION

In *The Black Atlantic*, Gilroy (1993) uses the word 'diaspora' to refer to the effect that ethnic identity and culture can have on others. While ethnic identities are frequently based on the notion of being different, they can provide others with symbols that can be mixed together to create 'hybrid cultures'. In this sense, 'diaspora' refers to how ethnic cultures come to influence others as a result of migration. As members of an ethnic group move from nation to nation, their culture spreads and may be adopted by people from other ethnic groups. For example, in the UK we have seen the adoption of black musical styles by white youths, the adoption of black styles by Asian youths, the adoption of white styles by black youths and so on. This transportation of cultural styles can include music, styles of dress, patterns of speech and even political ideas and symbols. The formation of identity and culture is an ever-changing process influenced by all involved.

Exercise 13.10

Choose a band or another contemporary musical act that 'plays' with ethnic identity and influences. Describe how it does this, referring to samples of the music played and images of how the musicians dress. Use the internet to help you with your research.

However, it is important to recognize that the experiences of diasporic individuals are not all the same, but are tempered by religion, social status, economic circumstances and, above all, are gendered. In exploring the experience of Muslim women living in the USA and Canada, Mishra and Shirazi (2010) argued for a complex interaction between traditional Islamic frameworks and living in a predominantly Western and white society in the post-9/11 context. The reactions of different groups and individual women were very different and contingent on a number of factors. While religious identity remained strong for some of these women, they did not accept submissively patriarchal interpretations of the Qur'an or traditional Muslim dress, but negotiated their way through competing pressures to develop their own 'third space' (Bhaba, 2004) by developing more hybrid identities. The outcome of globalizing processes is therefore neither assimilation nor acceptance of fixed differences, but rather the creation of social space in which new hybrid identities are negotiated by agency and resistance. The wearing or non-wearing of the *hijab* is taken as being symbolic of this hybridity, because Muslim women choose to wear or not wear it on social as well as religious grounds and it is not a dichotomous split between 'religious oppressed' wearers and 'non-religious', modern non-wearers.

Globalization, ethnicity and the postmodern and poststructural critique

The rise of hybrid identities is linked to issues of globalization (see Chapter 14). Robins (1997) notes that while 'globalization' refers to the global narrowing of space and time it does not, paradoxically, refer to the loss of local identities or cultures. Rather, it refers to the spread of the 'local' to the global stage. In other words, we become more aware of the difference of others through the spread of regional and local differences across time and space. We are not moving towards a common global culture shared by all, but rather towards greater awareness of the variety of ethnic identities. The end result of globalization is not global similarity, but increased awareness of global difference.

For Robins, this globalization of difference raises questions about present notions of identity and those of the future. International travel and the popularity of tourism as an activity, the expansion of global communications, the globalization of popular culture and media, and the creation of world markets through the spread of multinational corporations call into question previous notions of national identity, ethnic identity and the boundaries between groups. Such questioning of the boundaries of identity is both disorientating and liberating. It can lead to increased anxiety and conflict, or to increased tolerance and harmony. In a similar argument, Back (1994) notes that those living in the West are experiencing global musical styles based on a pastiche of many cultural and ethnic symbols.

Exercise 13.11

There is an advertisement for the British bank HSBC promoting its understanding of other cultures as being beneficial for its customers, identifying it as 'the global local company'. This could be cited as an example of globalization highlighting global difference, not similarity.

Watch a range of television or online advertisements for global brands and companies.

1. Note which have been dubbed or personalized into a national, regional or local accent, or created specifically with one culture in mind.
2. Note which products are advertised in ways that translate globally.
3. Which of your lists is longer? Is this evidence of global similarity or difference? Write a couple of paragraphs in response to these questions, using examples.

Cohen (2006), though not positive about all the effects of global migration, believes the increase in the global movement of people has resulted in cosmopolitanism – people with an awareness of a wide range of cultures and with a greater acceptance of others. Cosmopolitan individuals may themselves feel aligned with more than one culture, thus becoming individuals with a more complex ethnic identity. Global hybridity, and a sense of cosmopolitanism, are cited as evidence of the onset of postmodernity in contemporary society. In this view, postmodernity has opened up global boundaries and blurred previously rigid distinctions (geographical and symbolic, real and imagined) between cultures, and has brought with it a plurality and diversity of ethnicity, culture and identity. We are more aware of the 'other' than ever before, and are able to borrow from this 'other' styles and symbols to use in fresh and creative ways. As Cohen (2006: 5) says, 'Despite more guards, more laws and more restrictions, the symbolic and real boundaries that divide societies are eroding. This is a result of ideas, images, money, music, electronic messages, sport, fashion and religions that can move without people, or without many people – forms, if you like, or virtual migration.' According to Morley (1994) the postmodern interpretation of globalization as liberation from traditional cultural and ethnic boundaries must be accompanied by a word of warning. What many postmodernists ignore is that there has always been a global awareness of others and of difference, especially as a result of the colonial and imperial past of many European nations. When postmodernists write of the increased awareness of others in the contemporary age, what they are really referring to is the increased recognition by those in the rich, industrialized First World of the experiences and cultures of those in the Third World. As a result of slavery, religious missionary work and colonialism, the ordinary members of Third-World societies have been aware of the difference of Western others for much longer than ordinary Westerners have been aware of them. In this sense the interconnectedness of global cultures and identities is not new at all.

bell hooks (1996) writes of the development of a 'postmodern blackness'. By this, hooks means that while postmodern views are frequently those of white, middle-class academia, the idea of cultural hybridity raises important issues for black people and can provide an important voice for them, particularly black women. Within sociology there is much talk about the opening up of people's awareness of difference, but the views of black female sociologists are still relatively unheard compared to those of their male and white counterparts. hooks suggests that postmodern ideas and postmodern society offer a context within which black people can think about their culture, history and themselves, and in doing so can value who they are. They can use this to struggle against racist ideologies that seek to devalue black identity.

What writers such as Hall (1992) have found useful about postmodernism when applied to issues of ethnic identity is the idea that identity has become 'fractured' or 'fragmented' into a vast plurality of possible identities – what we called a 'new ethnicity' earlier in the chapter. This is referred to as a process of 'decentring'. In other words, identity is a matter of personal creation, it is not fixed or handed down by others but is a mixed-up view of who they are. This reflects people having more than one identity and reflecting on this identity confusion.

However, Pilkington (2002) argues that we should not exaggerate the differences between ethnic groups, as 'there is a very real danger that the boundaries between them will be overdrawn and the cultural distinctiveness exaggerated'. This is one viewpoint within the multiculturalism debate.

Multiculturalism

Taking the term literally, a multicultural society is one characterized by diversity; one comprised of many different cultures existing side by side. The term has become politically sensitive in recent years, provoking debates about the impact of multicultural social policy.

Multiculturalism has been interpreted in different ways:

- by postmodernists as acceptance of diversity;
- as the respect of, and toleration of difference;
- as embracing cultural diversity and promoting segregation; or
- as promoting cultural assimilation with the 'blending' or amalgamation of cultures.

Multiculturalism can be argued to have had a big impact on culture and identity. However, it is all too easy to become bogged down in the debate and political sensitivities of the issue. The debate can appear to be between two opposites: assimilation and integration on the one hand, and multiculturalism on the other. It is not that simple, however. The Parekh Report (Parekh, 2000) says that it is possible to recognize diversity as well as to challenge racism and inequality. What does it mean for identity?

Pilkington (2002 and 2005) has attempted to bring together an analysis of social and political events in the UK, and a consideration of multiculturalism and diversity. We shall return to his work on national identity in Chapter 14, but here we shall focus on what his arguments bring to an understanding of ethnic identity. Pilkington refers to the 2001 riots in northern British towns, and Muslim segregation after the terrorist attacks in London in 2005. He cites Modood's (2007) argument that the move to multiculturalism resulted in fragmentation. In defence of multiculturalism, Smits (2011) argued that it was possible to have a multicultural (Australia) or bi-cultural (New Zealand) society, in which the differences between ethnic groups are recognized, while all groups subscribe to common civic values such as social justice and egalitarianism. However, the interpretation of multiculturalism as a force for social cohesion or to promote diversity and highlight difference is criticized by some.

ETHNIC IDENTITY AND CHOICE

How much choice do individuals have when it comes to their ethnic identity? Hall's (1992) 'decentring' and the resulting identity confusion has been developed by a range of other theorists. As we have seen, Eriksen (2002) argued that we are generally born into our ethnic identity; it is ascribed. According to globalization theorists, people do have a choice and there is an increasing plurality of identity.

Spencer et al. (2007) studied the experiences of migrants from former communist countries such as the Czech Republic, Poland and Estonia as they came to work in Britain following their countries joining the EU. They found that because of a lack of choice or power, these migrants to the UK retained their national or ethnic identities and didn't display plural identities. They found that most migrants spent very little time with British people. Many of the migrants planned to return to their home countries once the economic situation improved. After two years, one in four migrants surveyed spent no time with British people, instead staying within their community of other migrants. Spencer *et al.* found that this was not just through choice, but rather the feeling that British people didn't want friendship. As a Ukrainian woman commented, 'They do not let you into their circles' (ibid.: 58). Factors such as low wages, long working hours (many working at more than one job) and unfamiliarity with British law, support agencies and welfare available could explain their social and cultural isolation. This study highlights how ethnic identity develops in relation to other ethnic groups and within a specific context. Many migrants found it difficult to relate to others. Some migrants had been unaware that Britain is a multicultural country and had negative attitudes towards minority ethnic people. It is not certain how widespread these views were relative to those of British people. Some formed more positive attitudes through experience in the UK:

> I had not thought that this place was so multicultural. I did not know that there were black people. For me it was a disaster as I had seen them only 2–3 times in my life. I was also warned I should not use this word 'negro' but just to say 'black'. (Ukrainian woman, hospitality worker, aged 25). (Ibid.: 71)

Some ethnic minority groups therefore retain their sense of 'homeland' identity and retain a distinctive subcultural identity. This is related to their attitudes on moving to the UK, as well as their experiences while working there. In this case, the migrations were short-term and primarily for economic reasons, thus could be attributed partly to choice. This is evidence that while there may be a softening of the boundaries between ethnic groups, there is not necessarily an automatic integration of culture and identity in a global society.

Brown *et al.*'s (2007) findings were the result of a 12-month longitudinal study in 20 schools, and looked at how the children of immigrants felt about themselves and their ability to relate to others. The children felt most content in schools with high levels of social diversity, where they were more confident in socializing with others. They found that from the age of 5 children were aware of social categories and had developed ideas about their own cultural identity. Ethnicity appears to be an element of choice in identity from a young age and is enhanced if individuals feel comfortable to do so.

The study of ethnicities shows how complex identity can be in contemporary society. This raises issues not only for ethnic identity but also for national identities – a theme taken up in the next chapter.

CONCLUSION

As we have seen, notions of race, ethnicity and 'black' and 'white' are highly problematic and are open to considerable debate and discussion. There are a range of factors to consider in terms of ethnicity and identity:

▪ A focus on 'ethnicity' as opposed to race has resulted in ethnographic studies researching how individuals assign themselves an ethnic identity. This has highlighted the values, beliefs and attitudes of different ethnic groups and how they are active in creating their identities. It has been beneficial to take the focus away from biological differences of 'race'. However, some argue that biological ancestry is still significant in ethnicity.

As we have seen from the work of Hall and Gilroy, notions of ethnic identity are based on resistance and difference, and are frequently matters of hybridity. Ethnicity is a creation – it is based on political struggles and personal experiences. There is an element of individual choice, but how much choice individuals have depends on inequality and power. There are not the same opportunities for all ethnic groups in all countries.

It is often not useful to see ethnicity as distinct from other aspects of identity – gender, class and age. The relative importance of each factor will depend on the social situation, and to some extent, the individual. The study of ethnicities shows how complex identity can be in contemporary society. Ethnicities are not necessarily distinct in a global society, the boundaries between them can blur.

As Gilroy (1993) notes, the formation of ethnic identities is dynamic.

Experiences will differ from country to country as well as between urban and rural areas. Garland and Chakraborti (2000) note that there may be greater social exclusion and marginalization of ethnic minority groups in rural areas. There are opportunities for the formation of ethnic minority subcultures in urban areas, which are not available in more isolated rural communities.

It is difficult to reflect on the role of ethnicity without relating it to nationality as well as to the local. This raises issues not only for ethnic identity but also for national identities – a theme taken up in the next chapter.

Important concepts

Ethnicity • Diaspora • Globalization • Hybrid cultures • Race
• Symbolic ethnicity

Exam focus

(a) How has globalization changed the way in which we see ethnic identities in the contemporary world?
(b) With reference to ethnicity, discuss the way in which identity is a form of resistance in society.

Critical thinking

1. Are people free to choose whatever ethnic identity they wish?
2. Why do some choose to accentuate their ethnic identity whereas others try to downplay it?
3. The introduction to the Parekh Report (Parekh, 2000) talks about 'understanding that all identities are in a process of transition'. To what extent is this the case for ethnic identities?

4. Are there any truly multicultural societies?
5. Has ethnic hybridity become the norm?
6. Ethnic minority culture reflects power inequalities. Discuss to what extent this is the case.
7. 'Some identities give power.' Do some ethnic identities have greater social, economic and cultural capital?

Chapter 14

Community, Nation and Globalization

After studying this chapter, you should:

- be able to define the concepts of community, nation and globalization
- be able to identify how community and nation can establish identity
- understand the importance of notions of 'time' and 'space' for issues of identity
- understand the role of symbols in the creation of community and national identity
- be able to apply theoretical perspectives to the issue of globalization

INTRODUCTION

It is more than 150 years since the word 'sociology' was first used, and we could be forgiven for thinking that both society and sociology are very different from what they were in the days of the founders – Comte, Durkheim, Marx and Weber. For some sociologists, the founders' project of 'modernity' (see Chapters 3 and 7) has come to an end and we now live in a time of postmodernity (see Chapter 7), whereas for others great social change has taken place in our late-capitalist or postindustrial society, but not as envisaged by the postmodernists.

A central feature of contemporary sociology, whether attempting to deny modernity or to update it, is the idea of globalization, which has had profound implications for culture and identity. The onward march of globalization has implications for how we conceive the communities to which we belong, and for the ways that nations maintain their distinctive identities in an age where ordinary people are being exposed to new cultural ideas from places that were once far away, but now seem ever nearer because of air travel and mass communications.

Bauman (2004) reflects on the impact of globalization and social change on identity; 'The frailty and forever provisional status of identity can no longer be concealed. The secret is out.' What is the impact on community and national identity? Are these forms of identity 'frail' and 'provisional'? We shall examine a range of points of view.

MODERNITY AND THE DECLINE OF COMMUNITY

Along with the rise of science, rationality and technology, a key feature in the image of modernity held by the founders was urbanization: the creation of towns and cities, and migration from rural areas to these new industrial centres. Modernity was fundamentally tied to industrialization, and urbanization played a vital role in this. Workers were needed in the new factories, and agricultural production declined. The move to towns and cities heralded the dawn of a new age – one that would have a profound effect on traditional culture and identity.

ⒾⒶ

Exercise 14.1

In what ways do you feel that the modern-day community has changed from earlier forms? For each of the following aspects of society, compare and contrast the community of today with the community of the past.

- Religious practice
- Nature of the family

- Family meals
- The relationship between work and home

ⒾⒶ

Exercise 14.2

1. Conduct an open-ended, oral-history-based interview with an elderly person whom you know. Try to establish how modern life in towns and cities is different from before. Use your answer to Exercise 14.1 as the basis for the questions you ask.
2. Considering your experience of conducting primary research, reflect on the advantages and disadvantages of the interview method.

Many of the founders of sociology considered that the industrial age was accompanied by a 'decline of community'. An early expression of this idea is contained in the work of Tönnies (1963), who was writing at the end of the nineteenth century. Tönnies drew a distinction between traditional society (based on 'Gemeinschaft') and modernity (based on 'Gesellschaft'). These are two different ways of organizing social life, relationships and the creation of individual self-identity.

Gemeinschaft means 'community'. In rural areas, individuals were bonded into close-knit communities where everyone knew everyone else and had personal contact in all areas of life. Relationships were based on daily, face-to-face interaction:

The prototype of all unions of Gemeinschaft is the family. By birth man enters these relationships: free rational will can determine his remaining within the family, but the very existence of the relationship itself is not dependent on his full rational will. The three pillars of Gemeinschaft – blood, place (land), and mind, or kinship, neighbourhood and friendship – are all encompassed in the family. (Tönnies, quoted in Kumar, 1986: 80)

Gesellschaft means 'contractual association'. In other words, in an industrial society, relationships are based on impersonal forces. Instead of daily, face-to-face interaction with everyone, there are limited interactions with just some of the people, based on role specialization, where some people have work relationships, others family relationships and yet others neighbourly relations. Tönnies, who characterized Gesellschaft as a state of isolation and tension between individuals, seemed to regret the decline of community. Even though Gesellschaft allows people the freedom to choose the relationships they wish in their lives outside work, it none the less isolates them from those around them.

Emile Durkheim explored a similar theme to Tönnies in his book *The Division of Labour in Society* (1938), where he made a distinction between two types of 'solidarity' (see Chapter 3); that is, ways of organizing individuals into a cohesive group: mechanical solidarity, found in rural areas where individuals were bonded by similarity and the sharing of tasks, and where everyone knew everyone else; and organic solidarity, which emerged with industrialization and urbanization and was based on the division of labour and specialized, work-related roles. The latter was a new form of solidarity which was based not on similarity, but on difference. Society became interconnected because people came to rely on others to perform tasks and roles they could not perform themselves. Though Durkheim was concerned about a potential increase in 'anomie', he believed that this new form of community would reinforce solidarity, rather than reduce it.

ⒾⒶ

Exercise 14.3

How would you measure Tönnies' claim that there has been a 'decline of community'? List potential ways of operationalizing the concept of 'community decline'.

The 'dark side' of city life

The idea that urban areas might not be conducive to a sense of community and self-identity can be found in the work of Simmel (1950) (see Chapter 4). Simmel sees urban areas as having both advantages and disadvantages. On the one hand, they allow greater freedom of expression, but on the other they bring about a feeling of isolation and loneliness since individuals feel most isolated when surrounded by a multitude of strangers. Simmel was concerned with the impersonal and anti-communal nature of life in the city.

According to Kumar (1986), the views of the founders and other classical sociologists about the communal nature of city life differed dramatically, offering different ways of looking at the city and its effects on identity, relationships, community and culture. Consequently, there developed over time very different ways of thinking about 'community' and different definitions of the concept.

ⓊⒾ
Ⓐ

Exercise 14.4

Consider the five quotations below from a range of classical thinkers (quoted in Kumar, 1986). Identify which quote or quotes can be associated with the three general positions listed after the quotations. Explain why you have allotted the quotations as you have.

1. Marxist thinker, *Friedrich Engels*: 'We know well enough that the isolation of the individual – a narrow-minded egotism – is everywhere the fundamental principle in modern society. But nowhere is this selfish egotism so blatantly evident as in the frantic bustle of the great city. The disintegration of society into individuals, each guided by his private principles and each pursuing his own aims has been pushed to its furthest limits in London. Here indeed human society has been split into its component atoms.'
2. *Ferdinand Tönnies*: 'The city consists of free persons who stand in contact with each other, exchange with each other and cooperate without any Gemeinschaft...these numerous external contacts, contracts, and contractual relations, only cover up as many inner hostilities and antagonistic interests.'
3. *Georg Simmel*: 'The reciprocal reserve and indifference and the intellectual life conditions of large circles are never more strongly felt by the individual in their impact upon his independence than in the thickest crowd of the big city. This is because the bodily proximity and narrowness of space makes the mental distance only the more visible. It is obviously only the obverse of this freedom if, under certain circumstances, one nowhere feels as lonely and lost as in the metropolitan crowd. For here as elsewhere it is by no means necessary that the freedom of man be reflected in his emotional life as comfort.'
4. *Louis Wirth*: 'The city consequently tends to resemble a mosaic of social worlds in which the transition from one to another is abrupt. The juxtaposition of divergent personalities and modes of life tend to produce a relativistic perspective and a sense of toleration of differences.'
5. *Emile Durkheim*: 'great cities are the uncontested homes of progress; it is in them that ideas, fashions, customs, new needs are established and then spread over the rest of the country...life is there transformed with extraordinary rapidity: beliefs, tastes, passions are in perpetual evolution. No ground is more favourable to evolutions of all sorts'.

- Position one: the city as unrestrained individualism.
- Position two: the city as both enslavement and liberation.
- Position three: the city as opportunity.

Problems with defining 'community'

For the founders – and in particular for Durkheim and Tönnies – the concept of community was almost interchangeable with the idea of solidarity. Being in a community implied the subordination of the individual to the wider group. This view has come under attack in contemporary sociology for three reasons:

It suggests a romanticized and nostalgic 'golden age' of community where everyone was bonded together. This is an unrealistic image.

Living in a community might not be the same thing as experiencing solidarity. Within communities there is conflict, as well as the opportunity for creative social action.

To claim that 'community' has died is an extreme view. It may have changed, but many consider that a sense of community still exists in society. Perhaps it makes more sense today to speak of communities. Parekh (2000) argues that, in a diverse, multicultural society, it is more appropriate to talk about a 'community of communities'.

Howard Newby (1980) identifies three main approaches to how different sociologists have tried to define the idea of community:

- Community can be seen as being defined by geographical boundaries between different territories.
- Community can be seen as a localized area: a network of interrelationships.
- Community can be seen as people's sense of 'togetherness'.

Despite the problems with the idea of community, we should emphasize the effect that one's place in the community and one's relationships with others have in the formation of self-identity. As Durkheim notes in *The Elementary Forms of the Religious Life* (1982), group membership and the experience of community are vital to knowing who you are as well as knowing who you are *not*. Thus membership of a group gives one a sense of having a place into which one can fit. This idea of membership of groups is not just the concern of functionalist sociologists. Interactionist sociologist, William Foote Whyte (1955) wrote of the feeling of 'street-corner community' held by youths in Chicago's Italian slum areas during the Second World War. He notes that community membership and self-identity were a matter of everyday life and interaction, and that this included hanging around on street corners engaging in banter.

①Ⓐ

Exercise 14.5

List six ways in which life and life-styles differ between urban and rural areas.

①Ⓐ

Exercise 14.6

Consider your answer to Exercise 14.5 above. Write a couple of paragraphs on the consequences that living in cities might have on identity formation.

Bauman (1990) argues that notions of community or togetherness are about sameness and otherness. Bauman suggests that while groups may be divided into 'us' and 'them', one cannot exist without the other:

'Them' are not 'us', and 'us' are not 'them'; 'we' and 'they' can be understood only together, in their mutual conflict. I see my in-group as 'us' only because I think of some other group as 'them'. The two opposite groups sediment, as it were, in my map of the world on the two poles of an antagonistic relationship, and it is this antagonism which makes the two groups 'real' to me and makes credible that inner unity and coherence I imagine they possess. (Ibid.: 41)

Bauman sees this sense of difference as helping us to structure who we feel ourselves to be – our identity. This difference is both symbolic and relational: it is a sign of the exclusivity of our group in our consciousness, but it also relates to the people one does and does not associate with in day-to-day life in society.

In *Liquid Times* (2007), Bauman cites one of the negative consequences of globalization being the constant change that communities face. Inequalities are more visible and human bonds become weaker. Communities are seen increasingly as networks of weak links. This is reflected in Putnam's *Bowling Alone* (2000). Putnam's argument is that, in the USA, community networks and the bonds between people are weakening. People are less involved with others (even going bowling on their own compared to with others) and this weakening of social networks can result in weaker self-identities.

Anthony Cohen (1989) rejects the notion of 'community' as a physical geographical boundary. Instead, he thinks in terms of 'imagined' or 'symbolic communities' – an approach that owes a great deal to postmodern views of society. This is not to say that the boundary concept is not useful in understanding what communities are and how they contribute to the formation of identity. However, for Cohen, such boundaries are not geographical features, nor are they imposed by politicians and the state. Rather, they are in the mind of the beholder. Such boundaries are 'inherently oppositional' in that they structure the world into groups, based on their difference from each other. In this sense, communities are symbolic creations – they enable further symbols to be learned, acquired and manipulated, through interaction with others who share a common idea of reality: 'Our argument has been, then, that whether or not its structural boundaries remain intact, the reality of community lies in its members' perception of the vitality of its culture. People construct community symbolically, making it a resource and repository of meaning, and a referent of their identity' (ibid.: 118).

Similar to the ideas of Cohen, Anderson (1983) suggests that 'nation' and 'nationhood' are symbolic constructions. This is true if we think about the expanse of the geographical area that is home to a 'nation'. Any sense of national identity and togetherness must be largely symbolic or 'imagined', since no national is ever likely to know each and every other national with whom s/he identifies.

The symbolic nature of national identity has also been considered by sociologist Timothy Crippen (1988). Crippen is influenced by Durkheim's *The Elementary Forms of the Religious Life* (1982), in which Durkheim makes a distinction between the 'sacred' and the 'profane'. Whereas the sacred are symbols that are treated as distinct and special, the profane are ordinary symbols of 'this world'. According to Durkheim, while sacred symbols undergo a process of renewal from time to time, they are a vital feature of group membership, since they represent the group and its identity. Crippen (1988) argues that the principal sacred symbols at the time he was writing are those connected with nation, nationalism and national identity.

Berking (2003) calls for a return to the use of 'community' within sociology as a useful concept in a postmodern world. As culture becomes global, subject to reinterpretation and constant change, people no longer have a solid basis from which to form their identities. Looking to communities could be the way to conceptualize these fluid hybrid identities.

Exercise 14.7

In an extended version of the table below, summarize in note form the ideas on community discussed so far in this chapter.

	Date when writing?	Basic concepts	Argument
Tönnies			
Durkheim			
Simmel			
Engels			
Wirth			
Bauman			
Cohen			
Anderson			
Crippen			
Putnam			

Exercise 14.8

List the strengths and the weaknesses of the ideas of each of the following writers:

- Tönnies
- Durkheim
- Simmel
- Bauman
- Cohen
- Anderson

NATIONAL IDENTITY

As we have discussed above, nations and nationality can be seen as social constructions. Their importance as components of identity cannot be underestimated. Globally (and historically), nationality is a significant cause of conflict.

Exercise 14.9

From your own knowledge, or using the internet to research, identify three global examples of conflicts linked to national identity.

McCrone (2002, 2006), in his analysis of national identities in modern Britain, notes that there is a close link between ethnicity and nationality. When researching national identity he refers to 'identity markers' that enable individuals to claim a particular nationality; these include: 'place of birth, ancestry, place of residence, length of residence, upbringing/education, name, accent, physical appearance, dress, behaviour and commitment/contribution to place'. There is an overlap here with many of the 'markers' of ethnicity. Keep theories and researchers from the previous chapter in mind as we cover this topic.

McCrone (2002, 2006) highlights the role of a sense of 'place' in identity, one component of national identity. Easthope (2009: 73) reminds us that

> Indeed, bonds to place need not be positive. People also identify against places, establishing their own sense of self by contrasting themselves with different places and the people in them. This is the thesis of Said's *Orientalism* (1979), and there has been much scholarly interest in the connection between places (particularly home-places) and hostilities, especially at the national scale.

(See Chapter 13 for more on Said's Orientalism thesis.)

Ⓤ Ⓐ

Exercise 14.10

How important is place to your identity? Identify all the places (these could be locations, regions or nations) that are important to your identity.

The founding fathers of sociology predicted that affiliation with national identity would decrease and become less important as society developed. Early research in this area by Gellner (1983) and Elias (1978) – *The Civilising Process*, first published in 1939; see Chapter 2) links national identity to modern civilization. National identity was seen to be a result of modernization and the need for a state to intervene in the running of a large-scale urban society that was more complex in nature. However, critics argue that national identity pre-dates the Industrial Revolution.

Has national identity declined with globalization?

Pilkington (2002) links the development of national identity to that of mass communication. To form a national identity, people have to have a sense of those who are different. Pilkington argues that globalization has resulted in people fearing that global organizations (for example, the EU) will take power and control from nations, at the same time as strengthening ethnic minority identities which compete or conflict with a national identity (see Chapter 13). This can be seen in the increasing presence of anti-immigrant far right parties in Europe.

It can be argued that globalization might have a variety of impacts on national identity in different areas:

- It could make national identity stronger, as people want the security of a nation-state bureaucracy.
- It could weaken identities, with the 'homogenization' of culture and the development of global cultural symbols (Pilkington, 2002).
- It could lead to the development of 'cosmopolitanism', a universalistic and inclusive identity, in contrast to narrower, exclusive national identities.

▨   Alternatively, people could turn to local identities to gain a sense of belonging and security in a time of change.

▨   It could result in more flexible and hybrid identities.

Held (1991) suggests that the future of the nation as a self-contained political entity, and of national identity itself, has become uncertain. Whereas for some, globalization signals the end of national divisions in respect of political and economic action, cultural reproduction and consumption, and self-identity, others predict the maintenance of distinct differences between the 'imagined communities' that nations represent. For Held, while economic and cultural distances are being reduced, nationalist feelings may strengthen in response to a perceived loss of autonomy. McCrone (1998), in *The Sociology of Nationalism*, discusses the diverse forms of nationalism and argues that no single theory can fully explain it. He concludes that belief in nationalism is stronger than ever. While globalization has undermined nationalism, the ideology of nationalism continues because of its flexibility; it is adaptive. O'Donnell (2007), in his discussion of British national identity, concludes that the identities of the British are becoming progressively less confined by national boundaries. Communities of identity, which for some engender deeper and more meaningful feelings than national identity, are to be found worldwide, a reality to which the British government must adjust. In common with other forms of identity, national identities can be seen as being characterized by increased hybridity and choice. Berdsey's (2006) research into sports supporters and national affiliation among British Asians brings to light this hybridity and the complexity of 'identity politics'. Increasing numbers of British Asians support the England football team but choose to support a cricket team from the Indian subcontinent. Berdsey maintains that this trend reflects the role of cultural heritage for young British Asians as well as settlement within the British nation.

The development of a cosmopolitan outlook in a globalizing world, in opposition to nationalism, is also cited as a cause of the weakening of national identities (see Brett and Moran, 2011). Following Kaufmann (2004), they distinguish between political cosmopolitanism, which is related to global governance and cultural cosmopolitanism, which is in opposition to national identities. The tension between national identities and cosmopolitanism is important, because in societies where there are many differing ethnic minorities and continued inward migration, the balance between these outlooks will be a factor in how welcoming or hostile is a host society. In the case of Australia, however, Brett and Moran (2011) found that there was no simple dichotomy between nationalism and cosmopolitanism in the outlooks held by their sample of 42 interviewees. Rather, national identity, imagined as an open culture with a stress on individualism, was mobilized by individuals to provide a welcome to a mix of different individuals, rather than to migrating communitarian ethnic groups. It was the mixture of national and cosmopolitan identities that led to an openness towards inward migrants.

In his analysis of the options open to Danes in terms of their national identity in a global context, Jenkins (2010: 2) does not see the national identity as declining in response to globalization, but changing:

What it means to be Danish will, in the long run, be decided by the democracy of the marketplace, by people – with their wallets, their taste buds, their holiday destinations, their television channel selectors, and their educational, leisure and labour market decisions – voting for something broader and wider than their parents knew. It is not reversible, it will gather pace, but whatever the result looks like, it will still be 'Danish'.

A range of factors impact on the resilience and form of Danish nationality and how much meaning it holds for the Danes. These include politics, history, religion and the education system. Jenkins' work highlights how generalizations should not be made from one nation to another.

Exercise 14.11

Using the internet, research nationalist movements in three countries. Are they minority interest groups or do they have a widespread following?

THE IMPORTANCE OF TIME AND SPACE

Anthony Giddens' 'structurational sociology' allows us to reconsider the notion of community, with reference to the structures that both enable and constrain us in our life (see Chapter 6). Giddens (1984) suggests that while we are born into a ready-made social reality that shapes and structures what we do, within such structures we have the freedom to think, reflect and shape our identity. Daily acts of social action and interaction occur in both time and space. Giddens states that:

- Action has a tempo associated with it that governs its duration.
- Action and interaction are 'located' at different times – some actions are considered normal at some times but not at others.
- Actions take place in spaces: some actions are considered normal in some spaces but not in others.
- Individuals are born into a space that structures and shapes their early lives, and initially the individuals have no choice as to where or what this particular space will be.

Giddens suggests that by considering the ways in which action and interaction are structured by time and space, we are led to reconsider the notion of community. He stresses that we should not 'romanticize' the notion of community, especially when discussing the past, but should think about the importance for society of local regions and the places/spaces in which humans act and interact.

Giddens points out that pre-modern societies were more 'fixed' in their space than is the case today. Most people did not – could not – travel very far, nor did they have much contact with other cultures. They were structured by their place – their 'locale'. Today, time and space have been reduced because of the growth of transportation and communication networks, and consequently our sense of place is very different. Yet even though we may view the world differently, we still conduct our interactions within spaces – within locales – that dictate the pattern our interactions will take. Giddens thus replaces the notion of community with the idea of 'locale' – in both time and space.

A locale is a space that gives a context to the actions that occur within it. These spaces can be macro (large-scale) or micro (small-scale). They can also be political spaces, such as a particular government's legal territory, or physical spaces, such as a house or the various rooms in a school. In defining the idea of locale Giddens refers to 'regionalization', an idea influenced by the dramaturgical writings of Erving Goffman (1971b) (see Chapter 6). What this means is that the spaces in which we interact – the locale – are organized into different areas or regions. Some of these regions allow us to act in some ways, others in different ways. This depends very much on whether the region in question is 'front stage' or 'back stage', to use Goffman's terminology: on whether it is public or private. The example Giddens himself gives is of an ordinary house. Different spaces, or rooms, are used for different actions and interactions at different times of the day and even on different days of the week. For example, how we behave in the privacy of the bathroom or our bedroom is not necessarily the way we behave in communal areas such as the living room. Sometimes rooms are used for different activities at different times. A front room might be a study or even homework room in the early evening, but not later on when other family members arrive. All the rules that are associated with the different regions of the locale define what we should do and how we should do it. In this sense they contribute to who we think we are.

①Ⓐ

Exercise 14.12

Using a copy of the table below, speak to a number of your friends or colleagues to conduct a survey and record how their rooms are used in day-to-day life.

How/when are the following rooms used, and by whom?	Respondent 1	Respondent 2	Respondent 3	Respondent 4	Respondent 5
Kitchen					
Parents' bedrooms					
Children's bedrooms					
Front room					
Back room					
Dining room					
Garden					

Place, mobility and identity

Easthope (2009) researched young people from Tasmania, Australia, who had travelled and lived abroad before returning to the state. Easthope aimed to assess the impact of movement and place on their identity. She argues (ibid.: 78) that within society today, 'Mobility and place are fundamental aspects of the human condition and the concept of identity cannot be fully understood without reference to this dialectic.' Mobility can give an awareness of difference and the 'other' and, in combination with a sense of place, are important factors in identity development. She questions whether mobility is resulting in 'dislocated identities': 'We cannot say that we are moving away from the importance of place attachment totally, nor can migrants be categorized into "modern" and "postmodern" ideal identity types. People can, and do, draw from both facets of identity construction simultaneously.' (ibid.: 78).

UNDERSTANDING GLOBALIZATION

The concept of globalization has become highly significant for sociologists and has been a theme throughout this text. It provides us with a way to think about how human societies are interconnected in time and space. Waters (1995: 5) defines globalization as 'A social process in which the constraints of geography on social and cultural arrangements recede and in which people become increasingly aware that they are receding.'

Waters notes that while the word global has existed for at least 400 years, the word that describes the process of becoming global – globalization – did not come into use until about 1960. When first used, the word stood for the worldwide spread of interconnected economic relations and markets. However, globalization is not just an economic force, it is also a cultural one. Ideas, attitudes, mass media, cultural commodities and symbols have spread across vast and once unbridgeable temporal and spatial distances. Globalization is about the reduction of time and space, and it has profound consequences for the establishment of one's identity.

ⓘⒶ
Exercise 14.13

Consider the following items, and for each one provide examples of how globalization has affected it, and consequently also our social lives.

- Clothing
- Food
- Music
- Television
- Religion
- Travel
- Communications
- Finance
- The environment

According to postmodernists, the process of globalization can be seen as either liberating or constraining. The plurality of cultural meanings on offer due to globalization means that individuals can 'pick and mix' from them, and thus modify their identity in line with the ever-changing and expanding world. People could choose to embrace multiple identities. Pilkington (2002) argues that globalization could lead to 'cultural homogenization', the consumption of cultural products globally (films, fashion, music) resulting in increased similarity. But it can also result in people becoming fascinated by difference and wanting to access culturally distinctive products globally. The rapid expansion of cultural influences might create uncertainty – it might lead to confusion, chaos and cultural disorder, in which a stable sense of identity will be difficult to maintain.

Exercise 14.14

Which of the above positions do you agree with the most: the ideas of Held (that nationalist feelings strengthen in a global society) or the postmodern view (that nationalist identities are weak and fluid)? Explain your view in approximately 150 words.

Some writers suggest that increased global interconnectedness has led to the expansion of order and democracy in the world. Media critic McLuhan (1964; McLuhan and Fiore, 1967) wrote as early as the 1960s about the creation of a 'global village' and a 'global culture' based on new technology – a very early prediction of the global power of today's internet. However it may be an exaggeration to suggest that the internet represents a new 'global culture'.

Exercise 14.15

Are you a member of an online community? Identify three online 'communities'. How are the members related? Do the members have similar backgrounds?

How is your local community represented online? Are there any political interest groups, protest groups, social or leisure activities?

Online communities and identity

The growth of new communication technologies and their potential either to build up 'virtual' identities or to increase the social isolation of users of online communications has been documented by many sociologists (see, for example, Räsänen and Kuovo 2007). Many studies have found that the characteristics of real-time peer groups can also be seen in virtual communities (see Caplan and Turner, 2007), but that there are important differences between the two, especially that the virtual environment is a community of choice, which is also anonymous. Lehdonvirta and Räsänen (2010), in their study of young users in Spain, Japan and the UK, found that it was those who had high levels of sociability offline who employed online group activities as 'an additional source of identification' (ibid.: 14). Moreover, online interactions allowed these individuals a greater flexibility in experimenting with different identities than in offline peer groups restricted by place.

Schmidt's (2007) review of blogging practices has shown that blogs (regularly updated personal websites which commonly have an interactive element with comments, opinions and links) can promote a blog-community identification. Knitting blogs (Wei, 2004, in

Schmidt, 2007) and blogs used by the goth community (Hodkinson, 2006) show how subcultural identity can be expressed through blog use. The internet is used by groups as another medium for expressing culture and identity, and maintaining social ties. User-ranked news sites such as Reddit and Digg involve individuals posting stories and articles they find interesting, with comments, to which the community respond with their own opinions, comments and rankings. Users can portray their identity and interests through their use of the sites.

New Right thinker, Fukuyama (1992) suggests that globalization is bringing about a 'new world order' where the ideological differences between East and West are being settled. This new world order is symbolized by the collapse of the Berlin Wall and the spread of free-market economic principles into former communist states. Many Marxists are critical of this image of globalization and see it as little more than the expansion of capitalist ideology across the globe. It is viewed as a process of global 'Americanization'. Marxists also question who have the opportunity to 'pick and mix' cultural meanings and identity. This is open only to those who have the financial resources and status to manipulate the new technology, and who have the freedoms of the 'global village'. Furedi (2004) notes that the 'experts' who assist people in the development and adaption of identities in the global world are not neutral. They have a vested interest in individuals becoming reliant on their guidance and support.

Globalization and 'reflexive modernity'

Giddens (1996) describes the contemporary age not as one of postmodernity, but of 'reflexive modernity' (see Chapter 7). A new age has succeeded modernity in one sense, but it should not be confused with the ideas associated with the intellectual movement of 'postmodernity', such as the decline of truth and the rise of relativity. Giddens suggests that our new times are characterized by the feelings of 'ordinary social actors' that society has changed rapidly and the future has become uncertain. This is very unlike modernity, which was based on absolute notions of truth and certainty. In this new age we are beginning to think about the uncertainties of existence. It is an age in which we must be 'reflexive' about our lives, our relationships, our future and our very sense of self. Giddens suggests that, because of the changing nature of time and space, identity is no longer what it was in pre-modern times, when one's sense of place was much more fixed and localized. Because of globalization we are now aware of the risks and dangers of modern living (also see Beck's theory of risk in Chapter 7).

Two key features of reflexive modernity are the creation of a post-traditional social order and the acceleration of globalization. Giddens suggests that while the dynamic of globalization has existed for some time it is experienced differently today. We – as ordinary social actors – experience this process as both a constraint and a force for liberation, or as an all-enveloping process of decentring and independence. Giddens feels that few people are unaware that their lives are part of a wider, global process, and that their day-to-day actions are influenced by remote events. However, not only are our individual actions influenced by globalization, our actions in turn influence the spread of globalization itself:

> Less evident is the reverse side of the coin. The day-to-day actions of an individual today are globally consequential. My decision to purchase a particular item of clothing,

for example, or a specific type of foodstuff, has manifold global implications. It not only affects the livelihood of someone living on the other side of the world but may contribute to a process of ecological decay which itself has potential consequences for the whole of humanity. (Giddens, 1996)

Giddens suggests that in the period of reflexive modernity, globalization has become not so much a matter of impersonal forces, but something that shapes our very self-identity. It has become 'intimate' to the very centre of our being – who we are, and who we wish to become. Giddens describes globalization not as being 'out there' in relation to humans, but as 'in here'. By this, he means that globalization affects our intimate day-to-day lives and our self-identity. It enables us to think about other cultures and to locate ourselves within a much wider, larger 'locale' – the world itself. Since society is 'post-traditional', individuals now have to work as never before to construct those aspects of social life that were previously handed down. We have to create personal and intimate relationships, take control of our future and develop our own identity. This means that we live in a state of uncertainty, yet it is a state in which we can become free: free from tradition, free to decide who we are.

In contrast, Bauman (2007) highlights the negative consequences of global society, including the problems individuals have in developing a stable sense of identity. Individuals increasingly live in fear of the negative things that might happen (such as safety in your home and local area, and avoiding illness) and over which they have no control. Identity development, according to Bauman, is marketed to us increasingly as a fun leisure activity, although identities will always be in a state of flux, and a continual project until we find a stable source to which we can anchor our identity.

CONCLUSION

It is difficult to dispute that we live in a global age, and that this has been recognized by individuals in society. The concept of globalization has certainly enjoyed a rapid rise in interest among sociologists. Globalization raises questions about how individuals experience time and space, and how they experience and create culture and identity. Just how globalization should be interpreted is still a matter of debate. Some see it as a source of liberation and creativity; while others view it as presenting the human race with further risks and damage. Whatever the outcome of this debate, we can be certain that globalization will remain an important feature of society as we move into the future.

Those who argue that identity has taken on more flexible and hybrid forms see identity as an incomplete 'project' subject to constant revision and amendment. This provides opportunities for individuals: 'people are faced with the "freedom and burden" of designing their own identity' (Williams and McIntyre 2001: 397, quoted in Easthope 2009: 65). However, the resources you have individually or as a community will impact on whether these opportunities give increased choice, or bring increased constraints.

Important concepts
Community • Cultural homogenization • Globalization • Gemeinschaft • Gesellschaft • Nationalism • Urbanization

---

Exam focus

(a) Assess the importance of location as a source of identity.
(b) To what extent do you agree that community is in decline as a source of identity?
(c) Can national identities survive in a global society?

Critical thinking

---

1. Does a global culture exist?
2. 'Globalization has reduced the strength of local and national identities.' Do you agree? If not, why not?
3. Has a 'European' identity emerged with the development of the European Union?
4. Do individuals have the choice to create their own identity?
5. 'The concept of national identity ... can be seen as the hinge between structure and action' (Bechhofer and McCrone, 2010). To understand national identity fully is it necessary to consider a variety of sociological theories and approaches?

Appendix: Exam Guidance and Strategies for Essay Writing

Exam guidance

Sociology exam questions, particularly longer-answer, essay-type questions require you to not only show your knowledge and understanding, but also to show that you can interpret data, apply theories and research, analyse arguments and evaluate text. The key to success is to initially consider the question carefully. What skills does it require you to show?

- Make sure you understand the 'command' words used at the start of each question; that is, you should understand the differences and/or similarities between words such as evaluate, outline and assess, and phrases such as 'to what extent'.
- Use sources (if applicable) directly – make reference to them, and discuss and evaluate them. This includes named research studies as well as reference to theorists and theories. Don't just list them. Apply them to the specific issues in question.
- Use key sociological concepts for depth and detail. Try to define or explain them within the 'flow' of what you are writing – this will add considerably to the depth of your answer.
- Answer the question directly. Provide a conclusion at the end that directly addresses the actual point of the question – that is, whatever it is that the 'command' word at the start of the question asks you to do.
- Link studies to theories or particular sociologists. Try to compare different types of sociology for evaluation purposes.
- Make evaluative criticisms of the data or source/stimulus provided (when relevant or applicable) and of studies and sociological ideas.
- Use command words such as: alternatively, in comparison, consequently, an example is, however, to evaluate, to signpost your interpretation, analysis, application and evaluation.
- Demonstrate different interpretations of the same question, or even ideas or concepts from the viewpoint of more than one sociological theory.

- Demonstrate the interconnectedness of all sociological ideas and debates, in that an idea or concept applied in one topic area can be applied to another area – but ensure that you make its relevance clear and link it to the question.
- Ensure you have a strong introduction and conclusion that weigh up the evidence and address the different sides of, or solutions to, the concepts in question.

Strategies for essay writing

If you find yourself getting tangled up in ideas, concepts and arguments when planning essays it is a good idea to step back and impose a logical framework on your planning. This will enable you to reflect whether you have enough content and whether you are truly responding to the question set. Try using the format below to structure your plan. Over time you will develop your own essay writing style and start to ask yourself these questions intuitively.

Put the question into your own words. What is it asking you to do?	
List relevant concepts, research and theories	
Outline arguments and evidence for the view in the question	Outline arguments and evidence against the view or theory in the question
What is your conclusion? Have you answered the question?	

Essay checklist

- Have you answered the question?
- Have you referred to all relevant theories and evaluated them?
- Have you used sociological concepts appropriately?
- Are all points made supported by relevant research?
- Have you considered (and evaluated where appropriate) the methodology of research?
- Does your argument flow from the start of your response to the conclusion?

Bibliography

Abbott, P. and Wallace, C. (1997) *An Introduction to Sociology: Feminist Perspectives*, 2nd edn (London: Routledge).

Adam, B. Beck, U. and Van Loon, J. (2000) *The Risk Society and Beyond: Critical Issues for Social Theory* (London: Sage).

Adorno, T. W. (1991) *The Culture Industry* (London: Routledge).

Adorno, T. W. and Horkheimer, M. (1979) *The Dialectic of Enlightenment* (London: Verso).

Adorno, T. W. and Horkheimer, M. (1993) 'The Culture Industry: Enlightenment as Mass Deception', in S. During (ed.), *The Cultural Studies Reader* (London: Routledge).

Alexander, C. E. (2000) *The Asian Gang: Ethnicity, Identity, Masculinity* (Oxford: Berg).

Alexander, J. (1985) *Neofunctionalism* (London: Sage).

Alexander, J. C. (1990) 'Analytic Debates', in J. Alexander and S. Seidman (eds), *Culture and Society: Contemporary Debates* (Cambridge: Cambridge University Press).

Allen, C. (2005) 'From Race to Religion: The New Face of Discrimination', in T. Abbas (ed.), *Muslim Britain: Communities Under Pressure* (London: Zed Books).

Althusser, L. with E. Balibar (1968) *Reading Capital* (London: NLB).

Althusser, L. (1969) *For Marx* (Harmondsworth: Penguin).

Althusser, L. (1971) *Lenin and Philosophy and Other Essays* (London: NLB).

Althusser, L. (1976) *Essays in Self-Criticism* (London: NLB).

Anagnostou, Y. (2009) 'A Critique of Symbolic Ethnicity: The Ideology of Choice?', *Ethnicities* 9(1).

Anderson, B. (1983) *Imagined Communities* (London: Verso).

Anderson, E. (2009) *Inclusive Masculinity: The Changing Nature of Masculinities* (London: Routledge).

Anderson, T. (2010) 'Thinking Allowed', BBC Radio 4, 30 June, available at: www.bbc.co.uk/radio4; and 'Fan Girls Online', 29 September, available at: http://www.girlsonline-project.com.

Anderson, W. T. (ed.) (1996) *The Fontana Post-Modernism Reader* (London: Fontana).

Andrews, M. (2009) 'The Narrative Complexity of Successful Ageing', *International Journal of Sociology and Social Policy* 29(2): 73–83.

Ang, I. (1991) *Desperately Seeking the Audience* (London: Routledge).

Archer, L. (2011) 'Constructing Minority Ethnic Middle-Class Identity: An Exploratory Study with Parents, Pupils and Young Professionals', *Sociology* 45(1): 134–51.

Archer, M. S. (1982) 'Morphogenesis versus Structuration: On Combining Structure and Action', *British Journal of Sociology* 33(4): 455–83.

Archer, M. S. (1988) *Culture and Agency: The Place of Culture in Social Theory* (Cambridge: Cambridge University Press).

Archer, M. S. (1995) *Realist Social Theory: The Morphogenetic Approach* (Cambridge: Cambridge University Press).

Archer, M. S. (2007) *Making Our Way Through The World: Human Reflexivity and Social Mobility* (Cambridge: Cambridge University Press).

Aspinall, P., Song, M. and Hashem, F. (2008) 'Ethnic Options of "Mixed Race" People in Britain: Full Research Report', University of Kent, August. ESRC End of Award Report, RES-000-23-1507 (ESRC: Swindon).

Back, L. (1994) 'The Sounds of the City', *Anthropology in Action* 1(1).

Ballaster, R. (1991) *Women's Worlds: Ideology, Femininity and the Woman's Magazine* (London: Macmillan).

Barker, M. (1981) *The New Racism* (London: Junction Books).

Barthes, R. (1967) *Elements of Semiology* (New York: Hill & Wang).

Barthes, R. (1993) *Mythologies* (London: Vintage).

Barthes, R. (1996) *Image–Music–Text*, ed. S. Heath (London: HarperCollins).

Barwise, P. and Ehrenberg, A. (1988) *Television and Its Audience* (London: Sage).

Baudrillard, J. (1981) *For a Critique of the Political Economy of the Sign* (St Louis, MO: Telos).

Baudrillard, J. (1983) *In the Shadow of the Silent Majorities* (New York: Semiotext(e)).

Baudrillard, J. (1988) *Selected Writings*, ed. M. Poster (Cambridge: Polity Press).

Baudrillard, J. (1993) *Baudrillard Live: Selected Interviews*, ed. M. Gane (London: Routledge).

Bauman, Z. (1990) *Thinking Sociologically* (Oxford: Blackwell).

Bauman, Z. (1996) 'From Pilgrim to Tourist – A Short History of Identity', in S. Hall and P. du Gay (eds), *Questions of Cultural Identity* (London: Sage).

Bauman, Z. (2000) *Liquid Modernity* (Cambridge: Polity Press).

Bauman, Z. (2004) *Identity* (Cambridge: Polity Press).

Bauman, Z. (2007) *Liquid Times: Living in an Age of Uncertainty* (Cambridge: Polity Press).

Bechhofer, F. and McCrone, D. (2010) 'Choosing National Identity', Sociological Research Online 15(3), available at: http://www.socresonline.org.uk/15/3/3.html.

Beck, U. (1992) *Risk Society: Towards A New Modernity* (London: Sage).

Beck, U. (1999) *World Risk Society* (Cambridge: Polity Press).

Becker, H. (1973) *Outsiders: Studies in the Sociology of Deviance* (New York: Free Press).

Beer, D. and Burrows, R. (2007) 'Sociology and Web 2.0: Some Initial Considerations', Sociological Research Online 12(5). Available at: http://www.socresonline.org.uk/12/5/17.html.

Beer, G. (1985) *Darwin's Plots: Evolutionary Narrative in Darwin, George Eliot and Nineteenth-Century Fiction* (London: Ark).

Bell, D. (1973) *The Coming of Post-Industrial Society* (New York: Basic Books).

Benjamin, W. (1970) *Illuminations* (London: Collins).

Bennett, A. (1999) 'Subcultures or Neo-tribes? Re-thinking the Relationship between Youth, Style and Musical Taste', *Sociology* 33(3).

Bennett, A. and Kahn-Harris, K. (eds) (2004) *After Subculture: Critical Studies in Contemporary Youth Culture* (Basingstoke: Palgrave Macmillan).

Bennett, T. (1991) *Outside Literature* (London: Routledge).

Berdsey, D. (2006) ' "If I Ever Play Football, Dad, Can I Play for England or India?": British Asians, Sport and Diasporic National Identities', *Sociology* 40(11).

Berger, P. and Berger, B. (1971) *Sociology: A Revised Approach* (Harmondsworth: Penguin).

Berger, P. L. and T. Luckmann (1967) *The Social Construction of Reality: A Treatise in the Sociology of Knowledge* (Harmondsworth: Penguin).

Berking, H. (2003) ' "Ethnicity is Everywhere": On Globalization and the Transformation of Cultural Identity', *Current Sociology* 51(3).

Bernstein, B. (1970) 'Education Cannot Compensate for Society', in P. Worsley (ed.), *Modern Sociology: Introductory Readings* (Harmondsworth: Penguin).

Bernstein, B. (1972) 'Language and Social Context', in P. Giglioli (ed.), *Language and Social Context* (Harmondsworth: Penguin).

Bernstein, B. (1996) *Pedagogy, Symbolic Control and Identity* (London: Taylor & Francis).

Best, S. and Kellner, D. (1998) 'Beavis and Butt-head: No Future for Post-Modern Youth', in J. S. Epstein (ed.), *Youth Culture: Identity in a Postmodern World* (Oxford: Blackwell).

Bhaba, H. (2004) *Location of Culture* (London: Routledge).

Billington, R., Hockey J. and Strawbridge, S. (1998) *Exploring Self and Society* (London: Macmillan).

Blaikie, A. (1999) *Ageing and Popular Culture* (Cambridge: Cambridge University Press).

Blumer, H. (1969) *Symbolic Interactionism: Perspective and Method* (London: University of California Press).

Blumler, J. G. and Katz, E. (eds) (1974) *The Uses of Mass Communication: Current Perspectives on Gratifications Research* (London: Sage).

Bocock, R. (1993) *Consumption* (London: Routledge).

Bordo, S. (1990) 'Feminism, Postmodernism and Gender-Scepticism', in L. J. Nicholson (ed.), *Feminism/Postmodernism* (London: Routledge).

Bourdieu, P. (1977) *Outline of a Theory of Practice* (Cambridge: Cambridge University Press).

Bourdieu, P. (1990) *In Other Words* (Cambridge: Polity Press).

Bourdieu, P. (1993) *Sociology in Question* (London: Sage).

Bowles, S. and H. Gintis (1976) *Schooling in Capitalist America* (London: Routledge & Kegan Paul).

Bradley, H. (1996) *Fractured Identities: Changing Patterns of Inequality* (Cambridge: Polity Press).

Brah, A. (1992) 'Difference, Diversity and Differentiation', in J. Donald and A. Rattansi (eds), *Race, Culture and Difference* (London: Sage).

Brett, J. and Moran, A. (2011) 'Cosmopolitan Nationalism: Ordinary People Making Sense of Diversity', *Nations and Nationalism* 17(1): 188–296.

Brown, R., Rutland, A. and Watters, C. (2007) *Identities in Transition: A Longitudinal Study of Immigrant Children*, ESRC End of Award Report, RES-148-25-0007 (Swindon: ESRC).

Buckley, C. A., Pitt, E., Norton, B. and Owens, T. (2010) 'Students' Approaches to Study, Conceptions of Learning and Judgements about the Value of Networked Technologies', *Active Learning in Higher Education* 11(1): 55–65.

Buss, D. M. (2003) *The Evolution of Desire: Strategies of Human Mating* (New York: Basic Books).

Butler, J. (1990) *Gender Trouble: Feminism and the Subversion of Identity* (London: Routledge).

Callaway, H. (1984) 'Women's Perspectives: Research as Re-vision', in P. Reason and J. Rowan (eds), *Human Inquiry* (New York: Wiley).

Camarota, S. A. (2011) '*A Record-Setting Decade of Immigration: 2000–2010*', Center for Immigration Studies, October 2011. Available at: http://cis.org/2000-2010-record-setting-decade-of-immigration; accessed 11 March 2012.

Campbell, C. (2009) 'Distinguishing the Power of Agency from Agentic Power: A Note on Weber and the Black Box of Personal Agency', *Sociological Theory* 27(4).

Caplan, S. E. and Turner, J. S. (2007) 'Bringing Theory to Research on Computer-Mediated Comforting Communication', *Computers in Human Behavior* 23(2): 985–98.

Charlsworth, S. J. (2000) *A Phenomenology of Working Class Experience* (Cambridge: Cambridge University Press).

Cixous, H. (1980) 'Sorties', in E. Marks and I. de Courtivron (eds), *New French Feminisms: An Anthology* (Brighton: Harvester).

Cixous, H. and Clement , C. (1986) *The Newly Born Woman* (Manchester: Manchester University Press).

Chittenden, T. (2010) 'Digital Dressing Up: Modelling Female Teen Identity in the Discursive Spaces of the Fashion Blogosphere', *Journal of Youth Studies* 13(4): 505–20.

Clarke, J. (1976) 'The Skinheads and the Magical Recovery of Community', in S. Hall and T. Jefferson (eds), *Resistance Through Rituals* (London: Hutchinson).

Clarke, J., Gall, S., Jefferson, T. and Roberts, B. (1976) 'Subcultures, Cultures and Class', in S. Hall and T. Jefferson (eds), *Resistance Through Rituals* (London: Hutchinson).

Cohen, A. P. (1989) *The Symbolic Construction of Community* (London: Routledge).

Cohen, A. P. (1994) *Self-Consciousness: An Alternative Anthropology of Identity* (London: Routledge).

Cohen, P. (1972) 'Subcultural Conflict and Working Class Community', Working Papers in Cultural Studies No.2, Centre for Contemporary Cultural Studies, University of Birmingham.

Cohen, R. (2006) *Migration and Its Enemies: Global Capital, Migrant Labour and the Nation-State* (Aldershot: Ashgate).

Cohen, S. (1987) *Folk Devils and Moral Panics: The Creation of the Mods and Rockers* (Oxford: Basil Blackwell).

Cohen, S. and Taylor, L. (1992) *Escape Attempts: The Theory and Practice of Resistance to Everyday Life*, 2nd edn (London: Routledge).

Collins, P. H. (1990) *Black Feminist Thought: Knowledge, Consciousness, and the Politics of Empowerment* (New York: Routledge).

Collins, P. H. (2004) *Black Sexual POlitics* (New York: Routledge).

Comte, A. (2003) *Positive Philosophy of Auguste Comte, Part I* (1855), trans. H. Martineau (Kessinger Publishing).

Comte, A. (1957) *A General View of Positivism*, trans. J. H. Bridges (first published 1857) (New York: Robert Speller & Sons).

Connell, R. W. (1987) *Gender and Power* (Cambridge: Polity Press).

Connell, R. W. (2001) *The Men and the Boys* (Cambridge: Polity Press).

Connell, R. W. (2005) *Masculinities* (Cambridge: Polity Press).

Cooley, C. H. (1927) *Life and the Student* (New York: Alfred A. Knopf).

Côté, J. E. and Levine, C. G. (2002) *Identity Formation, Agency and Culture: A Social Psychological Synthesis* (Hillsdale, NJ: Lawrence Erlbaum Associates).

Crenshaw, K. (1991) 'Mapping the Margins: Intersectionality, Identity Politics, and Violence Against Women of Color', *Stanford Law Review* 43(6).

Crippen, T. (1988) 'Old and New Gods in the Modern World: Towards a Theory of Religious Transformation', *Social Forces*, 67 (December).

Crook, S., Pakulski, J. and Waters, M. (1992) *Postmodernization: Change in Advanced Society* (London: Sage).

Darwin, C. (1871) *The Descent of Man and Selection in Relation to Sex* (New York: Prometheus).

Davidson, M. (1992) *The Consumerist Manifesto: Advertising in Postmodern Times* (London: Routledge).

de Beauvoir, S. (1972) *The Second Sex* (London: Vintage).

Deleuze, G, and Guattari, F. (1987) *A Thousand Plateaus: Capitalism and Schizophrenia* (Minneapolis, MN: University of Minnesota Press).

Derrida, J. (1973) *Speech and Phenomena: And Other Essays on Husserl's Theory of Signs*, trans. D. B. Allison (Evanston, IL: Northwestern University Press).

Derrida, J. (1977) *Of Grammatology* (Baltimore, MD: Johns Hopkins University Press).

Derrida, J. (1978) *Writing and Difference* (Chicago, IL: University of Chicago Press).

Deutsch, N. L. and Theodorou, E. (2010) 'Aspiring, Consuming, Becoming: Youth Identity in a Culture of Consumption', *Youth and Society* 42(2): 229–54.

Dillon, M. (2010) *Introduction to Sociological Theory: Theorists, Concepts and Their Applicability to the Twenty-first Century* (Chichester: Wiley-Blackwell).

Douglas, M. (1966) *Purity and Danger* (London: Routledge).

du Gay, P., Hall, S., Janes, L., Mackay, H. and Negus, K. (1997) *Doing Cultural Studies: The Story of the Sony Walkman* (London: Sage).

Dunn, J. (1988) *The Beginnings of Social Understanding* (Oxford: Basil Blackwell).

Durkheim, E. (1938) *The Division of Labour in Society* (Glencoe, IL: Free Press).

Durkheim, E. (1970) *Suicide: A Study in Sociology* (London: Routledge & Kegan Paul).

Durkheim, E. (1972) *Selected Writings*, ed. A. Giddens (Cambridge: Cambridge University Press).

Durkheim, E. (1982) *The Elementary Forms of the Religious Life*, 2nd edn (London: George Allen & Unwin).

Easthope, H. (2009) 'Fixed Identities in a Mobile World? The Relationship between Mobility, Place and Identity', *Identities* 16(1): 61–82.

Elias, N. (1970) *What is Sociology?* (New York: Columbia University Press).

Elias, N. (1978) *The Civilising Process* (Oxford: Basil Blackwell).

Elias, N. and E. Dunning (1986) *Quest for Excitement: Sport and Leisure in the Civilizing Process* (Oxford: Basil Blackwell).

Eliot, T. S. (1948) *Notes Towards a Definition of Culture* (London: Faber & Faber).

Epstein, J. S. (ed.) (1998) *Youth Culture: Identity in a Postmodern World* (Oxford: Blackwell).

Eriksen, T. H. (2002) *Ethnicity and Nationalism: Anthropological Perspectives* (London: Pluto).

Erikson, E. (1970) ' "Identity Crisis" in Perspective', in E. H. Erikson, *Life History and the Historical Moment* (New York: W. W. Norton) 1975.

Faludi, S. (1992) *Backlash* (London: Chatto & Windus).

Fausto-Sterling, A. (2000) *Sexing the Body: Gender Politics and the Construction of Sexuality* (New York: Basic Books).

Featherstone, M. (1991) 'The Body in Consumer Culture', in M. Featherstone, M. Hepworth and B. S. Turner (eds), *The Body: Social Process and Cultural Theory* (London: Sage).

Featherstone, M. (1992) 'Postmodernism and the Aestheticization of Everyday Life', in S. Lash and J. Friedman (eds), *Modernity and Identity* (Oxford: Basil Blackwell).

Featherstone, M. (1994) *Consumer Culture and Postmodernism* (London: Sage).

Featherstone, M. and Hepworth, M. (1991) 'The Mask of Ageing and the Postmodern Life', in M. Featherstone, M. Hepworth and B. S. Turner (eds), *The Body: Social Process and Cultural Theory* (London: Sage).

Fenton, S. (1999) *Ethnicity: Racism, Class and Culture* (Basingstoke: Palgrave Macmillan).

Ferguson, M. (1983) *Forever Feminine* (London: Heinemann).

Firestone, S. (1979) *The Dialectic of Sex*, 2nd edn (London: Women's Press).

Fiske, J. (1989) *Reading the Popular* (London: Unwin Hyman).

Foucault, M. (1984) *The Foucault Reader*, ed. P. Rabinow (London: Penguin).

Foucault, M. (1989a) *Madness and Civilisation: A History of Insanity in the Age of Reason* (London: Routledge).

Foucault, M. (1989b) *The Archaeology of Knowledge* (London: Routledge).

Foucault, M. (1989c) *The Birth of the Clinic: An Archaeology of Medical Perception* (London: Routledge).

Fox, K. (2004) *Watching the English* (London: Hodder & Stoughton).

Frankenberg, R. (1993) *White Women Race Matters: The Social Construction Of Whiteness* (Minneapolis, MN: University of Minnesota Press)

Freud, S. (1923) 'The Ego and the Id', Vol. 19 of J. Strachey (ed.), *The Standard Edition of the Complete Psychological Works of Sigmund Freud* (London: Hogarth Press).

Freud, S. (1930) 'Civilization and its Discontents', Vol. 21 of J. Strachey (ed.), *The Standard Edition of the Complete Psychological Works of Sigmund Freud* (London: Hogarth Press).

Frosh, S., Phoenix, A. and Pattman, R. (2001) *Young Masculinities* (Basingstoke: Palgrave)

Fukuyama, F. (1992) *The End of History and the Last Man* (New York: Free Press).

Furedi, F. (2004) *Therapy Culture: Cultivating Vulnerability in an Uncertain Age* (Abingdon: Routledge).

Gans, H. (1974) *Popular Culture and High Culture* (New York: Basic Books).

Gans, H. (2009) 'Reflections on Symbolic Ethnicity: A Response to Y. Anagnostou', *Ethnicities* 9.

Garfinkel, H. (1967) *Studies in Ethnomethodology* (Englewood Cliffs, NJ: Prentice-Hall).

Garland, J. and Chakraborti (2000) N. ' "Race" Space and Place: Examining Identity and Cultures of Exclusion in Rural England', *Ethnicities* 6: 159.

Gauntlett, D. (1998) Media/Gender/Identity Resources. Available at: http://www.theory.org.uk/ctr-quee.htm.

Gauntlett, D. (2002) *Media, Gender and Identity: An Introduction* (London: Routledge).

Geaves, R. (2005) 'Negotiating British Citizenship and Muslim Identity', in Abbas, T. (ed.), *Muslim Britain: Communities Under Pressure* (London: Zed Books).

Gellner, E. (1983) *Nation and Nationalism* (Oxford: Basil Blackwell).

Giddens, A. (ed. and trans.) (1972) *Emile Durkheim: Selected Writings* (London: Cambridge University Press).

Giddens, A. (1976) *New Rules of Sociological Method: A Positive Critique of Interpretative Sociologies* (London: Hutchinson).

Giddens, A. (1978) *Durkheim* (London: Fontana).

Giddens, A. (1984) *The Constitution of Society: Outline of the Theory of Structuration* (Cambridge: Polity Press).

Giddens, A. (1990) *The Consequences of Modernity* (Cambridge: Polity Press).

Giddens, A. (1991) *Modernity and Self-Identity: Self and Society in the Late Modern Age* (Cambridge: Polity Press).

Giddens, A. (1992) *The Transformation of Intimacy: Sexuality, Love and Eroticism in Modern Societies* (Cambridge: Polity Press).

Giddens, A. (1993) *The Giddens Reader*, ed. P. Cassell (Basingstoke: Macmillan).

Giddens, A. (1994) *Beyond Left and Right: The Future of Radical Politics* (Cambridge: Polity Press).

Giddens, A. (1996) *In Defence of Sociology: Essays, Interpretations and Rejoinders* (Cambridge: Polity Press).

Giddens, A. and Diamond, P. (2005) *The New Egalitarianism* (Cambridge: Polity Press).

Gilmore, D. (1990) *Manhood in the Making: Cultural Concepts of Masculinity* (New Haven, CT: Yale University Press).

Gilroy, P. (1987) *There Ain't No Black in the Union Jack* (London: Hutchinson).

Gilroy, P. (1993) *The Black Atlantic: Modernity and Double Consciousness* (London: Verso).

Gilroy, P. (1997) 'Diaspora and the Detours of Identity', in K. Woodward (ed.), *Identity and Difference* (London: Sage).

Giroux, H. A. (1983) *Theory and Resistance in Education* (New York: Bergin & Garvey).

Giroux, H. A. (1994) *Disturbing Pleasures* (New York: Routledge).

Giroux, H. A. (1998) 'Teenage Sexuality, Body Politics, and the Pedagogy of Display', in J. S. Epstein (ed.), *Youth Culture: Identity in a Postmodern World* (Oxford: Basil Blackwell).

Gladwell, M. (2000) *The Tipping Point* (London: Little, Brown).

Goffman, E. (1968) *Asylums: Essays on the Social Situation of Mental Patients and Other Inmates* (London: Pelican).

Goffman, E. (1971a) *Relations in Public: Microstudies of the Public Order* (Harmondsworth: Penguin).

Goffman, E. (1971b) *The Presentation of Self in Everyday Life* (London: Penguin).

Goldschmidt, W. (1990) *The Human Career: The Self in the Symbolic World* (Oxford: Basil Blackwell).

Goldthorpe, J. H., Lockwood, D., Bechhofer, F. and Platt, J. (1968) *The Affluent Worker: Industrial Attitudes and Behaviour* (Cambridge: Cambridge University Press).

Gramsci, A. (1971) *Selections from the Prison Notebooks*, ed. Q. Hoare (London: Lawrence & Wishart).

Gramsci, A. (1977) *Selections from Political Writings: 1910–1920*, ed. Q. Hoare (London: Lawrence & Wishart).

Gramsci, A. (1978) *Selections from Political Writings: 1921–1926*, ed. Q. Hoare (London: Lawrence & Wishart).

Greer, G. (2000) *The Whole Woman* (London: Anchor Books).

Grosfoguel, R. (2004) 'Race and Ethnicity or Racialized Ethnicities?: Identities within Global Coloniality', *Ethnicities* 4(3).

Habermas, J. (1981) *The Theory of Communicative Action* (London: Heinemann).

Habermas, J. (1987) *Toward a Rational Society* (incl. 'Technology and Science as "Ideology"'(1968)) (Cambridge: Polity Press).

Habib, S. (2010) *Islam and Homosexuality* (Santa Barbara, CA: Praeger).

Hakim, C. (1995) 'Five Feminist Myths about Women's Employment', *British Journal of Sociology* 46(3).

Hakim, C. (1996) *Key Issues in Women's Work: Female Heterogeneity and the Polarisation of Women's Employment* (London: Athlone Press).

Hall, S. (1988) *The Hard Road to Renewal: Thatchersim and the Crisis of the Left* (London: Verso).

Hall, S. (1990) 'Cultural Identity and Diaspora', in J. Rutherford (ed.), *Identity: Community, Culture, Difference* (London: Lawrence & Wishart).

Hall, S. (1992) 'The Question of Identity', in S. Hall, D. Held and T. McGrew (eds), *Modernity and Its Futures* (Cambridge: Polity Press).

Hall, S. (1993) 'Encoding, Decoding', in S. During (ed.), *The Cultural Studies Reader* (London: Routledge).

Hall, S. (1996) *Stuart Hall: Critical Dialogues in Cultural Studies*, ed. D. Morley and K. H. Chen (London: Routledge).

Harris, D. (1996) *A Society of Signs?* (London: Routledge).

Hartmann, H. (1981) 'The Unhappy Marriage of Marxism and Feminism', in L. Sargent (ed.), *The Unhappy Marriage of Marxism and Feminism* (London: Pluto Press).

Hayward, K. and Yar, M. (2006) 'The "Chav" Phenomenon: Consumption, Media and the Construction of a New Underclass', *Crime Media Culture* 2: 9.

Heaphy, B. (2008) 'The Sociology of Lesbian and Gay Reflexivity or Reflexivity Sociology?', *Sociological Research Online* 13. Available at: http://www.socresonline.org.uk/13/1/9.html

Heaphy, B. (2011) 'Gay Identities and the Culture of Class', *Sexualities* 14(1): 42–62.

Heath, A. *et al.* (2008) *Are Traditional Identities in Decline?*, ESRC Research Report RES-148-25-0031 (Swindon: ESRC).

Hebdige, D. (1979) *Subculture: The Meaning of Style* (London: Methuen).

Held, D. (1991) 'Democracy, the Nation State and the Global System', in O. D. Held (ed.), *Political Theory Today* (Cambridge: Polity Press).

Heller, A. and Feher, F. (1988) *The Postmodern Political Condition* (Cambridge: Polity Press).

Hetherington, K. (1998) *Expressions of Identity: Space, Performance, Politics* (London: Sage).

Hewitt, R. (1986) *White Talk, Black Talk* (Cambridge: Cambridge University Press).

Hey, V. (1997) *The Company She Keeps: An Ethnography of Girls' Friendship* (Buckingham: Open University Press).

Hicks, J. and Allen, G. (1999) *A Century of Change: Trends in UK Statistics Since 1900* - Commons Library Research Paper, Published 22 December 1999 Research papers RP99/111 Available at http://www.parliament.uk/briefing-papers/RP99-111.

Hill, R. (2010) 'Thinking Allowed', BBC Radio 4, 30 June 2010; available at: www.bbc.co.uk/radio4. And http://www.york.ac.uk/inst/cws/researchst/roseyh.htm, accessed 29 September 2010.

Hochschild, A. (1983) *The Managed Heart: Commercialization of Human Feeling* (Berkeley, CA: University of California Press).

Hockey, J. *et al.* (2007) *Masculinities in Transition: Identity, Home and Workplace*: Full Research Report. ESRC End of Award Report, RES-000-23-0441 (Swindon: ESRC).

Hodkinson, P. (2002) *Goth. Identity, Style and Subculture* (Oxford: Berg).

Hodkinson, P. (2004), 'The Goth Scene and (Sub)Cultural Substance', in A. Bennett and K. Kahn-Harris (eds) (2004), *After Subculture: Critical Studies in Contemporary Youth Culture* (Basingstoke: Palgrave Macmillan).

Hodkinson, P. (2006) 'Subcultural Blogging: Online Journals and Group Involvement Among UK Goths', in A. Bruns and Y. Jacobs (eds), *Uses of Blogs* (Oxford: Peter Lang).

Hollis, M. (1977) *Models of Man* (Cambridge: Cambridge University Press).

Holmes, David (2005) *Communication Theory: Media, Technology and Society* (London: Sage).

Hood-Williams, J. (1996) 'Goodbye to Sex and Gender?', *The Sociology Review*, 20.

hooks, b. (1996) 'Postmodern Blackness', in W. T. Anderson (ed.), *The Fontana Post-Modernism Reader* (London: Fontana).

Hughey, M. W. (2011) 'Backstage Discourse and the Reproduction of White Masculinities', *The Sociological Quarterly* 52(1): 132–53.

Irigaray, L. (1985) *Speculum of the Other Woman* (Ithaca, NY: Cornell University Press).

Irigaray, L. (1992) *The Irigaray Reader*, ed. M. Whitford (Oxford: Basil Blackwell).

Irigaray, L. (1993) *An Ethic of Sexual Difference* (London: Athlone Press).

James, S. and A. Busia (eds) (1993) *Theorising Black Feminisms. The Visionary Pragmatism Of Black Women* (London: Routledge).

Jameson, F. (1983) 'Post-modernism and Consumer Society', in H. Foster (ed.), *Post-modern Culture* (London: Pluto).

Jay, M. (2010) 'Liquidity Crisis: Zygmunt Bauman and the Incredible Lightness of Modernity', *Theory, Culture and Society* 27(6): 95–106.

Jenkins, R. (1992) *Pierre Bourdieu* (London: Routledge).

Jenkins, R. (1996) *Social Identity* (London: Routledge).

Jenkins, R. (2010) *Being Danish: Paradoxes of Identity in Everyday Life* (Copenhagen: Museum Tusculanum Press).

Jenkins, R. (2010) *Being Danish* abstract. Available at:www.dpu.dk/fileadmin/www.dpu.dk/aktuelt/kalender/beingdanish/arrangementer_2010_20100429155359_richard-jenkins-being-danish_abstract.pdf.

Jones, S. (1994) *The Language of the Genes* (London: Flamingo).

Katz, S. and Marshall, B. (2003) 'New Sex for Old: Lifestyle, Consumerism and the Ethics of Ageing Well', *Journal of Ageing Studies* 17(1): 136.

Kaufmann, E. (2004) 'The Rise of Cosmopolitanism in the Twentieth Century West: A Comparative-Historical Perspective on the United States and European Union', *Global Society* 17(4): 359–83.

Kellner, D. (1992) 'Popular Culture and the Construction of Postmodern Identities', in S. Lash and J. Friedman (eds), *Modernity and Identity* (Oxford: Basil Blackwell).

Kerr, C., Dunlop, J. T., Harbison, F. and Myers, C. A. (1973) *Industrialism and Industrial Man* (Harmondsworth: Penguin).

King, A. (2010) 'The Afghan War and "Postmodern" Memory: Commemoration and the Dead of Helmand', *British Journal of Sociology* 61(1).

Kirby, M. (1999) 'New Approaches to Social Inequality', *The Sociology Review* 8(3).

Kristeva, J. (1981) *Desire in Language* (Oxford: Basil Blackwell).

Kristeva, J. (1986) *The Kristeva Reader*, ed. T. Moi (Oxford: Basil Blackwell).

Kroeber, A. L. and C. Kluckhohn (1963) *Culture: A Criticial Review of Concepts and Definitions* (New York: Vintage Books).

Kumar, K. (1986) *Prophecy and Progress: The Sociology of Industrial and Post-Industrial Society* (Harmondsworth: Penguin).

Lawler, S. (2005) 'Introduction: Class Culture and Identity', *Sociology* 39(5).

Le Bon, G. (2008) *The Crowd: A Study of the Popular Mind* (Lawrence, Kansas, USA: Digireads.com)

Lea, J. and Young, J. (1993) *What Is to Be Done About Law and Order?* (London: Pluto).

Lehdonvirta, V. and Räsänen, P. (2010) 'How Do Young People Identify with Online and Offline Peer Groups? A Comparison between UK, Spain and Japan', *Journal of Youth Studies* 14(1): 91–108.

Lenhart, A. (2007) 'Social Networking Websites and Teens: An Overview', *PEW Internet and American Life Project*, 7 January.

Lévi-Strauss, C. (1969) *The Elementary Structures of Kinship* (Boston, MA: Beacon Press).

Lévi-Strauss, C. (1972) *The Savage Mind* (London: Weidenfeld & Nicolson).

Lévi-Strauss, C. (1977) *Structural Anthropology 1* (Harmondsworth: Penguin).

Lévi-Strauss, C. (1978) *Structural Anthropology 2* (Harmondsworth: Penguin).

Lincoln, S. (2004) 'Teenage Girls' "Bedroom Culture": Code versus Zones', in A. Bennett and K. Kahn-Harris (eds), *After Subculture: Critical Studies in Contemporary Youth Culture* (Basingstoke: Palgrave Macmillan).

Lindsay, C. (2005) ' "McJobs", "Good Jobs" and Skills: Job-Seekers' Attitudes to Low-Skilled Service Work', *Human Resource Management Journal* 15(2).

Lindsay, C. and R.W. McQuaid (2004) 'Avoiding the 'McJobs': Unemployed Job Seekers and Attitudes to Service Work', *Work, Employment and Society* 18(2).

Locher, D. A. (1998) 'The Industrial Identity Crisis: The Failure of a Newly Forming Subculture to Identify Itself', in J. S. Epstein (ed.), *Youth Culture: Identity in a Postmodern World* (Oxford: Basil Blackwell).

Lyotard, J.-F. (1984) *The Postmodern Condition: A Report on Knowledge*, 2nd edn (Manchester: Manchester University Press).

Mac an Ghaill, M. (1994) *The Making of Men: Masculinities, Sexualities and Schooling* (Milton Keynes: Open University Press).

Mackinnon, C. (1982) 'Feminism, Marxism, Method and the State', in N. O. Keohane, M. Z. Rosaldo and B. C. Gelpi (eds), *Feminist Theory: A Critique of Ideology* (Brighton: Harvester Wheatsheaf).

Malacrida, C. and Low, J. (eds) (2008) *Sociology of the Body* (Don Mills, ON, Canada: Oxford University Press).

Malinowski, B. (1922) *Argonauts of the Western Pacific* (London: Routledge & Kegan Paul).

Malinowski, B. (1954) *Magic, Science and Religion and Other Essays* (New York: Anchor Books).

Mama, A. (1989) 'Violence against Black Women: Gender, Race and State Responses', *Feminist Review* 32: 30–48.

Mannheim, K. (1960) *Ideology and Utopia: An Introduction to the Sociology of Knowledge* (London: Routledge & Kegan Paul).

Marcia, J. E., (1966) 'Development and Validation of Ego Identity Status', *Journal of Personality and Social Psychology* 3: 551–8.

Marcuse, H. (1964) *One-Dimensional Man* (London: Routledge & Kegan Paul).

Marcuse, H. (1969) *Eros and Civilization* (London: Routledge & Kegan Paul).

Martin, G. (2009) 'Subculture, Style, Chavs and Consumer Capitalism: Towards a Critical Cultural Criminology of Youth', *Crime Media and Culture* 5: 123.

Marx, K. (1989) *Readings from Karl Marx*, ed. D. Sayer (London: Routledge).

Marx, K. and Engels, F. (1974) *The German Ideology*, 2nd edn (London: Lawrence & Wishart).

Marx, K. and Engels, F. (1984) *Basic Writings on Politics and Philosophy*, ed. L. S. Feuer (London: Fontana).

Marx, K. and F. Engels (1985) *The Communist Manifesto* (London: Penguin).

Maynard, M. (1998) 'Feminists' Knowledge and the Knowledge of Feminisms', in T. May and M. Williams (eds), *Knowing the Social World* (Buckingham: Open University Press).

McAllister-Groves, J. (1995) 'Learning to Feel: The Neglected Sociology of Social Movements', *Sociology Review* 43(3).

McCormack, M. and Anderson, E. (2010) '"It's Just Not Acceptable Any More": The Erosion Of Homophobia and the Softening of Masculinity at an English Sixth Form', *Sociology* 44(5): 843–59.

McCrone, D. (1998) *The Sociology of Nationalism* (London: Routledge).

McCrone, D. (2002) 'Who Do You Say You Are? Making Sense of National Identities in Modern Britain', *Ethnicities* 2(3).

McCrone, D. (2006) 'A Nation That Dares Not Speak Its Name? The English Question', *Ethnicities*. 6(6).

McDowell, L. (2003) *Redundant Masculinities? Employment Change and White Working Class Youth* (Oxford: Blackwell).

McLuhan, M. (1964) *Understanding the Media* (London: Routledge).

McLuhan, M. and Fiore, Q. (1967) *The Medium Is the Message* (London: Allen Lane).

McRobbie, A. (1983) 'Teenage Girls, Jackie and the Ideology of Adolescent Femininity', in B. Waites, T. Bennett and G. Martin (eds), *Popular Culture* (London: Croom Helm).

McRobbie, A. (1986) *Postmodernism and Popular Culture*, ICA Documents 4/5 (London: ICA).

McRobbie, A. (1994) *Postmodernism and Popular Culture* (London: Routledge).

McRobbie, A. (2010) 'Thinking Allowed', BBC Radio 4, 30 June; available at: www.bbc.co.uk/radio4.

McRobbie, A. and Garber, J. (1976) 'Girls and Subcultures', in Hall and Jefferson (eds), *Resistance through Rituals: Youth Subcultures in Post-War Britain* (London: Hutchinson).

Mead, G. H. (1934) *Mind, Self and Society* (Chicago, IL: University of Chicago Press).

Mercer, K. (1990) 'Welcome to the Jungle: Identity and Diversity in Postmodern Politics', in J. Rutherford (ed.), *Identity: Community, Culture, Difference* (London: Lawrence & Wishart).

Mercer, K. (1994) *Welcome to the Jungle: New Positions in Black Cultural Studies* (New York: Routledge).

Mercer, K. (1995) 'Black Hair/Style Politics', in E. Carter, J. Donald and J. Squires (eds), *Cultural Remix: Theories of Politics and the Popular* (London: Lawrence & Wishart).

Merton, R. K. (1989) 'Social Structure and Anomie', in D. H. Kelley (ed.), *Deviant Behaviour: A Text-Reader in the Sociology of Deviance*, 3rd edn (New York: St Martin's Press).

Miles, S. (2001) *Social Theory in the Real World* (London: Sage).

Miller, W. B. (1962) 'Lower Class Culture as a Generating Milieu of Gang Delinquency', in M. E. Wolfgang, L. Savitz and N. Johnston (eds), *The Sociology of Crime and Delinquency* (New York: John Wiley).

Millet, K. (1970) *Sexual Politics* (New York: Doubleday).

Mills, C. W. (1959) *The Sociological Imagination* (London: Oxford University Press).

Mishra, S. and Shirazi, F. (2010) 'Hybrid Identities: American Muslim Women Speak', *Gender, Place and Culture* 17(2): 191–209.

Modood, T. (1988) ' "Black" Racial Equality and Asian Identity', *New Community* 14(3).

Modood, T. (1992) 'British Muslims and the Rushdie Affair', in J. Donald and A. Rattansi (eds), *Race, Culture and Difference* (London: Sage).

Modood, T. (2007) *Multiculturalism* (Cambridge: Polity Press).

Moore, A. (2010) ' "I" and "We" Identities – an Eliasian Perspective on Lesbian and Gay Identities', *Sociological Research Online* 15. Available at: http://www.socresonline.org.uk/15/4/10.html.

Moran, C. (2011) *How to Be a Woman* (London: Ebury Press).

Morgan, D. H. J. (1996) *Family Connections: An Introduction to Family Studies* (Cambridge: Polity Press).

Morley, D. (1980) *The Nationwide Audience* (London: BFI).

Morley, D. (1994) 'Postmodernism – the Highest Stage of Cultural Imperialism?', in M. Perryman (ed.), *Altered States: Postmodernism, Politics and Culture* (London: Lawrence & Wishart).

Morris, D. (1968) *The Naked Ape* (London: Corgi).

Muggleton, D. (2000) *Inside Subcultures: The Postmodern Meaning of Style* (Oxford: Berg).

Muggleton, D. and Weinzierl, R. (eds) (2003) *The Post-Subcultures Reader* (Oxford: Berg).

Muir, R. and Wetherell, M. (2010) *Identity, Politics and Public Policy* (London: Institute for Public Policy Research).

Mulvey, L. (1975) 'Visual Pleasure and Narrative Cinema', *Screen* 16(3).

Murray, C. (1984) *Losing Ground* (New York: Basic Books).

Narumi, H. (2010) 'Japanese Street Style', in V. Steele, P. Mears, Y. Kawamura and H. Narumi (2010) *Japan Fashion Now* (London: Yale University Press).

New, C. (1993) 'Structuration Theory Revisited: Some Reflections on Agency', *Social Science Teacher* 22(3).

Newby, H. (1980) 'Community', Study section 20 in *An Introduction to Sociology* (Milton Keynes: Open University Press).

Nicholson, L. (1999) *The Play of Reason: From the Modern to the Postmodern* (Buckingham: Open University Press).

Norris, C. (1992) *Uncritical Theory: Postmodernism, Intellectuals and the Gulf War* (London: Lawrence & Wishart).

Norris, C. (1993) *The Truth about Postmodernism* (Oxford: Basil Blackwell).

Oakley, A. (1972) *Sex, Gender and Society* (London: Temple Smith).

Oakley, A. (1982) *Subject Women* (London: Fontana).

O'Donnell, M. (2007) 'Review Debate: We Need Human Rights Not Nationalism "Lite": Globalisation and British Solidarity', *Ethnicities* 7: 248.

O'Hara, M. (1996) 'Constructing Emancipatory Realities', in W. T. Anderson (ed.), *The Fontana Post-Modernism Reader* (London: Fontana).

Parekh, B. (2000) *Commission on the Future of Multi-Ethnic Britain: The Parekh Report* (Runnymede Trust Report) (London: Profile Books). See also http://www.runnymedetrust.org/projects/meb/report.html.

Park, R. (1929) 'The City as a Social Laboratory', in T. Smith and L. White (eds), *Chicago: An Experiment in Social Science Research* (Chicago, IL: University of Chicago Press).

Park, R. (1950) *Race and Culture* (Glencoe, IL: Free Press).

Park, R. and E. Burgess (eds) (1925) *The City* (Chicago, IL: University of Chicago Press).

Parsons, T. (1951) *The Social System* (Glencoe, IL: Free Press).

Parsons, T. (1971) *The System of Societies* (Englewood Cliffs, NJ: Prentice-Hall).

Pattillo-McCoy, M. (1999) *Black Picket Fences: Privilege and Peril among the Black Middle Class* (Chicago, IL: University of Chicago Press).

Payne, G. and Grew, C. (2005) 'Unpacking "Class Ambivalence": Some Conceptual and Methodological Issues in Unpacking Class Cultures', *Sociology* 39(5).

Pearce, F. (1989) *The Radical Durkheim* (London: Unwin Hyman).

Pearson, G. (1983) *Hooligan: A History of Respectable Fears* (London: Macmillan).

Pedrozo, S. (2010) 'To Be "Cool" or Not to Be "Cool": Young People's Insights On Consumption and Social Issues in Ro de Janeiro', *Journal of Youth Studies* 14(1): 109–23.

Peirce, C. S. (1991) *Peirce on Signs: Writings on Semiotic by Charles Sanders Peirce*, ed. J. Hoopes (Chapel Hill, NC: University of North Carolina Press).

Philo, G. (1990) *Seeing and Believing: The Influence of Television* (London: Routledge).

Pilkington, A. (2002) 'Cultural Representations and Changing Ethnic Identities in a Global Age', in M. Holborn (ed.) *Developments in Sociology: An Annual Review*, Vol. 18 (Harlow: Causeway Press/Pearson Education).

Pilkington, A. (2005) 'Social Cohesion, Racial Equality and Ethnic Diversity' in M. Holborn (ed.) *Developments in Sociology: An Annual Review*, Vol. 21 (Harlow: Causeway Press/Pearson Education)

Pilkington, A. (2008) 'From Institutional Racism to Community Cohesion: The Changing Nature of Racial Discourse in Britain', *Sociological Research Online*. Available at: http://www.socresonline.org.uk/13/3/6.html.

Pilkington, A., Housee, S. and Hylton, K. (eds) (2009) *Race(ing) Forward: Transitions in Theorizing Race in Education* (Birmingham: Higher Education Academy Network, University of Birmingham).

Poole, F. J. P. (1994) 'Socialization, Enculturation and the Development of Personal Identity', in T. Ingold (ed.) *Companion Encyclopedia of Anthropology: Humanity, Culture and Social Life* (London: Routledge).

Postman, N. (1985) *The Disappearance of Childhood: How TV Is Changing Children's Lives* (London: W. H. Allen).

Prins, B. (2006) 'Narrative Accounts of Origins: A Blind Spot in the Intersectional Approach?',*European Journal of Women's Studies* 13(3).

Puar, J. K. (2005) 'Queer Times, Queer Assemblages', *Social Text* 23(3–4).

Pullen, L. (2009) 'Read Write Web', Interview with Jolie O'Dell, 7 June 2009. Available at: http://www.readwriteweb.com/archives/the_sociology_of_twitter_with_liz_pullen.php.

Putnam, R. D. (2000) *Bowling Alone: The Collapse and Revival of American Community* (New York: Simon & Schuster).

Rahman, M. (2010) 'Queer as Intersectionality: Theorizing Gay Muslim Identities', *Sociology* 44(5), 994–61.

Räsänen, P. and Kuovo, A. (2007) 'Linked or Divided by the Web? Internet and Sociability in Four European Countries', *Information Communication and Society* 10(2): 219–241.

Reddington, H. (2003) ' "Lady" Punks in Bands: A Subculturette?', in D. Muggleton and R. Weinzierl (eds), *The Post-Subcultures Reader* (Oxford: Berg).

Richardson, D. (1993) 'Sexuality and Male Dominance', in D. Richardson and V. Robinson (eds), *Introducing Women's Studies* (London: Macmillan).

Richardson, D. (2010) 'Youth Masculinities: Compelling Male Heterosexuality', *British Journal of Sociology* 61(4): 737–56.

Richardson, J. (1990) 'Race', in M. Haralambos (ed.), *Developments in Sociology: An Annual Review*, Vol. 3, (Harlow: Causeway Press/Pearson Education).

Roberts, K. (2001) *Class in Modern Britain* (Basingstoke: Palgrave).

Robins, K. (1997) 'What in the World's Going On?', in P. du Gay (ed.), *Production of Culture/Culture of Production* (London: Sage).

Robinson, V. (2008) 'Men, Masculinities and Feminism', in D. Richardson and V. Robinson (eds) *Introducing Gender and Women's Studies*, 3rd edn (Basingstoke: Palgrave Macmillan).

Robinson, W. P. (1996) *Social Groups and Identities: Developing the Legacy of Henri Tajfel* (Oxford: Butterworth-Heinemann).

Rorty, R. (1989) *Contingency, Irony and Solidarity* (Cambridge: Cambridge University Press).

Rorty, R. (1996) 'Ironists and Metaphysicians', in W. T. Anderson (ed.), *The Fontana Post-Modernism Reader* (London: Fontana).

Ross, A. (1994) 'Andrew Ross' Weather Report', *Artforum*, 10–12 May.

Rowe, J. W. and Kahn, R. L. (1998) *Successful Aging* (New York: Pantheon Books).

Ruspini, E. (2007) 'Changing Femininities, Changing Masculinities: Social Change, Gender Identities and Sexual Orientations, *Sociological Research Online* 12(1). Available at: http://www.socresonline.org.uk/12/1/ruspini.html.

Said, E. W. (1978) *Orientalism* (London: Penguin).

Said, E. W. (1995) *Orientalism: Western Conceptions of the Orient*, 2nd edn (London: Penguin).

Saucier, P. K. (2011) 'Cape Verdean Youth Fashion: Identity in Clothing', Fashion Theory: The Journal of Dress, Body & Culture 15(1): 49–66.

Saunders, P. (1990) *Social Class and Stratification* (London: Routledge).

Saussure, F. de (1983) *Course in General Linguistics* (London: Duckworth).

Saussure, F. de (1990) 'Signs and Language', in J. C. Alexander and S. Seidman, *Culture and Society: Contemporary Debates* (Cambridge: Cambridge University Press).

Savage, M., Bagnall, G. and Longhurst, B. (2001) 'Ordinary Ambivalent and Defensive: Class Identities in the Northwest of England', *Sociology* 35(4): 875–92.

Savage, M., Barlow, J., Dickens, P. and Fielding, T. (1992) *Property, Bureaucracy and Culture: Middle-Class Formation in Contemporary Britain* (London/New York: Routledge).

Schmidt, J. (2007) 'Blogging Practices: An Analytical Framework', *Journal of Computer-Mediated Communication* 12(4).

Schutz, A. (1967) *The Phenomenology of the Social World* (Evanston, IL: Northwestern University Press).

Schutz, A. (1970) *On Phenomenology and Social Relations: Selected Writings* (Chicago, IL: University of Chicago Press).

Segal, L. (1997) 'Sexualities', in K. Woodward (ed.), *Identity and Difference* (London: Sage).

Seidler, V. (1989) *Rediscovering Masculinity: Reason, Language and Sexuality* (London: Routledge).

Seidman, S (1997) *Difference Troubles: Queering Social Theory and Sexual Politics* (Cambridge: Cambridge University Press).

Simmel, G. (1950) *The Sociology of Georg Simmel*, ed. K. H. Wolff (New York: Free Press).

Simmel, G. (1955) *Conflict and the Web of Group Affiliation* (New York: Free Press).

Simmel, G. (1957) 'Fashion', *American Journal of Sociology* 62: 541–8.

Simon, W. (1996) 'The Postmodernization of Sex and Gender', in W. T. Anderson (ed.), *The Fontana Post-Modernism Reader* (London: Fontana).

Skeggs, B. (2005) 'The Making of Class and Gender through Visualizing Moral Subject Formation', *Sociology* 39(5).

Smith, D. (2007) 'Identity Crisis, Or Just Confusion?', ESRC, *The Edge*, 24 (Spring). Available at: http://www.esrc.ac.uk/_images/The%20Edge%2024_tcm8-8231.pdf.

Smith, J. (1997) *Different for Girls: How Culture Creates Women* (London: Chatto & Windus).

Smits, K. (2011) 'Justifying Multiculturalism: Social Justice Diversity and National Identity in Australia and New Zealand', *Australian Journal of Political Science* 46(1): 87–103.

Soja, E. W. (1996) 'Los Angeles 1965–1992: From Crisis-Generated Restructuring To Restructuring-Generated Crisis', in A. J. Scott and E. W. Soja (eds), *The City: Los Angeles and Urban Theory at the End of the Twentieth Century* (London: University of California Press).

Spencer, H. (2003) *The Principles of Sociology*, (New Jersey: Transaction Publishers). Originally published 1898.

Spencer, H. (1971) *Herbert Spencer: Structure, Function and Evolution*, ed. S. Andreski (London: Nelson).

Spencer, S., Ruhs, M., Anderson, B. and Rogaly, B. (2007) *Migrants' Lives Beyond the Workplace: The Experiences of Central and East Europeans in the UK* (York: Joseph Rowntree Foundation).

Stuart, A. (1990) 'Feminism: Dead or Alive?', in J. Rutherford (ed.), *Identity: Community, Culture, Difference* (London: Lawrence & Wishart).

Sumner, C. (1994) *The Sociology of Deviance: An Obituary* (Buckingham: Open University Press).

Sutherland, E. (1924) *Principles of Criminology* (Chicago, IL: University of Chicago Press).

Swingewood, A. (1977) *The Myth of Mass Culture* (London: Macmillan).

Tajfel, H. (ed.) (1982) *Social Identity and Intergroup Relations* (Cambridge: Cambridge University Press).

Tajfel, H. and Turner, J. C. (1986) 'The Social Identity Theory of Intergroup Behavior', in S. Worchel and W. G. Austin (eds) ,*Psychology of Intergroup Relations* (Chicago: Nelson-Hall).

Thornton, S. (1995) *Club Cultures: Music Media and Subcultural Capital* (Cambridge: Polity Press).

Tiger, L. and R. Fox (1972) *The Imperial Animal* (London: Secker & Warburg).

Tomlinson, L. (1998) ' "This Ain't No Disco"... Or Is It? Youth Culture and the Rave Phenomenon', in J. S. Epstein (ed.), *Youth Culture: Identity in a Postmodern World* (Oxford: Blackwell).

Tönnies, F. (1963) *Community and Society*, ed. P. Loomis (New York: Harper & Row).

Turner, B. S. (1984) *The Body and Society: Explorations in Social Theory* (Oxford: Basil Blackwell).

Twine, F. W. (2010) 'White Like Who? The Value of Whiteness in British Interracial Families', *Ethnicities* 10(3).

Tyler, I. and Bennett, B. (2010) ' "Celebrity Chav": Fame, Femininity and Social Class', *European Journal of Cultural Studies* 13(3): 375–93.

Walby, S. (1989) 'Theorising Patriarchy', *Sociology*. 23(2).

Walby, S. (1990) *Theorising Patriarchy* (Oxford: Basil Blackwell).

Waters, M. (1995) *Globalization* (London: Routledge).

Weber, M. (1961) *From Max Weber: Essays in Sociology* (London: Routledge).

Weber, M. (1968) *Economy and Society: An Outline of Interpretive Sociology*, 3 vols, ed. G. Roth and C. Wittich (New York: Bedminister Press).

Weber, M. (1985) *The Protestant Ethic and the Spirit of Capitalism* (London: Unwin).

Weeks, J. (1990) 'The Value of Difference', in J. Rutherford (ed.), *Identity: Community, Culture, Difference* (London: Lawrence & Wishart).

Weinstein, D. (1991) *Heavy Metal: A Cultural Sociology* (New York: Lexington).

Whelehan, I. (2000) *Overloaded: Popular Culture and the Future of Feminism* (London: The Women's Press).

Whyte, W. F. (1955) *Street Corner Society: The Social Structure of an Italian Slum* (Chicago, IL: University of Chicago Press).

Williams, R. (1963) *Culture and Society 1780–1950* (Harmondsworth: Pelican).

Williams, R. (1983) *Keywords: A Vocabulary of Culture and Society* (London: Fontana).

Willis, P. (1977) *Learning to Labour* (Farnborough: Saxon House).

Willis, P. (1979) 'Masculinity and Factory Labour', in J. Clarke, Critcher, C. and Johnson, R. (eds), *Working Class Culture* (London: Hutchinson).

Willis, P. (1990) 'Masculinity and Factory Labour', in J. C. Alexander and S. Seidman (eds), *Culture and Society: Contemporary Debates* (Cambridge: Cambridge University Press).

Willis, P. with James, S., Canaan, J. and Hurd, G. (1993) *Common Culture: Symbolic Work at Play in the Everyday Cultures of the Young* (Milton Keynes: Open University Press).

Wirth, L. (1938) 'Urbanism as a Way of Life', *American Journal of Sociology* 44: 1–24.

Woodward, K. (ed.) (1997) *Identity and Difference* (London: Sage).

Yang, J. (2010) 'The Crisis of Masculinity: Class, Gender, and Kindly Power in Post-Mao China', *American Ethnologist* 37(3): 550–62.

Yinger, J. M. (1976) 'Ethnicity in Complex Societies', in L. A. Coser and O. N. Larsen (eds), *The Uses of Controversy in Sociology* (New York: Free Press).

Zingsheim, J. (2011) *Mutational Identity: (Re)creating Ourselves through Pop Culture and Pedagogy* (Charleston, USA: BiblioBazaar).

Zweig, C. (1996) 'The Death of the Self in the Postmodern World', in W. T. Anderson (ed.), *The Fontana Post-Modernism Reader* (London: Fontana).

Zweig, F. (1961) *The Worker in an Affluent Society: Family Life and Industry* (London: Heinemann).

Author Index

Subject Index